D1593708

Books by Jacques Ellul

Autopsy of Revolution (1971)

A Critique of the New Commonplaces (1968)

The Political Illusion (1967)

Propaganda: The Formation of Men's Attitudes (1965)

The Technological Society (1964)

These are Borzoi Books
published in New York by Alfred A. Knopf

AUTOPSY
OF REVOLUTION

AUTOPSY

OF

REVOLUTION

BY

JACQUES ELLUL

TRANSLATED FROM THE FRENCH BY PATRICIA WOLF

New York: Alfred A. Knopf

1971

THIS IS A BORZOI BOOK
PUBLISHED BY ALFRED A. KNOPF, INC.

Copyright © 1971 by Alfred A. Knopf, Inc.

All rights reserved under International and Pan-American
Copyright Conventions. Published in the United States by
Alfred A. Knopf, Inc., New York, and simultaneously in Canada
by Random House of Canada Limited, Toronto. Distributed
by Random House, Inc., New York. Originally published in
France as *Autopsie de la Révolution* by Calmann-Lévy, Paris.
Copyright © 1969 by Calmann-Lévy.
ISBN: 0-394-47131-8
Library of Congress Catalog Card Number: 73-154944
Manufactured in the United States of America

First American Edition

Contents

Preface

Revolts, revolutions, uprisings, rebellions, agitation, civil wars, *coups d'état:* these are the very fabric of history.[1] They are part of human existence. Not an accident but a constant, not disruption but movement produced in the unhurried stream of history.

---

[1] Let us take a few examples. The seventeenth century: 1601–10, the "period of strife," a series of revolts in Russia; 1610, Sikh uprising; 1620–30, Chinese revolt against the Mings; 1631, uprising in Dijon and in Aix-en-Provence; 1635, Bordeaux insurrection; 1636, rebellion of the *Croquants;* 1637, revolt of Awa Kousa in Japan; 1639, revolt of the *Nu-pieds;* 1640–4, rebellions against the Mings leading to the downfall of that dynasty; 1640, Catalonia's revolt against Spain, lasting until 1652; in the same year, 1640, outbreak of the Portuguese Revolution, which persisted, latent or explosive, until 1668; 1641, a year of widespread turmoil, peasant revolts in Ireland, Switzerland, Germany, and Russia; 1643, revolt of the Rouergue; 1645, revolt of Montpellier; 1647, Masaniello's year-long rebellion in Naples against the Spanish viceroy; 1648, also a year teeming with revolutions: England's revolution, which began in 1640 but developed notably between 1648 and 1653, and which has been said to be perhaps "the first great bourgeois revolution of modern times"; the Fronde in France, from 1648 to 1652; the Ukraine uprising from 1648 to 1654; popular risings in Russia in this same year, in Moscow, Koslov, Tomsk, etc.; the Hindu rebellion of the Mahrattas against the Mongol invaders, also in 1648; in 1649, resumption of the Moscow rebellion; 1650, Novgorod uprising and William of Holland's *coup d'état;* 1653, peasant war in Switzerland; 1662, revolt in the Boulonnais and revolt of Moscow over a monetary problem; 1664–70, the great rebellion of Audijos; 1670–1, the great revolt of Stenka Razin and the peasant rising in Bohemia; 1673–81, widespread revolt in north-

There is nothing extraordinary in revolution that conflicts with a norm or standard governing the behavior of peoples, powers, and civilizations. Let us not rely on outlines of history that speak of 1649, 1785, or 1917, for when we take a closer look at events, we find evidence of this permanence of revolution among mankind. It is useless to look for divisions between periods of order and of disorder. Revolution is not so much the driving force as one of the elements in the invisible thread from which the fabric of civilization is woven.

But we are at once restrained by a concern of a formal nature for a definition. What are we saying when we use the word "revolution"? What will these four syllables mean to the next man? "The duty of every Christian is to be a revolutionary," proclaimed Camilo Torrès. This is obvious. But does it mean that he must be a Hitlerite or a Marxist, an anarchist or a Stalinist? What revolution can a Christian hope for or espouse? Whom shall he believe among those who proclaim themselves revolutionaries? Definitions are not enough, especially those in the dictionary. Revolution is something one endures, believes in, plunges into, and achieves. Each era, each human society

---

eastern China; 1675, another year of abundance: so-called *papier timbré* (stamp tax) revolts in Brittany and Bordeaux, mounting rebellions of the Sikhs and Mahrattas, and immediately afterward the religious revolt of the Camisards; 1679, the Irish Revolution.

Let us take another period, from 1770 to 1850. There again we find uprisings, rebellions, revolts, and revolutions throughout the world. 1768, Geneva's democratic revolution; 1772, revolution within the Swedish monarchy; 1775–83, the American Revolution on the heels of her war against Great Britain; 1780–83, multiple risings in England and Ireland, great revolt of the Indians of Peru; 1781, revolt of New Granada, revolution in Fribourg and once again in Geneva in 1782; 1783–7, revolution with numerous orientations in the United Provinces; 1787–90, revolution of the Austrian Low Countries; 1788–94, revolt in Guiana, Polish Revolution; 1789, beginning of the French Revolution, democratization of the regime in Sweden; 1791, Polish Revolution; 1792, renewal of the Belgian Revolution, Rhenish Revolution, widespread revolt in the Antilles; 1794, uprisings in Ireland; 1795, revolution in Holland and in Geneva, risings in London, Birmingham, etc., in Constantinople and Smyrna; 1796, revolution of the Italian States; 1797, mutiny of the English fleet; 1798, revolution in Switzerland and Ireland; 1799, revolt of the Ionian Islands and Malta; 1810, revolution of the Spanish colonies which was to end in the recognition of their independence in 1825; also from 1810 to 1829, war of independence of the Balkan peoples; 1820, the Italian and Spanish revolutions; 1821, the Greek Revolution, and in 1830, the great flames of revolution in France, in Belgium, and in Poland . . . prelude to 1848.

has its own, always different yet always similar, always a reflection of others yet unique every time, like love. Should we stop talking about it to prevent it from becoming a household word? A valid question. Still, it is merely a human reality, neither sacred nor remote; but to begin to understand it we must simply accept it just as men have lived it and discussed it each time.

So instead of looking for a definition at the start, I shall insist upon practicing nominalism, which seems to me an excellent point of departure for most sociological studies. We must accept as revolution what men of a certain period experienced as revolution and so named it themselves, sometimes in different terms. It is utterly absurd and pretentious to state that the revolution of 1830 was not a revolution. Those who made it experienced it as a decisive revolution. We must regard historical reality in the way men perceived it at the time, in the way they believed it and transmitted it to us. And, similarly, instead of undertaking a global sociology of revolutions, I shall confine myself to the existence of widely diverse historical phenomena. It is not my purpose in this essay to construct either a sociology of various revolutions or, even less, a general history of revolution. My attitude is related to our times. The study of history or sociology can only provide a reference point for considering the present condition of revolution and the likelihood of revolution in the making. Under these circumstances, the problem for the reader will be to understand that we are here dealing concurrently with patterns and with history, which seems to be contradictory. Thus, in the first three chapters, it might appear that history is involved: the first ends with 1789, the second deals with the developments of 1789, and the third discusses revolutions after that date. But this is not altogether true. For the first chapter also presents the more or less direct relationship between revolt and revolution. The second aims at defining the intellectual thrust of revolution, while the third concerns a category of specific revolutions, those which take place "within the stream of history." And both of these orientations are necessary in order to comprehend the current situation. So we are dealing simultaneously with history and with concepts. I know that this combination is open to serious criticism. But here again I believe that sociological phenomena must be approached by various means. The important thing, in relation to our past, is to bear in mind the specificity of the times and to avoid projecting (as much as we ever can) our current attitudes upon the past, making it serve only to justify them.

AUTOPSY
OF REVOLUTION

[1]

FROM REVOLT TO REVOLUTION

Revolution Against History

Revolt

In his celebrated essay "The Rebel," Camus distinguished metaphysical revolt from historical revolt. He began by searching out the meaning of metaphysical revolt. He expressed the sensitivity of a human being. But he was led to this by literary works—so that his admirable analysis, which is undoubtedly valid on a certain level, does not return to human reality; and while the debate over Prometheus can go on forever, it has nothing in common with the *Croquants*—not even anything unconscious and involuntary. If one does not believe that literature is an act in itself, and perhaps the sole act (but not to believe this is not to be in temper with the times—I am obliged to accept this and am resigned to it!), then one must take the position that there is no revolt that is not historical, and that metaphysical revolt, ultimately a spiritual state or the adoption of a philosophical posture, has absolutely no

significance except for the person who experiences and com-
municates it. The only possible analysis of revolt is historical.
It is the only method of inquiry that will perhaps enable us to
find at least a partial answer in a human attitude toward life.
It is not valid to descend from the metaphysical to the historical. But the latter may perhaps evoke the former, or, better
still, in the pretentious vocabulary of our times, the "historial"
of revolt. In any event, it is impossible to treat the two revolts
separately. One alone exerts the force of reality.

There appear to be two permanent factors in every historical
revolt: the sense of the intolerable, and accusation.

Revolt breaks out, man becomes a rebel, a community revolts when an act, a situation, or a relationship becomes intolerable. It was possible to endure injustice, want, hunger,
oppression, and scorn up to a certain point, up to a certain
moment; then, suddenly, sometimes as a result of a seemingly
insignificant occurrence—no more significant, at any rate,
than any number of others—the rebel says No. The limit has
been reached. Now it is no longer possible to continue in the
same direction. "We have fallen into poverty, we are oppressed, we are crushed with labor, we are insulted, we are not
looked upon as men, we are treated like slaves who must
endure their harsh and wretched lot in silence—and we have
borne all this—but we are being pressed down relentlessly into
the pit of misery . . . we are driven to desperation, Sire, we
have gone beyond the bounds of patience. We have reached
that terrible moment when it is better to die than to prolong
unbearable suffering." [1]

This tragic passage summarizes everything that can possibly
be said about revolt. Now the daily pattern of existence has
become intolerable. This day-to-day, hand-to-mouth situation
cannot continue any longer—the final drop of water in the
brimming glass . . . when patience and the capacity to en-

---

[1] The workers of St. Petersburg petitioning the czar in January 1905; quoted
by Decouflé, *Sociologie des révolutions*, 1968, p. 29.

dure suffering have reached their limit. The rebel senses somehow that if the situation continues, he is bound to perish. If
he says No, it is not because of any principles or concepts but
because he cannot go on living *this way*. He is simply preserving himself. "He is fighting for the integrity of a part of
his being." He is at the edge of despair. Camus is clearly aware
of this, at the outset, when he writes: "It means that things
have gone too far. This far, yes, but no farther. . . . There is
a point beyond which you shall not go. . . . The No affirms
the existence of a boundary." But then, unfortunately, he
wanders off into arguments which lead him to the conclusion
that revolt necessarily implies the feeling of being right. There
is impatience only in the etymological sense of the word—no
more than that, I think. Yet this crushing pressure that brings
man to raise himself also brings him into history. This No,
hurled at a given instant, is in fact hurled in history. The
details are also part of history. It is not because the British
fleet (and, similarly, later the Russians on the *Potemkin*)
mutinied at Spithead in 1797 "owing to bad food and to inadequate leaves" that this event is without current significance. Today it is the practice among intellectuals, imbued as
they are with Leninism, to minimize revolt and to conceive
of revolution in different terms—majestic and profound. "In
order to be able to reconstruct and to mold history in its own
image, the revolutionary plan must begin by integrating and
interpreting it completely; popular revolt is indifferent to
history and breaks out only in response to a daily existence
that has become intolerable: the lack of this basic dimension is
what differentiates it . . . from the revolutionary plan." [2] In
any event, it is not because the rebel has no theoretical understanding of class relations or no broad conception of history,
etc., that he is somewhat removed from the latter. I would
readily say that the capacity to integrate history dehumanizes
revolution altogether, and that the popular upheaval of revolt
remains the expression of humanity. Not of metaphysical man

---

[2] Decouflé, op. cit.

but of man in his history. And what appears to me to bear out this reality is in fact the perpetual affirmation of it. "Things can no longer go on this way," in other words, a point has been reached beyond the two basic drives mentioned above: man revolts because the "no longer" is now the impossible. But it has nothing to do with feeling. From now on there is no purpose in seeking an *explanation* of the revolt or a reason for the ringleader's or the rebel's attitude. Countless volumes on the life of Spartacus or of Saint-Just, with all their attempted psychological nuances, testify to the futility of the search. And the failure of *Thomas Münzer* by Bloch and of the very recent *Nat Turner* by Styron [3] reveals the limitations, *in this area,* of both social psychology and psychoanalysis. All these men are enduring the impossible; history has gone along this way but cannot continue to do so. The logic of the situation, the unwieldiness of the machine, and the viscosity of reality clearly anticipate what is going to happen: there will be increasing oppression, increasing starvation. And this anticipation based on certainty is what the rebel rejects. He is involved directly in the stream of history. He realizes that he is more wretched today than he was ten years ago and that things can only get worse. Therefore he regards his history as an inevitable tragedy, as destiny—and it is out of despair that he says No. No to what? Simply to today's hunger? In fact, to tomorrow's hunger. And this is why revolt is firmly anchored to history; but it is a history that is being rejected.

All too frequently, of course, when we speak of freedom in defining revolt, its meaning is corrupted by our experience of history. For us, freedom has become the grist of philosophy or of political science. Hannah Arendt's book brings out this misunderstanding. But prior to the eighteenth century, freedom had another significance, a directly human one: escape from the unbearable, from the design of destiny whose immediate face was the oppressor. So the struggle against the oppressor is

---

[3] E. Bloch, *Thomas Münzer*, Fr. edn., 1966; William Styron, *The Confessions of Nat Turner*, 1968.

only secondary, indirect. Revolution is always constructive: it must open the way to exultant tomorrows; revolt is a titanic earth-rending upheaval in the face of an unknowable future. For this reason rebels often are conspirators, sworn comrades. Revolutionaries are not oath-takers. For, as Starobinski aptly expressed it: "Through the prime act of oath taking, the individual has accepted the death of his personal existence: he has committed himself to an ultimate choice in which man's essence is fulfilled—freedom, but at the cost of sacrificing everything unessential, namely everything that is not freedom —or death." Thus despair is in the very heart of revolt, in its initiation and its development. Revolutions are always acts abounding in hope. Death may occur; it is accidental. In revolt, death is at the very heart of the upheaval.

The echo of every revolt: "Wherever fear of hunger and fear of prison exist such as we know them, there is no room for fear of hell," one of the Ciompi ringleaders in Florence said. This bears out Emmanuel Mounier's statement on the risk involved in every revolt: "The joy of sacrifice and the perilous exaltation of death resides in them. Death is a ready answer that absolves one from seeking other answers." How often, in fact, has a revolt perhaps collapsed because the rebel, instead of looking for a satisfactory answer, has fixed its price no higher than the death of the first oppressor and his own death. Yet how often, too, was nothing else really possible in the quest for absolute freedom in the face of absolute suffering, as Marx would put it, for a revolt at the start can never sustain, never endure, never exact that which is less than eternal.

This is demonstrated by the numerous Negro slave revolts in the United States, organized by Gabriel Prosser in Richmond (1800), Bole Ferebee (1807), Denmark Vesey (Charleston, 1822), David Walker (1829), Nat Turner (Virginia, 1831) and Charles Deslones (1838).[4] Futile revolts that be-

---

[4] Aptheker, *American Negro Slave Revolts, 1526–1860,* 1958.

wilder us by the intense despair they convey in the single fact
that they inevitably lead to the gallows.

In comparison with the fashionable modern doctrines of
revolution, the efficient apparatus of Leninists and of others,
all of which aspire to interpret history in one way or another,
the rebel resembles a poor clod who refuses the history he has
already endured and can plainly foresee, which is in store for
him, clear as the light of day, tomorrow, as certain as the rising
sun. And this is why revolt is at once reactionary and mystical.
It is always reactionary in the sense that it rejects its immediate
past but favors a former and assuredly more satisfactory past:
"to restore the old order of things and thereby ease the
people's burden." "A return to the old customs. . . . They are
willing to pay the customary old taxes. . . . They are content
to have a king who rules according to custom." "What is
needed is a return to the good times of the States," said the
French rebels of the seventeenth century, but the Russian
rebels expressed it no differently: they wanted a true czar,
one who would restore the ancient rights of the peasants.[5] And
in the sixteenth century there was the same problem: the
German peasants rose "in order that things might be restored
to exactly the same state they once were in when men were
still free." [6] Similarly, in the Middle Ages, the revolt of the
Goliards, although it might appear to involve all of society,
turned out to be just as conformist and reactionary.[7] Does this
mean that it was not historical? We think of history only as
forward movement. For the people of that era, history was a
return to good times. Truth was to be found in the past. There
was no refusal to move forward, simply the desire to approach
a restoration of times when men had been free and had had
enough to eat. They had to abolish the inexorable degradation
of their condition. What was intolerable, finally, was to float
with the current. The normal flow of history had to be altered.

---

[5] These statements and numerous others are taken from the remarkable book
by R. Mousnier, *Fureurs paysannes,* 1967.

[6] E. Bloch, *Thomas Münzer, théologie de la révolution.*

[7] Vexliard, *Introduction à la sociologie du vagabondage,* 1956.

Yet, by the same token, there is almost always a mystical[8] element associated with this denial, for no one sees *how* to alter the normal course of this ill-fated adventure. One surprising question always remains when we study detailed descriptions of hundreds of these revolts: what did these peasants imagine when they rose in rebellion, hanged a tax-collector, put a chateau to the torch, or raided a caravan? Driven to desperation, they rose—and then what? We eventually learn that the revolt actually achieved nothing. But what could they really hope to gain? Did they not know that every rebellion, no matter where it occurs, inevitably meets with repression and every rebel with massacre or execution? And when a small victory is theirs, this band of insurgents suddenly falters, unable to proceed. The scholar will say: "They lacked a doctrine . . ." Agreed. This very fact made them rebels, against a destiny whose course they were trying to change, but without a plan for changing it. And because they rejected any further advance of history along the lines that their daily experience taught them to expect, they could not conceive of any tomorrow at all: revolt has no future, because this future can only be an aggravation of the present, and rebels are done with the present. This explains their passivity—when revolt is temporarily gaining ground or when it is collapsing. Either instance simply demonstrates the inability to create a future. But it also explains the mysticism that accompanies nearly every rebellion. There is no logical future, no conceivable positive transformation of the present, so one makes the leap to the end of time—a visualization of the ultimate future, of a society which has no community with the one being refused, and which is frequently a recovery of the ultimate and also visualized past. That blissful past before the fall. Revolt marches toward the Advent; it is a visionary quest for a totally free and equalitarian society, the kingdom of the millennium,

---

[8] Revolutionary messianism, outside the Western hemisphere, has been studied in detail (dealing with all the themes of revolt we mention here) by M. I. Pereira de Queiroz, "L'Homme et la Société," *Mouvements messianiques dans quelques tribus sud-américains*, 1968.

the restoration around Christ's tomb of the perfect society of
the poor, the revolt of John of Leyden or of Münzer and the
peasants, Joachim de Flore's rebellion, *"revolutio temporis*
returning to the *restitutio omnium,* the eschatological re-
version of all things to their pristine perfection," the revolt of
the *Nu-pieds* in Normandy and of the "army of suffering" that
sought to implement literally the equalitarian communism of
the Acts of the Apostles. And Métraux observes the same
characteristic in the revolt of the Indian masses: "The Empire
of the Incas shall be restored and gladness shall reign once
more throughout New Peru." It would be wrong to assume at
this point that any sort of fulfillment of history is occurring:
we are in the realm of myth, of projection into a mythical age
discovered spontaneously in the utmost suffering of the human
heart. In his intense despair, the rebel responds simultaneously
by rebelling and by casting himself into the myth. Only a sense
of greatness far surpassing human actions can compensate for
the experience of reality and for an act deriving from absolute
necessity, yet futile in essence. Thus revolt does not lead anywhere. Camus deludes himself when he counterbalances the
absolute No with a Yes. But this is metaphysics. Revolt does
not alter historical reality even if the causes of it are perfectly
legitimate or if it can provide its own objectives. But as
Mousnier points out, "the outcome of a rebellion on the one
hand, and its motives and objectives on the other, are different
matters." Even when revolt succeeds temporarily, it does not
know what to do with victory: this is Pancho Villa and Li
Tzu Chang (1644), who, having won absolute power, fail to
utilize it and collapse. Rebels never have more than a limited
view of the enemy at hand or of the misery that must be overcome, just as they are incapable of uniting regions that revolt
simultaneously. Rebels do not see beyond their own terrain
(the revolts of Spartacus, of the Jacques, of Münzer, of the
Torreben, of Le Gaoulé, etc.). And we should bear in mind
that because of these characteristics, revolt is definitely not a
small-scale revolution, or a near-successful one. These are

different categories. "Those peasants were raging savages, not revolutionaries" (Mousnier), "their outburst was not even an attempt at revolution." This also applies precisely to the great rising of the Peruvian Indians, instigated by Tupac Amaru in 1780.

Moreover, revolt may assume broad dimensions; it can fire a country—and even triumph. Revolt is not necessarily doomed to defeat or extermination; it may on occasion destroy the power and the social structures that incited it. But neither breadth nor victory can make revolt into a revolution. Between the rebellions of Spartacus and of Pancho Villa there is of course the gap separating failure from success, but there is a much closer relationship: an explosive adventure launched against an intolerable society, against a future void of hope— and Pancho Villa, as he takes power, soon does not know what to do. He is unable to organize or govern or make decisions. The same contrast exists between revolt and revolution as between the nomad and the man with fixed abode. The nomad can invade cities but then does not know what to do next. So he loots, burns, sacks, and remains a nomad, still camping in tents outside the cities he has just conquered. The rebel sometimes halts at that point where his rebellion is likely to succeed. He stops in the face of an impossible future. He does not know how to create history. There was a consultation before the arrest of Spartacus outside the gates of Rome, which was then defenseless and lay open to him. He had only to take the city. He did not take it—undoubtedly because of his confused state of mind, a characteristic of all rebels because they are not revolutionists. What would he have done with Rome, he who was only a leader of slave bands? He retreated from the image of power, from the necessity for organizing a society and from the order that he should have reestablished. He had no conception of government or administration. He must have realized this, so he returned to the mountains, letting victory slip from his grasp. His rebellion introduced no new principle into Roman society. But sometimes revolt strikes to the hilt.

And then we find a strange kind of destruction of societies. This is suggested by the Etruscans and the Mayans.

The Etruscan Empire, at the height of its power and before Rome was of consequence, underwent a serious crisis which was to cause its downfall. Neither the war with the Greeks nor even the invasion of the Gauls could have destroyed this power. During the first half of the fifth century B.C., revolts which cannot really be considered social or political broke out in most of the Etruscan cities. Strange revolts, threatening the Etruscan League, inciting conflicts in one city after another, bringing long periods of strife, and with very different regimes and leaders. These revolts succeeded in that they destroyed Etruscan order, federal unity, and economic activity. Successive waves of rebels took control but without ever establishing a new system and a coherent power, and it was amid this general turmoil that the Greeks finally won the war and Rome gained her independence. Revolt culminating in the destruction of Etruria—but not revolution. No one had sufficient vision to establish a new order, no one was capable of taking the situation in hand. Perhaps the same cause brought about the strange end of the Mayan Empire in 890, with the wholesale abandonment of cities and territories, which was not owing to war, epidemic, or famine. The hypothesis currently held by specialists in this field is precisely that of peasant rebellion against the reigning priesthood—a rising of peasants weary of forever raising more and more temples, a revolt against "the incredible folly of building that had invaded the priesthood . . . a folly that had assumed unbelievable proportions." So the revolt, victorious as it was, was not so much against wealth or power as against an excess of futile and ostentatious labor; it led, in victory, not to a new order but to the abandonment of these cities and temples and, shortly afterward, to the destruction of the Mayan society and its civilization, which was to emigrate. Thus the victorious revolt, obeying no laws but its own, faithful to its sources and to its origins, reached the moment of freedom which was to be rewarded by the death of that society in which it functioned.

There is nothing beyond victory. Victor or vanquished, the rebel moves only toward death. A choice he is unable to express, usually, but which means that for him death has become preferable to life. This unconscious choice, together with the desperate attempt to alter destiny, makes every revolt legitimate. The diversity of immediate motives does not change the profound reality of the sense of legitimacy that resides in the rebel. But the impossibility of the future has important consequences, and related to this is, first of all, the absence of a program. One plunges headfirst into rebellion, without knowing exactly what to do or where to go. There is the present impossibility of continued survival, and one moves in the unpredictable direction of the immediate and rejected past. In the course of revolt, numerous objectives certainly can appear. And this is indeed one of the characteristics of revolt: variability. Rebels hurl themselves at a tax-collector or at the bakeries to obtain bread; then, while the revolt remains self-sustaining for a while, it shifts direction, and temporary leaders propose actions that are always immediate and localized, but diverse. Very often it will get its second wind with the advent of repression: demonstrators have been arrested, so the revolt rebounds, demanding their freedom. They are to be tried, so it attempts to disrupt the trial. And occasionally, too, when authority (which is not really threatened) tries to gratify the rebels' demands, the revolt lashes back, just after positive measures have been adopted, to demand something totally different. This complete lack of decision is also evidence of the absence of a program and the inability to conceive of a planned and satisfactory future. Moreover, this is why revolt is "anti." It is almost never "pro." But this "anti" (which surges up in the face of a probable evolution) frequently strikes at what we would call progress. It is the result of everything we have already said about revolt and is confirmed by the facts: how many revolts have occurred because of, and in opposition to, a phenomenon of progress! We should not forget the periodic

rebellions of workers against machines. Those of 1832 are well
known, but there were also the revolts of the *Ongles bleus*
(blue fingernails) against the new crafts, the fifteenth-century
risings to protest the silk machines, the English rebellions
against the spinning jenny, the revolts of the Rhone workers
against the first steamboat. Inventions of the devil or fear of
unemployment: in each of these cases, revolt was aimed at
what we consider the symbol of progress. And we should
probably include among reactionary revolts all those that
arose in protest over crown taxes, the new tax during the
Middle Ages. The fiscal policies of the crown during the
fourteenth and fifteenth centuries incited mass risings all
over Europe, in Burgundy as well as in Scandinavia, in
Beauvais just as in Flanders, in England, and in Aragon. But
the opposition stemmed not so much from the burden of the
tax as from its novelty: the presence of the king's agents, who
were strangers. Revolt is rejection of a centralizing and remote
power.

An expression of backward attitudes, or lack of education,
perhaps; nevertheless revolt is there. Similarly, the rebellions
of the seventeenth century were motivated to a great extent
by the growth of the state—by its development, its administrative improvements, and expanded functions; but this
growth entailed spending, and in the people's eyes the spending was wasteful. They could no more understand administrative necessity or centralization than they could the necessity
of machines. "We are dealing with a retrograde and par-
ticularist political movement directed against the development
of the modern absolute state with its centralizing and consolidating functions" (but, on the other hand, Mousnier adds:
there is no trace of a social program), and this was true in
France (the *Nu-pieds*) as well as in Russia, with Stenka Razin
opposed to centralization and efforts to organize an administrative bureaucracy, and in China under the last of the Mings.

Similarly, Le Gaoulé [9] rose against the arrival of adminis-

---

[9] Petit Jean, *Le Gaoulé, révolte de la Martinique en 1717*, 1966.

trators responsible for establishing order out of the confusion in Martinique that followed Louis XIV's death. The administrators sought to rationalize the socioeconomic system, to integrate the economy, and to normalize the relations of power: they were regarded as disruptors of society in the service of the state, and this at once incited the reactionary rebellion. We should also bear in mind that the premises of the French Revolution were initially a reaction against a state seeking to improve itself: the famous struggle of the *parlements* against power constituted a defense of bourgeois privilege against the *progress* brought by the monarchy. The entire movement from 1780 to 1789 was one of reactionary revolution. The government effected remarkable reforms in all areas at this time, and its role was the progressive one. But the people refused to follow, bound by their traditional organization, their privileges, and their established situations: so power was termed despotic because it sought increasing rationality, even though the reforms it achieved were more liberal.

"Novelties" are intolerable in every country. Revolt is against progress.

The second major pole of revolt, the form of its existence, is accusation. For revolt to occur, there must be a clear and distinct identification of an enemy, of someone responsible for the general misfortune. Accusing someone else, pointing out injustice incarnate in another man, shifting one's own injustice and responsibility onto other shoulders, are essential facets of human nature and of the rebel's nature. This other party must be identifiable, cannot be too remote or too overwhelming. During the stage of accusing "somebody" or "them," revolt does not break out. However, the indignation toward the "somebody" or "them" can create a favorable climate for revolt. The mysterious "they" are blamed for monopolizing grain, for keeping money short, for requisitioning, for judging and condemning. . . . But as long as their face remains invisible, there can be no revolt. "They" must suddenly become someone. So an innocent traveler in no way connected with the accusations on the public tongue will suddenly catalyze, because he has misinterpreted some word or misread some scrap of paper, all this rancor and anger; he becomes a marked man, an expiatory victim, a scapegoat for the misfortunes of everyone.[10] This overwhelming misery and ruin must come from someone. Endured as a destiny we said, it is true, but a destiny for which someone is responsible. Pin the blame somewhere, preferably on whoever is closest at hand. Revolt cannot be appeased either by sociological analyses or by abstract objects held accountable for deprivation (the state), or by persons so remote that they are mythical (the king), or by groups that are more or less fluid (a class, for instance). Revolt lives in the immediate present, and it is here that the responsible person must be found; the accusation falls upon the man who is *here*. Just as the rebel sees the apocalypse on his horizon, in the movement that hurls him along, so his accusation takes a concrete form. The enemy, source of his grief, is bound to be at hand, within striking distance. For this enemy is indeed a scapegoat who must be sacrificed and must suffer for the sins of the people. And, in the end, the enemy massacred by the rebel, though flesh and blood, is no doubt the symbol of all and every execration. The fundamental act of accusing someone whose face is known involves three principle signs. We have said that the phenomenon of revolt is closely linked to the phenomenon of the state (without there being any all-encompassing relationship), and this applies to Western Europe as well as to Russia or even China. Whether it is a modern state in the process of establishing itself, with its authority bearing down relentlessly, whether it is an oppressive, tyrannical state attempting to expand its sway over free peoples ("the period of strife in Russia was fundamentally caused by the development

---

[10] What I say is in no sense imaginary; it happens frequently in every revolt—for example, the massacre of Poupine at the start of the *Nu-pieds* rebellion.

of the state"), or whether it is a well-organized state, as in China, but one whose excessive organization loosens its hold on reality and leaves it unable to control the economic and social world—what happens then is what we might call a crisis of the state that begets rebellion ("actions on the part of the state much more than social conflicts appear to be the motive for revolts"). Moreover, the state in China and in Russia seems to generate social conflicts in the period under discussion (the seventeenth century). "The revolts during the seventeenth century in France, Russia, and China were re-actions against the state" (Mousnier). This thesis is strongly supported by a historical analysis which I find indisputable. And I could apply it generally to many other periods of revolt without, of course, universalizing it. In the final analysis, the important point here is the following: the state is an abstraction. And if it is the true core of revolt, the crux of the problem, the rebel, owing to his need for a scapegoat, cannot react to it in this form. He then attacks the *agents* of the state—the one nearest at hand and, hence, the most despised. The servant of government becomes the very face of the state. Though he be merely a modest administrator, usually at a rather low level, he is the incarnation of everything hated, the immediate ex-perience, all the rest of which is mere abstraction. The army recruiter, the tax-collector, the provost, and the bailiff are the ones who will fall to the desperate wrath of the people. It has to be an individual. There is no such thing as revolt endured against an abstract state. And this is also why, traditionally, in the course of revolt the king or czar does not come under attack: he is much too remote and abstract. He is not a human being. This issue does not exist for the rebel.

The second sign of this profound reality of revolt is the minor role of social classes or even strata.[11] Today it is the fashion to interpret every insurrection, rebellion, or revolt in

---

[11] The term "social classes" is, in general, historically incorrect for designat-ing the social strata of societies prior to the eighteenth century. Cf. J. Ellul, *Revista di Storia amministrativa,* 1968.

terms of class conflict. Yet this is absolutely incorrect from a historical point of view. It would take feats of aerial gymnastics to fit the classes to the existing facts. Rebel groups frequently consist of people from social milieus which differ greatly and which, according to the class theory, ought even to be hostile to each other.

This is a firmly established fact: revolts and revolutions prior to the end of the eighteenth century are really not expressions of the class struggle. In the fourteenth century we find an alliance of "peasants-bourgeois-nobles" or "craftsmen-bourgeois" in all the revolutionary movements. The Cabochiens were bourgeois and workers, the Ciompi were nobles and workers, just as in most of the Italian cities of that period the aristocrats made common cause with the *populo minuto;* the League of Public Welfare was a coalition of nobles, but its base of support was the common people. The popular risings in Flanders were nearly always led by nobles, and Cazelles's detailed study depicts the nobility acting in concert with Étienne Marcel's movement.[12] "The nobility was not the scapegoat of the [French] Revolution; it was, on the contrary, its moving force. Those who incurred suspicion or were held in disgrace were the ones who had diverted the kingdom's wealth to their own ends. . . . Those who were looked to for salvation were the educated people . . . those with an established fortune." This is where hope lies for a rebel people. In addition, the clergy was often involved directly in the French Revolution, rarely hostile, sometimes in the front ranks. And they were not merely representatives of the lower clergy but included bishops as well. Once they had expressed their convictions, churchmen became "insurgents." The sixteenth century bears this out. One great historian, convinced as he was of the weight of social circumstances, recognized nevertheless that: "From the influence of social issues upon the religious wars, it would be all too easy for simple minds to

---

[12] Cazelles, "Les Mouvements révolutionnaires du milieu du XIV⁰ siècle," *Revue Historique,* 1962.

infer that the free workers or those who were bound to associations, the victims of an already capitalistic *patronal*
oligarchy, served to recruit the Protestant militias . . . and
that the guild masters supported the Guise faction, but the
truth is more complex: there were Protestant *patrons,* and
the populace of Paris, along with their trade associations,
proved to be one of the strongest forces in the League." [13]

The Fronde, for example, was a fusion of nobles and
bourgeois, lords and peasants, etc. In most of the seventeenth-
century revolts, we find bourgeois groups, now from the upper
bourgeoisie, now from the lower bourgeoisie, inciting the unrest. Peasants or "workers" followed suit. But we also find
revolts led by *gentilshommes* or by priests. And it is especially
important to note that the latter were at times the leaders, at
times the led. It would be entirely superficial to suppose, for
instance, that the lord of a district raised a rebellion for
personal motives and enlisted his peasants. Countless risings
occurred in just the opposite way. The peasants were the ones
who touched off the spark, who set a region in turmoil and
then looked around for someone to captain their battles. These
leaders might be priests, as in the revolt of the *Nu-pieds,* who
were backed, however, by large sectors of the *gentilshommes,*
or might be a local lord distinguished for his military reputation. And many a time the great lords intervened between
their rebellious peasants (whom they protected from oppression) and the central authority—as late as the seventeenth
century. At any rate, among the accusations hurled at the
rebels one theme keeps recurring: "We could easily quell them
if the protection of the *gentilshommes* did not set them in open
rebellion." And this situation was not peculiar to France.
Revolts in every period of history involved mixed social milieus
without any sharp divisions between economic and social
interests. Of course, a rising against local lords might occur, or
a rebellion of the peasant against the city (in general, and
regardless of the social condition of the city dweller), or strife

<hr>

[13] H. Hauser, *Sources de l'Histoire de France au XVIe siècle,* Vol. III, 1948.

between the bourgeois and the rich peasant. But there was
also participation of rich and poor alike in rebellion against a
common oppressor (for example, the alliance of the rich,
established Old Cossacks and the nomadic, poor Cossacks in
1660 against the evolving Russian state).

There is evidence, too, of a relationship, and sometimes a
solid bond, among the different "classes" within the rebel
movements of the eighteenth century. Almost everywhere the
nobles made common cause with the peasants. The clergy
took a major role and were often in the forefront of insurgence.
In a very detailed study, Hours [14] stresses that a climate of persistent violence existed corresponding to a generally rebellious
attitude: the grain revolts and the violence unleashed on the
tax-collectors or the army recruiters were not echoes of class
struggle but rather evidence of "vertical solidarities" among
the members of a single group.

One should certainly not believe that the "interpretation"
of revolutionary phenomena as an expression of class conflict
involves a more penetrating analysis reaching beyond the
appearance of events; it is, on the contrary, a very simplistic,
dogmatic, and unreal interpretation when it is generalized.

And what a maze of problems it presents when it comes to
the French Revolution! Was there not first of all a revolt of the
nobility against the monarchy, as well as a revolt of the rich
bourgeoisie (1787–8)? And it was this revolt, produced by
widely different currents, that generated the popular outbreak,
which in itself possessed no distinct class character. The
revolution of the aristocracy struck out, after 1787, against
royal absolutism, while the bourgeois (notably those of the
legal profession) opposed certain reforms which they considered unacceptable, and out of this grew great fear and the
rising of the Paris populace. It is doubtful that the two latter
movements could have come alive without the preceding
ones. It was, in fact, the revolt of the aristocrats that trans-

---

[14] Hours, "Émeutes et émotions populaires dans le Lyonnais au XVIIIe
siècle," *Cahiers d'Histoire*, 1964.

formed itself into widespread agitation.[15] Let us pose the question, Who began the revolts? In the sixteenth, seventeenth, and eighteenth centuries, it appears that very often it was not the most impoverished or the most disinherited; frequently there was pressure from leaders, princes, aristocrats, or the *parlement* of Paris, and thus neither material poverty nor class conflict was initially at the source. Mass uprisings were instigated by controlling classes—not that they assumed the leadership or fomented intrigue, but they created a climate, they leveled accusations, they pointed to the widespread existence of disorder, injustice, and poverty. Moreover, because revolt, as we have said, is normally reactionary, these controlling classes are the first to want to revert to a former status which seemingly afforded them greater privilege. But, at that juncture, the people intervened each time and made common cause with its "class enemies" against an enemy that was even more intolerable, even more evident. Evidence plays a major role in revolt: a class is not a concrete, identifiable enemy. It is an abstraction, and for a class to be a motive for revolution, a certain educational foundation must have been given the masses, a moral awakening must have occurred, an unmasking: the "theoretical-practical" designation of the real enemy.

Related to this is the belief on the part of modern historians that social inequality has not always been the cause of traditional revolt.

It is difficult today to understand that the social issue of exploitation never played an important part in revolts prior to the eighteenth century. For although it is true that "the people" periodically rebelled against their masters, we should not confuse the historical "people" with the poor. The struggle, for instance, between the plebeians and the patricians in Rome had nothing to do with the struggle between poor and rich. The notion that all revolutions have a social origin is a pure and simple assumption fostered by Marxism. It is historically

---

[15] Godechot, *Les Révolutions de 1770 à 1799*, 1965.

incorrect. The social issue has played a revolutionary role only since the end of the eighteenth century. To arrive at it, men had first to be convinced that poverty was not the destiny of mankind, that the division between "aristoï," "oligoï," and the rest was not "natural." In other words, economic growth had to appear and raise the issue of a destined deprivation, and the image of potential abundance had to fill the eyes of the multitudes: at that point poverty and the inequity of distribution became causes of revolution, not before.

One more factor exerts an obvious influence, although we cannot react to it concretely: value. We know the important role Camus assigned to value in rebel activity. Camus put no special emphasis on the act of accusation. He said, simply in passing: "Along with a feeling of repulsion for the intruder, there occurs in every revolt a total and instantaneous identification of man with a part of himself. Therefore he implicitly allows a value judgment to intervene. . . . He weighs that which is preferable against that which is not. Not every value leads to revolt. But every rebel movement tacitly invokes a value. A moral awakening, however confused it may be, emerges from rebellion: the sudden and blinding awareness that there is something in man with which man can identify. . . . If man is willing to die in the act of rebellion he thereby demonstrates that he is sacrificing himself for a good he considers far greater than his own fate. . . . He is thus acting in behalf of a value that is as yet confused but which he senses is a common bond among all men. . . . Yet the foundation of this value is the revolt itself. Human solidarity is built upon the act of revolt, and the latter in turn finds its sole justification in this complicity." This passage clearly defines Camus's position. And we can understand why the philosopher thinks this way: it is far more consoling to believe that this decisive act is performed in the name of a value. But unfortunately, this unconscious, confused, and implicit value, this value which, in the final outcome, is merely the rebel himself and his complicity, this value which is self-identification, is something the philosopher has deduced, has assumed, has in some way invented. I am not sure that one can really isolate it. If revolt is the physical refusal to continue, if it approaches the reaction of a donkey who lies down at the roadside because he cannot go one step farther—beat him all you want, he won't budge—if it is this refusal to go on living an impossible existence, then there is no value. There is simply an impossibility. But if we consider bourgeois and aristocratic rebellions, they are often a rejection of change, a turning inward, the repudiation of a risk or of a liberality. I can see no value. And if we look at the principal aspect of accusation, which is the designation of a scapegoat, again we have trouble identifying this value. I try to justify myself, try to declare my innocence of the wrong being done, so I condemn someone else. It is all well and good on Camus's part to stress the value of solidarity and of complicity in revolt. He forgets too soon that revolt is directed against, that it ruptures solidarity and therefore destroys, value. Pilate, in order to convict Jesus, yielded to a rebellion of the Jewish people. Admitting that this people possessed a value, and that its complicity with Barabbas constituted a value, the value nevertheless was created solely at the cost of the innocent victim's life. And I would certainly never call the victims of revolt innocent men. But even when revolt strikes true and condemns the real cause of oppression, suffering, and misfortune (which does not happen often, for how many witches were slain in rebellions and held responsible for pestilence or for drought . . .), there is the initial urge to shift one's sins onto another person, to purge oneself by an act of execration. Where is the value? I am afraid it is only in the philosopher's mind. Certainly a value frequently appears in rebel movements (at least in the Western world) when they have left a written legend: freedom. Not so much as a principle or a general declaration, but as a very concrete force on the most humble and mundane level—reaching out to rid the world of the ancestry of taxation. Freedom is the battle against taxes or tax officials, the will to preserve the ancient charters.

Until the seventeenth century, these constantly recurring

words—revolt, strife, rebellion, agitation—never describe attempts to create a new order, or the desire for a new form of
society or government, or even for the advent of a *new*
freedom, despite the fact that the "backlash" of freedom is
what has triggered all the turmoil.

This was the steady trend from the twelfth century until
the beginning of the eighteenth. At the same time the nomad
retains his desire to remain free to wander over the land.
Revolts of the serfs, revolts of the Cossacks and of the Indians
against the colonizers, slave rebellions and revolts of conquered peoples against their conquerors; the prodigious adventure of Ishi.[16] I believe that concrete freedom (which is not
a value) was the sole "concept" called forth specifically in the
course of rebellion until the concept of social injustice emerged
and completely transformed the perspective of revolt. But in
the historical period under consideration, I do not think we
can venture so far as to make value a creative nucleus, a decisive impulse, for revolt.

"Situation" and "occasion": revolt does not flare up unless
a particular situation is established and tends to continue. In
dealing with the problem of revolt, we always find a situation
in which man found himself and an occasion that provoked its
repudiation. Let us not speak of causes, whether immediate
or long-range; the cause lies in some secret reflex of the human
heart that contracts the entire organism into the momentous
No that we have discussed. But this No exists only in relation
to a given situation and as a function of a provocative occasion.
I am deliberately speaking of "situations" and not of structures,
so the problem becomes confused and invites debate.

For the past half century, historians have tried to define
"revolt" and "revolution" in terms of a set of structures. The
ideology of classes and of the class struggle has so colored
our thinking that we can no longer evaluate history in any
other light. Even if we escape this pitfall, the conviction re-

---

[16] Kroeber, *Ishi*, 1968.

mains that everything is traceable to a particular structure of social relations. So one seeks to define revolt within that system. Although this doctrine is still accepted by a majority of historians, extensive and painstaking studies now cast doubt on the validity of these interpretive formulas. Let us examine a few examples of this research in the area of structures.

Some say that "the spirit of revolt is hard put to manifest itself in societies in which inequities are great (the Hindu caste system), or, on the other hand, in those where equality is absolute (certain primitive societies). In society, the spirit of revolt can exist only among those groups in which a theoretical equality masks profound factual inequalities." This, however, is not correct and is simply a confusion between revolt and revolution. Many revolts occur in caste societies. And, as Gurvitch points out, magic is a type of revolt in "primitive" society. Similarly, Decouflé maintains that there is scarcely ever a revolutionary plan in societies in which "residual poverty" exists. The marginal poor (but not the excluded) would be incapable of attaining the minimal level of aspiration for creating the conditions essential to a revolutionary plan. But the network of alienations stemming from marginality—more insidious because they are more diffuse—implants a culture of poverty that rules out the development of a revolutionary plan. Acute as that analysis may be, it does not, in my opinion, correspond to the facts: revolt, pure and simple, has occurred in excluded groups without producing anything more, without a revolutionary plan (the case of the Hebrews in Egypt, for example, which I consider significant). Decouflé in particular draws two conclusions from the analysis which appear untenable to me: "Marginality produces in the marginal man a kind of explicit illegitimacy," whereas the whole history of revolt proves, on the contrary, that rebel groups have a heightened awareness of the legitimacy of their rebellion. But this is based on the affirmation that "the marginal poor are powerless to infuse themselves into revolt." Here Decouflé is surely confusing revolt with revolution. We reiterate that revolt has no plan. But what of the many revolts that do indeed involve the marginal poor (for instance, today's rebellion of black Americans) as well as the excluded poor? It would appear that there is likely to be, on the contrary, a greater propensity for revolt among the excluded poor in the case of generalized poverty, and a greater propensity for revolution in the case of residual poverty (in industrial societies): where there is a global expansion of a society's economy, revolution takes root, becomes organized, and shapes a revolutionary plan for itself among the marginal members of that society. It seems to me that history does not entirely confirm Decouflé's analysis.

Others try to explain revolution in terms of the contradiction between the judicial and the economic situations. Whenever the code of justice is improved while economic conditions remain the same, there is a tendency toward revolt, for economic deprivation becomes increasingly intolerable when one has the advantage of exercising political rights and can express oneself validly in the available legal forms. Conversely, when the economic status of a group rises but its legal status remains stationary, there is a tendency toward revolution. The classic example is that of the bourgeoisie at the end of the eighteenth century. Undoubtedly there is some truth in this, but it seems extremely vague and inadequate. These structures may serve advantageously, but they generate nothing. We would need to prove that all revolutions have occurred within a structure showing evidence of this lag, and, conversely, that every structure of this type induces a revolution: we are a long way from that. The equation is so flimsy that it is of scant use to us. The same criticism applies to Janne's [17] analysis of structure as a determinant of revolution: revolution supposedly flares up as the result of a twofold malfunction of an institutional nature—the inability of the controlling classes to

---

[17] H. Janne, "Un Modèle sociologique du phénomène révolutionnaire," *Annales, Économies, Sociétés, Civilisations,* 1960. We will examine this analysis in detail in the next chapter.

maintain their functional role and of the institutions of
authority to deal with social conflicts. This goes back to the
idea that revolution is unleashed not by the might of rebellion
but by the abdication of power (in its two forms: class and
government). But this malfunction derives, according to
Janne, from the failure of those institutions to assimilate
technological advances and to incorporate them into the
existing structures—Ogburn's concept of "cultural lag." It is
difficult to leap from a specific fact (revolution occurs when
power is already weakened and helpless) to an analysis of
structure, and especially to a generalization. Many revolts and
a number of revolutions have taken place in societies in which
the controlling class and the power structure retained command, in which no astounding technological progress heralded
the impending earthquake. And how does one account for the
relationship between nonassimilated technological progress
and revolution? Here again historical events provide no
certainty, no generalization, because ultimately revolution is
a function not of structure, but of conjuncture, and revolt even
more so. Of course one or another structure may be advantageous, but no essential relationship is established. To pin-
point reality, we must concentrate on the conjuncture, which
can be resolved into a situation and an event. In the relationship between situation and occasion lies the fulfilled potential
of revolt. By regarding as "situations" the factors frequently
called "structural," we can agree as to the distortions in the
judicial and economic sectors, class relations, failure to absorb
technological progress, weakening of central power, failure
of the controlling class to fulfill its role: these are situations
(such as the stirring of a sense of nationalism, class rivalries,
etc.) which, among many other factors, characterize an
ever-shifting picture of events. We simply cannot isolate from
the extraordinary diversity of history a *single* denominator
that is common to and valid for all these situations and would
stand for structure. On the other hand, if we are to understand the phenomenon of revolution, we must take into

account the entire society that produces it and not isolate a factor—political, social, or economic—as if it alone were the ultimate and determining one. We must look at all of them together and in relation to one another in order to see the true conditions under which revolt and revolution have been possible and have been fomented.

The situations are as numerous as the examples of distortion in the judicial or the financial systems. In 1636, the people of Saintonge were disadvantaged as to tax levies in relation to the Bordeaux populace. Elsewhere, the peasants regarded the city dwellers as invaders, merciless competitors for a culture or for a local industry. Whole regions were prostrated regularly by pestilence or famine. Economic recessions occurred, often accompanied by financial distress, a condition also produced by great natural disasters when they are recurrent: drought for several years running, or a series of severe winters. Then surely revolt stems from the famine and pestilence; but more than that, it is a rebellion against the heavens, against divine injustice and the impossibility of surviving in the face of uncertainty and the expectation of floods or hail. So revolt is preceded by solemn expiatory ceremonies, processions, and supplications; if they do not succeed, there is always the option of revolt. On the same plane, a serious epidemic creates a revolutionary situation, as did the Black Death (violence unleashed against the Jews, who were blamed, and also against the rich, who, on that particular occasion, became the target of hate for a starving populace); futile and short-lived outbreaks of fear and anger, foremost among them the *Jacquerie,* which was terrible but brief, blind and sporadic, an expression of general instability and hatred of everything outside itself. Economic crises, often rural in origin, and "the landless becoming the unemployed produced the *Jacques* of the French plains, the *Tuchins* of Languedoc, the Lollards of southern England, the *Maillotins* of Paris, the *Coquillards* of Burgundy" (Favier).

"Economic stagnation leads to rebellion," of course, for it

is experienced most directly. In the eighteenth century, Le Gaoulé too was the result of Martinique's economic disorder. As for the end of the eighteenth century, Godechot concludes that the countless revolts during that period were one aspect of the economic crisis: a crisis brought on by rising prices (in America, 1763–77), by meager harvests (in Europe, 1770–89), by the collapse of certain prices owing to overproduction (the wine industry in France, 1770–89), and, in general, whatever the cause, by economic stagnation. But a situation that obviously should not be overlooked was the sudden increase of wars: revolt thrives upon war, violence upon violence, either directly in the lands pillaged by armies or indirectly through augmented taxation. A military defeat or a lingering "martyrdom" on the battlefield is a situation that can spread and spark motion. We know now that the mutinies of 1917 are traceable to misery, to infantry demonstrations against the senseless decimation of its ranks, to exhaustion, and to the failure of hopes that had bolstered the May offensive, much more than to pacifist and revolutionary propaganda.[18]

But a religious crisis, a crisis of conscience, the loss of faith in accepted values or in a certain scale of values, may also become the dominant factor in a situation and color everything else. There is no proof that religious ferment is generated by socioeconomic influences; it may occur by itself and determine other ferment. Luther's act touched off a general explosion, and though his beliefs were perhaps no more than dimly understood in his time, his protest released smoldering unrest and soon took the form of violent revolution: that of Münzer and of Schaffhausen, widespread revolts in Switzerland and Germany, Anabaptists and *Schwarmgeister,* the devout of Münster, and Wullenwever in Lübeck. The Peasant Party leaders were a priest and a blacksmith. From 1521 to 1535 there was constant unrest, the scope of which some scholars insist on confining to that of a social rebellion, whereas it was

---

[18] Pedroncini, *Les Mutineries de 1917,* 1968.

first and foremost a religious one. But the loss of values
suddenly renders intolerable a social or economic situation
that was otherwise bearable. The social and economic factors
are the pretext and not the basis; they are the cause only in
so far as there is no longer any reason to go on living and
what made life bearable has disappeared. When there is a loss
of values, it is not reality we see but the utter absurdity of
everything. Nothing makes sense any longer, and consequently
the lot of all mankind also becomes intolerable. To interpret
these revolts as proof that religion is an ideological curtain
and the opium of the people is to admit absolute ignorance of
one of the aspects of revolution.

However you look at it, the revolt of the Netherlands against
Spain in 1580 was a religious phenomenon before it became
an economic or social one, and the opposing forces were in no
sense uncertain as to why they were fighting. When a group
comes to recognize the specificity of its values, when the
commonly accepted values disintegrate, then there is a situation that normally produces revolution. The same holds true
when we have a society that violence seems to permeate,
forming a general pattern, a "culture of violence," as Harris
characterizes the United States.[19] He shows how the "climate"
of American society has evolved all along from violence, and
that violence is widely condoned: witness the growth of
slavery in a "free" society, the relegation of Indians to reservations, the recognition of lynch law, segregation in churches
as well as in trade unions. Physical or other acts of violence
alone are not sufficient to produce a potentially revolutionary
situation, which is mainly the conflict between proclaimed
values and the direct experience of reality: the fact that a
society in which equality and freedom are constantly affirmed
and held aloft is in reality a society in which violence is
regularly practiced with the intent to curtail the rights of
some members and to deny the equality of others. It constitutes a highly explosive situation.

---

[19] Clarence J. Harris, *Aerospace Technology and Urban Disorders*, 1968.

Of course, we should not overlook the tension between social groups. Although this is not the key to revolution, we should bear in mind, for example, the monarchy's political game of relying now on the "third estate" for support, now on the aristocracy, and ultimately inciting conflicts among social groups. Specifically, at the end of the eighteenth century, and in every country, the struggle between heads of state and various aristocratic corps led either the kings to make common cause with the Third Estate against the nobles (Austria and Sweden) or the aristocracy to stir up the people against the king (France and America). All these situations, in one way or another, created conditions favorable to revolt. Equally favorable conditions were to be found later on in the remoteness of power and of the seat of power; a certain isolation; difficulties of communication; economic instability; the demands of the state, unmitigated by its control over its own agents;[20] or even the rapid growth of slave and serf populations (in Rome and in seventeenth-century Russia).

One condition that Mousnier helpfully has brought out is social mobility. The existence of such mobility often engenders revolt as a means of improving the lot of a particular social group. But it prevents revolt from developing into revolution. In contrast, a stationary society provokes revolution. But in this connection, I wish to emphasize the transformation (progressive, or authoritarian as in seventeenth-century Russia) of a mobile society into an immobile one,[21] that is, a society in which progress and fluidity are arrested by external factors, or by a social consensus tending toward a social equilibrium that is not open to challenge even if political antagonisms exist, for a social consensus is not identical with—nor does it correspond to—a political consensus. Such discord in respect to government is of minor importance in a society immobilized by a seemingly general type of consensus applying to the society itself. It is perhaps this rigidity that places the in-

---

[20] Mousnier, op. cit., p. 339.
[21] Hoffmann, "Paradoxes," in *À la Recherche de la France*, 1963.

dividual in a specific situation of prerevolt, and in a way it explains both the reactionary and the apocalyptic nature of revolt. In any event, we are aware of the importance of conjuncture to the phenomenon of revolt and may even ask whether revolts are not essentially a matter of conjuncture. Supposing someone were to say: "Events alone are enough to explain revolts (of the peasants in France, Russia, and China during the seventeenth century). Similar conditions would have produced them in any society, would have sown desperation anywhere and a subsequent chain of angry explosions, without social structures being at issue." He would be advancing a theory that is perhaps incorrect, but that would not raise an eyebrow.

Other investigations seem wholly to confirm this theory. But it is impossible to provide a general rule covering the relationship between revolt and a given situation. The latter can only be the favorable factor, as revolt remains a human act, in a certain situation and on certain occasions. And as we have already said, the conjuncture has two components: a situation (certain examples of which we have just given) and an occasion. The man living in an economic depression or in the wake of a vast epidemic rebels when the situation is complemented at a particular moment by an occasion. There would be no purpose in listing all such occasions; they are endless. For the French army fighting in Romania in 1918, the occasion consisted of the bitter cold weather, the absurdity of having to battle former allies and collaborate with the Germans, and the injustice of being kept under arms after the war was over. As for the mutiny of the Black Sea fleet, the occasion (really quite incidental) was the assignment of a coal-stoking detail for Easter Sunday. The impassioned summons of a prophet or a religious enthusiast (Münzer or Nat Turner), or an attempted murder that shocks the public are still other occasions. And how many times has revolt followed the rape of a Lucretia, provided the accident is exploited by a tribune! But a tribune is powerless to act unless some unforeseen circumstance arises: Étienne Marcel, Van Artevelde, Cola di Rienzi, Münzer, Wat Tyler, and John of Leyden are all "occasions." The confessions of Nat Turner reveal the gradual development of values in one of these ringleaders of rebellion, of revolt, of revolution. But his words are only the occurrence of a moral awakening, the manifestation of a slow process of maturation. Yet just as important as the action taken by a leader is the presence of marginal members of society, who provide either an example, or a nucleus of crystallization, or an incitement. This seems to play a significant role in occasioning revolt. The existence of bandits, for one example: yet, as Vexliard has pointed out, the term is ambiguous.[22] He cites historic illustrations of guerrilla fighters who carried on internal warfare, disaffected members of society who fled to the forests and mountains with common criminals. During periods of oppression, these bandit groups might win the sympathy of the poor, but they might also be regarded as oppressors. The bands operated under the command of a local leader whose personality was the cohesive force binding the members into a unit. But the gap between banditry and revolt is quickly bridged once the former assumes a political orientation (the *bagaude* in Gaul from the third to the fifth century). At this stage the outlaws attract and enlist the support of local populations, who swell the original nucleus into an army. The bandit leader becomes the leader of a political revolt. This also applies to the great Chinese rebellion of 1636–43. Bandits, army deserters, and peasants evading taxation ended up with a commander, Li Tzu Cheng, who formed a rebel army and became (for a brief time) emperor. And afterward, they all reverted to open lawlessness.

Tramps also play a part: sometimes, quite by accident, the presence of tramps occasions revolt. Vexliard describes the revolts from the sixteenth to the eighteenth century which were incited by popular sympathy for one or two tramps who

----

[22] Vexliard, op. cit., pp. 126 *ff*.

had been arrested and misused by the local soldiery. Riots followed, aimed at freeing a prisoner or preventing the imprisonment of beggars; [23] D'Argenson speaks of the "unreasoned compassion of the Paris populace" and the demonstrations in support of paupers which broke out everywhere. They are all the more significant because they represent, not the self-defense of the social body or a group's defense of its own interests, but, on the contrary, the defense of an outlaw, a nonmember, who, under normal circumstances, would be a target for suspicion. But should we lend credence to this "unreasoned compassion," or was it not instead a reaction against interference on the part of an agent of the State? In any event, the fact remains that the existence of these vagabonds (bandits, beggars, Cossacks, etc.) in a society constitutes a permanent occasion for potential revolt. [24] Here again the tramp plays only a passive role, whereas the vagabond, on the contrary, can assume a very active part in fomenting revolt. This may happen either in the case of a roving band, which, in the course of its movements, gathers up an entire population, or in the case of a man who becomes the key element: Bolotnikoff, Stenka Razin, and countless others since the era of Spartacus—a leader who launches a revolt the success of which depends on the over-all situation. But it may also be said that under the authority of an outstanding individual, a roving band will frequently balloon, with the support of local populations, into an army. This occurred constantly under the Roman Empire from the third century to the fifth, as it did in China from the thirteenth to the fifteenth, etc. The summons of a rebel and the presence of an armed band are ever-recurring occasions inspiring man to reject his destiny.

This may also apply to the contagion of a revolt, or what others call its solidarity. These phenomena have not actually been studied, but they surely exist: it is almost certain that after the revolt of Saintonge in 1636, the vanquished

---

[23] Vexliard, op. cit., p. 205.
[24] In regard to the Cossacks, see Mousnier, op. cit., pp. 164 *ff*.

Saintongeais fled to Périgord, and then, in 1637, the revolt of the *Croquants* broke out; that the Breton countryside revolted in 1675 on the heels of and in the image of the rebellions of Rennes and Bordeaux is equally certain. Since that time, how many sympathetic strikes, for example, have occurred? Yet we know very little about the scope or mechanism of this factor. Is there any justification for talking of revolutionaries plotting a conspiracy, or of the fervor that harried rebels have aroused in a place to which they have brought news of momentous events?

Generally speaking, it would appear that we may discount the influence of conspiracies. We know for certain that, barring exceptions, conspiracies do not provoke revolt. Although we once held the extensive influence of secret societies, of the Freemasons, and of a variety of intrigues to be the source of the French Revolution of 1789, we have wisely relegated all that to the archives of romanticism. Similarly, Godechot speaks of the rash of conspiracies in Hungary between 1790 and 1794, conspiracies of the Jacobins and others,[25] none of which had any effect. We also know that the notion of conspiracy was widely accepted as an explanation of the Commune, yet what a minor role it played! Lefèbvre has made an excellent analysis of the difference in influence between the Internationalists, who, as individuals, had a broad impact, and the International, which had practically none.[26] The permanent conspiracies mounted by Blanqui were never channeled into a revolt any more than was that of the *Synarques,* etc. Actually, conspiracy undoubtedly had a considerable effect on what is called "palace revolution": it is still the surest device for dispatching tyrants, but it has nothing in common with revolt. The conspirator is a man bound by his system and his problem, blind and insensitive to the general situation. Conspiracy is the most ill-advised path to revolution. Lenin explained that admirably. And it explains why Camus is in error when he gives equal

[25] Godechot, op. cit., p. 151.
[26] Lefèbvre, *La Proclamation de la Commune,* 1965.

weight to nihilist conspirators and rebel or revolutionary mobs. It is true that the former are "metaphysical rebels," but they are simply conspirators, much like those of the sixteenth century, for example, despite their philosophic stature. Conspiracy serves adequately to destroy a man or a building, but it leads no further. Very rarely does it set off a revolt, and when it does, I would venture that the revolt is the result of chance, of the fortuitous conjuncture of a situation and this accident. For the conspirator is completely unaware of the situation, having only a superficial contact with that sector of the population which is in a potential state of revolt.

However (as we have already noted in connection with the *Croquants*), the infusion into a given group of a handful of outside rebels or revolutionists may assume considerable significance. We have come to assess more accurately the influence of the hordes of foreign revolutionaries who poured into France just before 1789, bringing with them their roving style of life, their frustrated hopes, and their determination to rebel: forty thousand Dutchmen after the failure of the revolt of the Lowlands in 1787, nearly ten thousand Belgians, and all of the democratic Swiss leaders on the heels of the risings in Fribourg, Geneva, etc. (1781). Many of them reappeared in Mirabeau's circle. These are known facts. But an interesting question has been raised in connection with the influence exerted by returning French troops after the American War of Independence. About six thousand soldiers came back home filled with revolutionary ideas. The map of their native districts matches almost exactly the map of the rural insurrections of 1789. Pure coincidence? [27] Whatever the answer is, it appears certain that in a given situation involving a human group, it is the presence, the actions, or the idea of one or more persons that occasions revolt. Yet we must repeat that this is not to be interpreted as a "clique" or a "conspiracy" or "agitators," etc., for the real impact is involuntary and unpremeditated: it is the encounter between

---

[27] For all these questions, see Godechot, op. cit., pp. 110, 113, 273.

situation and occasion which these men represent *by their bodily presence* that produces revolt.

We may even speak of contagion—from afar, of course—in Hispaniola at the time of the Negro revolts in 1791, which were patterned after what was happening in France; and in 1794, when the blacks rebelled against the planters, they did so on the strength of the Convention's proclamation of liberty.

Apart from this, the occasion may also arise as a result of specific events: decisions of the central authority, a drastic increase in the *gabelle* (salt tax), elimination of the privilege of *quart bouillon*,[28] the all-too-frequent quartering of troops on the march, the intensification of religious repression, the recall of an *intendant* who has won popular sympathy, the imposition of the *papier timbré* (stamp tax), the tobacco monopoly, a decision affecting navigation rights, ordinances governing the press, the order to return Prussia's cannon to her, etc. In each instance we find an event that in itself is not especially significant and does not warrant rebellion. A government has the right to assume that a particular measure it takes will not provoke disorder if it is a routine measure and if a hundred such others have been obeyed without causing any trouble. Then, suddenly, over that particular one, a revolt erupts. The government is as much a stranger to the situation as the conspirator; hence it never knows for certain what the effect of a decision will be.

Finally, we ought to give special note to the impact of false reports, rumors, and hearsay: the unfounded rumor of a newly arrived tax-assessor or of a royal decision to extend a particular levy.[29] And one of the most curious phenomena of general panic touching off revolt was the extraordinary false reports that triggered the Great Fear: the appearance of bandits, troops of aristocrats organized to murder the peasants, rural bands bent on pillaging cities—a multiplicity of vague rumors

---

[28] Privilege granted to certain regions of France allowing them to lower the salt tax.

[29] Mousnier, op. cit., pp. 106–38.

(a "colossal false report," as Godechot [30] puts it), all of which were probably spontaneous (they passed on their fears in a chain, Godechot goes on to say). By and large, however, I believe that the human presence has a greater effect than events themselves in triggering revolt, once a favorable situation exists.

From Revolt to Revolution

We have already seen how complex and uncertain the distinction between revolt and revolution is when they are considered as part of history and when we refrain from constructing concepts one atop another. History assures us that traditionally we may distinguish a certain transition between revolt and revolution, and that the latter is the result of the former and derives ultimately from the rebel. But the concept of revolution is a new one. The "phenomenon" of revolution is without precedent in premodern history. Not until modern times have both the necessity to make revolutions and the spirit of revolution come on the scene. Until the last century there was certainly a strong bond between the two, revolution being intertwined with revolt. Let us first eliminate the erroneous distinctions. There is no essentially higher or lower level of violence. At the time of the Paris disorders in May 1968, someone wrote: "There was no progression from brick-throwing to tear-gas grenades to machine-gun fire. . . . Revolution did not occur." What simplism! There have been innumerable conspicuously violent revolts in which hundreds were killed, yet without revolution. Inversely, there have been revolutions involving relatively few victims. After all, prior to the Reign of Terror a revolution did indeed occur between 1789 and 1792, and even then there were few deaths. In the second place, success is not what makes the difference: thinking in terms of abortive revolts or successful revolutions is an error

---

[30] Godechot, op. cit., pp. 126, 303.

that has already been cited. Nor does the difference depend
on dimension, for a revolt that embraces an entire country
can perfectly well remain a revolt: in 1794, two thirds of
France rose against the revolutionary government, yet it was
a revolt. Inversely, a revolution can take place with a mini-
mum of disorder: Geneva's revolution, for instance. Finally,
we must not look too hard for social consequences. Certain
revolutions have had few profound economic or sociological
results: the revolution of 1830 is an example. Yet revolts have
ushered in important changes: the Negro revolts in the United
States in recent years have induced the government to make
spectacular reforms. From here on, we shall attempt to determine the points of resemblance and, ultimately, to see what
makes a revolution a revolution.

We must realize that if a revolution grows out of a revolt—
and it frequently does [31]—it also takes on the characteristics
of that revolt. *On this level,* therefore, the question of revolutionary spontaneity is not valid. It is historically proved that
revolution cannot develop, any more than revolt can, from a
plot or a conspiracy. Revolution is not the result of any sinister
scheme; it grafts itself onto a spontaneous movement, an incidental upheaval, without which it is an impossibility. We
shall return to the question of spontaneity on another level,
but the chief similarity to be borne in mind is that revolution,
like revolt, is directed (or was, at least, until the nineteenth
century) against history. We must never assume that revolt
is a reactionary movement and revolution progressive: revolution, too, is traditionally opposed to what evolution promises
mankind. It is the refusal to advance toward that future. The
celebrated Marxist formula: "Revolutions are the locomotives
of history" is a gross misstatement of fact. On the contrary, they
usually seek to impede the development of history.

Even in his day, Machiavelli recognized revolution as di-

---

[31] A number of movements cited earlier as revolts will be mentioned here in
their developmental stage as revolutions.

rected toward the past; he called revolution *"renovazione,"* and that renewal or fresh start was the only conceivable change for the better. For centuries, men attempting revolution were not in search of innovation. The very choice of the word "revolution," an astronomical term indicating the course of a star returning to its point of origin, is itself symptomatic. Revolution comes back to the predetermined point that has mistakenly been left. It appears that the first use of the word was to indicate the restoration of the English monarchy in 1660. Therefore, the revolution was not at all the act of Cromwell and his government, but the overthrow of the Rump Parliament. Similarly, in 1688, the expulsion of the Stuarts and the crowning of William and Mary came to be called a revolution.[32] Known as the "Glorious Revolution," it was in fact the reinstatement of the power of the monarchy in its pristine glory and splendor, which disorders had ruined.

Thus most revolutions prior to the nineteenth century had a double thrust: they were conservative, even reactionary, bent on maintaining a situation and, better still, on restoring a former one, real or imagined, or they represented the determination to obstruct a "normal," predictable future, evaluated in terms of the present. In order to obtain what? No one generally knew for certain; there was no definite goal, only that refusal. At any rate, both hypotheses imply an effort to deflect the course of history. This interpretation is, to be sure, unconventional. Anyone who regards the communal movement as a series of revolutions is prepared to interpret it as a class conflict, mercantile demands for independence from the *seigneurs,* and much more: a revolution of freedom, the organization of a "democratic" power to combat the manorial system, and, as a result, an elaboration of history. But all that is a modernistic view. On the one hand, the men of the communal movements needed to establish a seignorial type of society to protect their interests: we are likely to forget that freed cities came into the seignorial system by declaring

---

[32] See *Oxford English Dictionary* and *Encyclopedia Britannica*.

themselves *seigneuries* (at the utmost, one could say that this represented the revolt of a vassal against a lord, with the vassal seeking his independence); on the other hand, they had to deflect the normal course of history according to which the *seigneurs* would reap the profits from technical progress and commercial activities. It was simply a matter of who was going to benefit. We have come a long way from the objectives that we attribute to those rebel bourgeois. The same applies to the great revolution of Torreben in Brittany, when the grievances of the peasantry, drawn up like a revolutionary program, were submitted time after time: liberty for this or that hereditary province; sweeping reforms covering compulsory labor, legal proceedings, marriages, inheritances, etc. But in actual fact the seignorial and feudal system was not under attack, nor was the hierarchical society, and the revolutionaries were not determined to topple the political regime, for they made no claims against the sovereign and absolute state. Of course, they did protest the courts, the nobility, and the "new taxes," but they did not propose any specific redress or any reform. They accepted what was traditional and customary; they opposed innovation, excess, and change.

The English revolution (1640) followed the same pattern despite the king's death.[33] It called for the preservation of order and religion and the protection of property; the government might change and the group in power might represent different interests: its objective was not to rush headlong into a totally unfamiliar future, but to solidify the past and halt the normal flow of history.

Cromwell saw himself as a combined "policeman and shepherd," and though liberty was proclaimed throughout the realm, it bore the mark of a statism in no way inferior to that of Louis XIV. This is plainly seen in the conflict between Cromwell and the Levelers, who themselves might have passed for modern revolutionaries: they drew up an Agreement of

---

[33] Lutaud, *Les Niveleurs, Cromwell et la République,* 1967.

the People calling for a type of popular and socialist republic. Although the Levelers originated among the craftsmen,
the shopkeepers, and the soldiery, their leaders were of the
nobility and of the higher military ranks, so the question of
class struggle is really not involved. Later on, in Russia, it
would seem that with Stenka Razin there was an equally
valid revolution: freedom again was proclaimed wherever the
Cossacks rode—Cossack freedom. In every city, advisory as-
semblies were organized, leaders elected, democratic and
egalitarian republics declared, but they were never more remote! Yet the entire Cossack body of that revolution was in
agreement on two points: the czar was not responsible for
the people's grievances (he was betrayed by false coun-
selors) and they were achieving their revolution in the name
of the Virgin Mary and therefore desired to abolish only
whatever obstructed their free and *traditional* pursuit of a
nomadic military life. Afterward, one could say that that immense explosion "did nothing to alter the steady evolution of
the Russian state into an increasingly absolute and centralized
structure. . . . It did nothing to alter the evolution of Russian
society." [34] None of those revolutions was in any sense a rupture of history or a crisis that took history onto a new path.
But the Millenarians provide many more examples of this, for
we may speak of revolution when they founded institutions
and powers and when they freed territories from traditional
authorities. But what did they do afterward? The insurgent
peasants under Münzer wanted to return irrevocably to the
past, to primitive times, to an age when men were free and
equal, the day of beginnings, the ancestral world in whose
bosom men were treated justly. [35] At that time John of Leyden
founded an experimental Kingdom of God in Münster, but
he was acting entirely outside history. To describe his act as a
prelude to communism is a misconception: we are dealing
with a revolution against history, the object of which is to

---

[34] Mousnier, op. cit., p. 234.
[35] Bloch, op. cit.

establish here and now the Kingdom of God on earth. The telling factor is not the pooling of wealth; it is the royal proclamation of universal justice, the enactment of a rigid moral code, an evangelical absolutism—before going to the opposite extreme.[36]

This also describes the great experiment of Joachim de Flore or the Brothers in Poverty,[37] and there are endless other examples involving illuminati, politicians, peasants, and bourgeois, all promoting the same end: revolution outside history, against history in the making, the search for a way back to the past, the attempt to begin afresh. Of course, from a modern standpoint we may say that this was only true in so far as the recapture of history was concerned, history internalized by the group, the mass, whereas revolution occurs as a function of the history of men as individuals frustrated by the pattern of their existence and in opposition to history, which conceals these frustrations in legends extolling the right of might.[38] This interpretation cannot alter the fact that the intent of these revolutionaries always includes a denial of history and that revolution, in their eyes, is not a means of creating history but, on the contrary, one of rejecting it. So it is obvious that by pursuing this argument and taking different points of view, we are bound to prove that these revolutions ultimately found their place in history, and that, having had one or another result, they were unquestionably history, etc., but all that is a discussion of interpretation that obscures the concrete reality of the revolutionary movement that begins with man's revolt.

What are, then, the distinctions between revolt and revolution? It seems to me that there are two completely new elements: the theory and the institution. Revolt at its source is void of thought; it is visceral, physical. Revolution implies a

---

[36] D'Aubarède, *La Révolution des Saints,* 1946, pp. 1520–36.
[37] Aegerter, *Les Hérésies au Moyen Age,* 1939.
[38] Decouflé, op. cit., pp. 43–9.

doctrine, a plan, a program, a theory of some kind, though the term "theory" need not have a very precise meaning. At any rate, it is my impression that the existence of this preliminary thought is what identifies revolution. An idea may be expressed occasionally in the course of revolt, but it is always incidental and emerges from the developing revolt itself. Revolution, in one aspect or another, possesses lines of intellectual force which revolt does not have. Moreover, revolution seeks to institutionalize itself. As we have said, when revolt occasionally succeeds, it stops short, stunned by its success. What characterizes the transformation of revolt into revolution is the attempt to provide a new organization (for lack of a corporation!), and in human terms this implies the existence of what Decouflé aptly calls the "managers" of revolution. But though he uses the word a bit scornfully, I myself believe that there can be no revolution without this combination of rebels and managers. Revolt does not reach the level of revolution as long as there are only the masses and the rebels: there have to be organizers—to put things in order after the storm.

Plan, theory, doctrine, principles: I am well aware of the distinctions between these terms, but they do not warrant too close attention. "We have reached the moment when revolt, rejecting all and every tyranny, seeks to embrace the whole of creation. . . . The irrational demand for liberty is about to choose reason, paradoxically, for its weapon, the sole conquering force it considers purely human. . . . The revolt movement shifts abruptly at its very core. Revolution begins with an idea. It is, specifically, the infusion of an idea into a historical experience, whereas revolt is simply a movement leading from individual experience to an idea." [39] It is altogether true that an assassin bent on dispatching a king is not the slave of an idea. Rebels, along with regicides such as those who murdered France's Henry III and Henry IV or Paul

---

[39] Camus, op. cit., pp. 132–6.

Doumer, are resolved to attack a person, without intent to alter the regime or change the structure of society. Revolution, on the other hand, contains a concrete ideology and not an embittered millennialism. But we must recognize the fact that this ideology may express itself in various ways, vaguely or precisely, in narrow or in broad concepts. Many of these revolutions start with a rather uncertain yet firm ideology: what Sartre and many others qualify as a plan. It is both a goal and a picture, a guide and a projection, intelligible as well as communicable. Decouflé [40] has clarified this point by showing that there are two types of plans: the predetermined plan and the revolutionary plan that is its antithesis. The revolutionary plan is collective and formulates in a nondoctrinal and more or less rational manner the aspirations of a group. The significance of such a plan, whatever form it may take, is that it provides a beginning. Revolution "is the only political event that confronts us directly and inescapably with the problem of a beginning." [41] Revolution is not an attempt to transform what exists; it has nothing to do with reform. It is a fresh start from zero. The revolutionary plan does not consist either in applying an idealistic doctrine or in reforming one or another element of society: it invariably comes down to establishing a beginning. After that, everything assumes a new aspect, and whether there is a return to the past, to a Golden Age, or the inauguration of something totally new cannot change the phenomenon. Wherever this laying of the first stone occurs, there is revolution. Otherwise the event may be social, political, or tragic, but it does not bear the mark of revolution. In the eyes of those who make it, it is a completely new story, "a story that has never been told before." And in this sense we can say that revolution is linked to freedom because this decisive (and absurd) beginning presupposes a liberation for man, who will be hurled onto a new course and who is summoned to forsake his old patterns of behavior.

---

[40] Decouflé, op. cit., p. 19.
[41] Hannah Arendt has elucidated this question remarkably well.

He is set free by being placed at this beginning. The same holds true even when a revolution is reactionary and runs counter to history: the established beginning is not the point of departure from the experienced past. "On that day everything was possible. . . . The future was present . . . ; that is, time no longer existed, a flash of eternity struck," Michelet wrote in his *Histoire de la Révolution*. At the same time, unparadoxically, the past must be reclaimed, not as an experience, a rehearsal, or a pattern, but as the absolute point of departure: turning backward is a way of opening a new history in which the mistakes we now recognize and suffer from will not be repeated. To establish a beginning and to retrieve the past: this is the plan. The mode of expression it may take is of only minor importance; hence it is entirely false to assert that revolution is primarily what terminates a particular period or era. When turmoil brings down a regime, it is not a revolutionary event: the ferment throughout the city-states in fifteenth-century Italy, for example, put an end to the medieval communities and to political freedom, but there was no revolution. The latter may bring an era to a close, but that is not what makes it revolutionary: by its inaugural role, and not otherwise, it acts as a terminator, even when it voices the No in the course of history.

The plan may be expressed in programs. The *Croquants* of Poitou, acting in behalf of the peasants of Poitou, enacted an ordinance providing for a communal and fiscal system, etc. But their aspirations went no farther than the gates of the town. They did not foresee the overthrow of the seignorial system or of the monarchy. At that stage, they simply wanted to submit their grievances in their *cahiers*. We have already discussed the Peasants' Code of Torreben in Brittany, where a program for action and reform was later to be developed. The same was true during many of the Russian revolutions, for Stenka Razin formulated a genuine program. But there is surely a difference between the comprehensive plan, which involves the re-evaluation of history, and the specific program, which, though narrower, nevertheless determines a revolution's orientation. The plan is much broader, more evocative, more stimulating to the imagination, and arises from the soul of a people. The program is stringent, setting up objectives to prevent revolution from foundering on illuminism and mysticism. But it is always inadequate. Although revolt invariably centers on what is concrete, immediate, and palpable, once revolution is rooted in the hearts of men it cannot fail to support an element of myth and ideology: evidence that doctrines and programs of an intellectual nature need to be rounded out by the addition of myth. These are, strictly speaking, the ingredients of the "revolutionary plan." Revolution is bound to embody a journey to the absolute in the hearts of those who take part in it. They are bound to see it as the ultimate solution to history, so that long before they make it, they believe in it. It is a cult object, whereas revolt provides none. Revolt "rumbles": it is wrath, a sudden gust, an explosion—immediate. Revolution is an idol; it is the Holy Revolution, venerated and cherished before being set in motion. It absorbs all the religious emotion that disappears from surrounding society. It is the solemn bearer of man's hope. This is why revolt has room for humor (savage and macabre, yet still humor), but never revolution, all of whose heroes take themselves far too seriously to abide a momentary jest. They are celebrants in a sacred rite. The revolutionary plan is infused with those elements and bears their stamp.

But programs and myths are not the entire revolutionary plan. There must also be a statement of doctrine, on the theoretical level (which rarely occurs). Discounting apocalyptic visions, when a revolutionary plan takes the form of a doctrine, such as Rousseau's *Social Contract,* for example, we then have a third aspect of it, but not the sole or exclusive one. In this connection, what seems to me to typify revolution in contrast to revolt is the phenomenon of verbalization and conceptualization *in advance* of action. We want to do something and we start out to do it. From the outset it is not a random adventure. It is the exposure and expression of mental images cherished by a social group, the ripening consciousness of the collective unconscious, the recovery of a historical memory projected into the future. And that is why, in order to ascertain whether a society is likely to enter into revolutionary action, it is not enough to examine merely the power structure, economic institutions, class conflicts, etc. We must also ask whether the society is equipped to undertake the task of conceptualizing, projecting, and programing. And at this point we encounter the primary aspect of the question of spontaneity. The fact that revolt is generally a spontaneous phenomenon and that revolution can emerge from it does not resolve anything. For revolution necessitates thought, even preliminary thought. In the past, the intellectual preparation for revolution has been overemphasized as a result of the hypnotic effects of 1789 and eighteenth-century theories. Today we neglect this factor. I am not dealing here with spontaneity, a much-debated doctrine of revolution, but with the fact that there can be no pure spontaneity in revolution, in which there is always forethought, and hence an inspiration. It is not a question of propaganda, but of the various modes of expressing a common aspiration. For example, during the revolutions that broke out all over Europe after 1780, there was talk of "French propaganda": this was not altogether real. The transmission (spontaneous at that) of ideas across frontiers served the same purpose. This applies also to the communal movement during the Middle Ages, when merchants spread ideas wherever they took their goods, and groups seething with revolt that came in contact with those utterances were led not to adopt the same ideas but to express their own will more clearly. Of course, the latter often would coincide with the will of neighboring peoples because of the objective similarity of their situations. But revolutionary thinking becomes self-generating within a group, which explains why it is revolutionary and ceases to be the bearer of a pure and simple No addressed to Destiny. A factor that aids the

formulation of this doctrine, or program, or plan, is the existence of an adversary sufficiently universal but nevertheless
distinct. The state appears to be the most effective crystalliz-
ing agent for this thinking: that is why we find the state and
revolution developing side by side. As long as there are misery
born of natural causes, and either diffuse or immediate oppression, revolt is present. But when there are signs of organization, when political power becomes concentrated and defined, negative thoughts crystallize alongside and burning
misery finds an interpretation. Thus the state, which was,
as we have seen, an instigator of revolt, becomes the instrument for transforming revolt into revolution.

In addition to this ideological factor, revolution as such
implies an orientation toward organization and institutionalization. It is possible that the earliest evidence of concern for
institutionalizing freedom was in the American Revolution,
the objective of which was to consolidate in a constitution the
power born of revolution. Then and there the organizer
emerged as the central figure—the one through whom revolution fulfills its meaning. But the problem that confronted
Robespierre and reappears again and again, had to be faced
then: If the goal of revolution is the creation of revolutionary
institutions signaling the end of public freedom, is it desirable
to call a halt to revolution?

Revolution contained an idea; it should be put to work. So
let us try to organize things, to give them either a temporary
framework or a more expert structure. Revolution cannot
escape the transition to institutions and managerial control.
Moreover, the managers frequently have absorbed, if not
created, the doctrine. They are forever accused of being the
exploiters or betrayers of revolution; in actual fact, if they had
not been on the scene, the revolutionary stage would never
have been reached. Revolutions are not made by leaders or
agitators. Obviously, every revolt has its own leaders and
agitators. The makers of the French Revolution were not

Marat or even Saint-Just; they were Sieyès, Robespierre, and, later on, Napoleon. Blanqui was not the focus of the revolutions that occurred during the second half of the nineteenth century, nor was Bakunin, but rather a man who never fired a shot or inflamed a crowd, a professional and organizational man. Occasionally the managers are revolutionaries of the previous generation: examples of this are rare, but Toussaint L'Ouverture is a good one, a man who, once he attained power, developed from a rebel slave leader into a political leader, as well as a fine administrator able to restore economic stability who allayed the fears and then backed the interests of the very planters against whom the revolution had been made. When these two abilities function simultaneously, they leave a distinct mark on certain periods in the lives of men such as Matthew and John of Leyden, Caboche, Cromwell, Bolívar, and Lenin. Revolt becomes revolution at the moment when they begin the task of construction. This is also what qualifies as revolution the radical transformation effected by power itself when it stems from the confrontation between rebel groups and privileged groups.

We ought to bear in mind this passage from Duverger: "Until now, the effectiveness of a revolutionary party has depended solely on its ability to acquire strong organization and intense centralization. Leftists are therefore trapped by a fundamental contradiction: if they apply their ideas of a society founded on small autonomous groups, they will have to reject the development of a central party apparatus and thereby doom themselves to impotence. If they create such an apparatus for purposes of efficiency, they will not be upholding their principles. . . ." And I would add that their successful revolution will bear the mark of this type of apparatus, for it cannot be abolished: it organizes what follows.

When revolt ceases to flounder about and begins to become organized, revolution faces a twofold problem. First, the question of force: has revolt gone far enough, has it rallied sufficient strength to withstand all that society can muster

against it? We should not overlook the fact that it is during
the very transition from revolt to revolution, when an attempt
must be made to carry out not agitation but a transformation,
that the surrounding society will hurl its most violent defiance.
As long as there is just "a breeze from the Fronde," it does
not cause much stir.

Once revolution seems to be taking on a form, or for that
matter institutions—that is to say, when it acquires an
identity—the defiance is unleashed. At that moment the real
test of force occurs. When Münzer or John of Leyden installed
his kingdom and began organizing it, when the revolution
of 1848 founded its first institutions, when the Night of August 4 occurred, or the Peasants' Code of Torreben was proclaimed, or Soviet power was becoming systematized: then
came the all-out offensive. As long as there was merely revolt
—so many revolts have occurred, and it is known that in the
test of force, revolt as such inevitably is defeated, so there is
no purpose in worrying too much. But when the organizing and
founding power of revolt becomes visible, then the social
structure alerts and gears itself to meet the danger—because
its survival is at stake.

But the second question is even more complex: Will revolt
be able to break free from itself? Will it be equal to the task
of either ending the violence or finding its own objective?
We have already seen that revolt usually stops short after
victory and does not know what to do next. It is stunned; it
wanders around in circles, and then falls asleep or else revels
pathetically in pleasures or in blood. It is not easy to move
from revolt to revolution. To bring armed, rampaging men
under control and to reorganize them, to transform the exaltation of battle into the will to build and to reshape, and
above all to know how to direct the new-found power: all
that is a double task wherein lies the critical point of revolution; the second task is largely made easy in that, as we have
said, there is no revolution until there is a doctrine, which is
generally preliminary. But the problem here stems from

the fact that this doctrine usually does not correspond truly to the actual situation after revolt is ended. Marx could not be applied directly in 1917; it needed an interpreter of genius who could follow events closely and apply doctrine rigorously. Rousseau was inapplicable: in 1790, it required the tireless or inspired efforts of administrators to systematize some of his ideas. Anyone attempting to apply them directly is bound to fail. The revolutionary plan at its source is invariably un-adaptable to the situation. This is perfectly understandable: otherwise it would not be revolutionary! Precisely because the revolutionary plan defies the "normal" course of history, it is outside that course; it is the affirmation of the impossible in the face of necessity. But once revolt is in motion, the milieu acquires a new fluidity, and thenceforth the revolutionary plan is no longer totally unadaptable. Still, there is a considerable gap between the institutions or the original idea and its ex-pression at the crucial time. At any rate, if the theorists have kept their thinking abreast of events (and as true revolution-aries they would have to do so), the picture has changed a great deal by the time revolt has passed and is headed for success. But we must remember that this change has not fol-lowed the exact pattern set forth by the theorist and described initially in the plan. The revolutionary plan is not a rail switchman directing freight shipments at his own discretion along tracks that the train is obliged to ride; it is, on the contrary, an inspiration changed into a possibility from the impossibility it was at the start. But there must be men to take up the plan, the doctrine, and the theory afresh, reviving and reintegrating them into the revolutionary process of develop-ment, seeing to it that they mature spiritually and beget new and perfect creations. In this area the plan or doctrine has its second application. If neither exists at the start, revolution makes no innovations as it progresses. On this score, Marx's theory of revolutionary praxis is false. We will return to this point.

When a successful revolt attempts to organize, it loses

steam very rapidly. In the seventeenth century the victorious peasants were content to set up communes with an advisory assembly patterned after those which had long existed in the cities. That was not a revolution. To reanimate the initial doctrine, there must be men. Administrators alone are equal to the task of transmuting agitation into institutions without losing the basic gains already made. They appear to be traitors and reactionaries because they do not uphold pure doctrine and because of their absence from the firing line at the height of the struggle. We tend to forget that it is impossible to maintain that degree of tension indefinitely. Lenin accurately predicted the phases of withdrawal and *détente*. We also forget that if there are no institutional structures, revolution will founder and become immobilized: in the first instance, tetany of the social organism would set in; in the second, paralysis caused by atonia, and there is no completed revolution, which occurs only to the extent that the administrators extract every possible asset for the whole of society from the original plan and from the blind revolt. The spontaneous institutions that spring up in the course of revolt, as in the beginnings of revolution—anarchist committees in Spain in 1936, the soviets of 1905 and 1917, republican committees for the defense of the Commune, *sans-culotte* sections in 1793—quickly reveal their instability, inadequacy, and incoherence when not remanded to the control of revolutionary administrators who can utilize them to solidify the structure of popular power. At the same time, they are forced to modify the orientation of these institutions, for once revolt as such is victorious, agitation must give way to construction.

Of course, revolt, that rejection of an impossible destiny, is a liberating force: there is always an ill-defined attempted liberation. Revolution may have a hundred other objectives. Even when it springs from revolt, even when it raises the cry of liberty, there is an important difference: revolt is itself the liberating movement. Revolution seeks to organize the situation, to find a stable structure for freedom. Thus revolt is movement; revolution tends toward the establishing of stability.[42] Revolt can take its course under a monarchy or even under a tyrant, without attempting to alter the regime. Revolution is destined to create a new regime or political body. For revolution to exist, the drive to be free must seek to *establish* freedom. Revolution inevitably channels itself into institutions and constitutions.

The most difficult stage is reached when angry mobs press at any cost to sustain the unrest, to maintain the excitement, when rebels lose sight of their power and are completely out of touch with what is real and possible, seeing revolt thereafter as divinity on the march and confusing motion itself with revolution. That is the crucial moment, the mystical moment of revolt: liberty or death. It is undoubtedly the most exhilarating moment, but that sort of romanticism spells doom for revolution. Lenin does not deny this in condemning leftism, nor does Robespierre, though he excludes the Fanatics. Ideally, this marks the transition to the absolute. Historically, reaction is taking hold. But the great test in this situation is to determine the right moment, to estimate whether something else is still possible or whether it is not best, at the risk of losing everything, to consolidate the gains and advance no farther. This is the primary task of revolution's administrators and the one that ordinarily requires the greatest effort: on the psychological level, the transition from agitation to integration;[43] on the sociopolitical level, the transition from fighting structures to governing structures. If the attempt fails, the results may mean either that revolution amounted to no more than the substitution of one governing group for another; or else that, religion, tyranny, and the scaffold having been abolished and the rule of justice and brotherhood proclaimed, the failure to bridge the gap will lead to dictatorship, to the worship of a new god, to mass death sentences and bloodshed wherever potential obstacles exist—for revolution now must

---

[42] Hannah Arendt has made a remarkable analysis of this difference in her *Essay on Revolution,* pp. 43–7 (Fr. edn., 1967).

[43] Cf. J. Ellul, *Propaganda,* 1960 (trans. 1965), on the question of the transition from agitational propaganda to integrational propaganda.

strike out against persistent revolt. In the beginning it sought to encourage the spirit of revolt, which was its progenitor. But now that spirit must be crushed, and in crushing it, revolution does not die but succeeds. Historically, all revolutions that have attempted to endure indefinitely without institutionalizing revolt have ultimately erased every gain. "There is an immutable hostility between the revolt movement and revolutionary gains." But there is no revolution until those gains are made, until that institutionalization, that setting in motion, begins. This is also why, at a certain time, the rebel is bound to take arms against revolution. But it was indeed revolution, not reaction and a regression to the situation in 1788, that continued under the Directory and Napoleon. There is no doubt that if power had been transferred to the Fanatics, Europe's armed coalition would have won the field in 1795 and the Revolution of 1789 would have been erased, leaving no more of a trace than Stenka Razin left in Russia. But it is impossible to convince rebels of this, for they cling perpetually to the notion that their administrators have betrayed them. The problem is knowing when the administrator intends to undertake the mutation: if it is too soon, he is a traitor; if it is the perfect moment, he achieves revolution. Camus has written aptly: "To kill God and build a Church is the unremitting and conflicting pattern of revolt. Absolute freedom becomes a prison of bounden duties, a collective asceticism, a legend ultimately. The nineteenth century, the century of revolt, thus feeds into the twentieth century, the century of justice and morality when everyone beats his breast." At that point, revolution is completed and must begin anew.

Of course, the current of pure revolt, unmixed with revolutionary ideology, flows throughout history. When it rises in our time, it does not issue from a void. It had a name: anarchy. Anarchism is born of the impossibility of continuing with things as they are. It is endured by a single human being. It exalts violence and inspires greater fear than the threat of revolution—and greater admiration. "Ravachol was guillotined, but he was highly esteemed for having killed" (Emmanuel Berl). Beleaguered anarchism, scorned by the great revolutionists, taking cover behind the protective mask of doctrine, is the current of continuous revolt. Nechayev, above all, demonstrated that.

In this connection, there is a curious sociological category which has not been studied adequately, that of professional revolutionaries.[44] Yet they deserve special mention. They appeared at the time of the French Revolution (another example of its initiating function). They spent their lives studying, evolving the theory of revolution, and, incidentally, agitating. They throve upon revolution, intellectually as well as materially. As literary men at the end of the eighteenth century, they were part of the artistic Bohemia that flourished at the beginning of the nineteenth. Marx was the classic example of these professional revolutionaries, who were never employed and were veritable *"rentiers de la révolution."* Most of their time was spent in libraries and clubs. They did not prepare revolution directly; they analyzed the disintegration of society and classified the conditions favorable to revolution. But when revolution arrived, they were equipped to play a vital role: they became its administrators and organizers. They stood not for disorder but for order, and after the storm had passed, they reorganized the structures (for which they were intellectually geared) and are known universally as experts on revolution. So it was natural that they should take power. With Lenin, a different type emerged: the man of action dominated. That was the major antagonism between Plekhanov and Kautsky on the one hand and Lenin and Trotsky on the other.

Two Complementary Images

Let us now isolate two images from the revolt/revolution complex, chosen from many possible examples because they are unusually typical.

[44] Eisenstein, *The First Professional Revolutionist: F. M. Buonarotti* (1761–1837), 1958.

The first comes from the English revolt of 1381.[45] It is commonly described as a peasant rebellion, but it was much more. The ideas of Wycliffe and the Lollards were fervently preached in Essex and Kent. Justice was proclaimed, and all men were declared equal; those teachings were plainly archaic, yet they openly indicted corrupt magistrates and feudal lords as well as government officials. In this instance, the theme of religion created the climate of revolt, which followed on the heels of a series of stringent administrative and fiscal ordinances: leaving the village to find work elsewhere was forbidden, wages were taxed, and a poll tax was imposed, a special levy on the peasantry; in addition, the extortionate practices of sheriffs (to line their own pockets) were a contributory factor (less significant than was believed). Finally, the peasants rose in protest over the levying of taxes in restriction of trade. An incident, perhaps legendary, sparked Wat Tyler's rebellion in his native village of Kent. The flames spread instantly. Bands of peasants attacked manors and cities—somewhat selectively, it would appear, for they generally singled out the properties of magistrates and of the king's officers for looting and burning. A number of churches also were attacked, many public buildings were destroyed, and prisoners were freed who straightway joined the rebels. In cities and towns the peasants were actively supported by priests and knights; generally, the peasantry was not hostile to the middle class or to the nobility. In some cases, rich landowners raised rebellions, arousing the local populace and leading the insurgents (as, for example, in Cambridge). Military operations were frequently under the command of knights. So there was really no "class struggle" in so far as either motives or conduct were concerned. The scene in London was to confirm this: as Wilkinson relates, the rebels converged on the capital, and their invasion of royalty's seat was no act of treason, for the majority of Londoners flocked to their side, giving sympathy

---

[45] This event has been selected because it is largely unknown in France except through Petit-Dutaillis's study. See Lindsay, *The Peasants' Revolt of 1381*, 1950; Wilkinson, *The Peasants' Revolt of 1381*, 1940.

and aid. And the "common people" were not the only ones to
link their misery with that of the peasants: the rich burgesses
and aldermen looked most favorably on the insurgents, who
declared themselves *amici regis* and thus gained entry to the
city.

But the support of London's populace significantly altered
the objectives of the revolt, which were, for the peasants,
social and fiscal. The Londoners' complaints were essentially
political and concerned the king and his ministers, for the
bourgeoisie did not share the grievances of the peasantry. Yet
they presented a united front and, on that occasion, they
unanimously called for indictment of officials who were
"traitors to the people and to the king." They demanded
punishment of the offenders and declared their loyalty to the
throne. In their eyes, revolt unquestionably was compatible
with fealty to the crown: they simply wanted to "inform the
king of certain things he did not know." That alliance, however, transformed a local peasant rebellion into something
completely different: extensive as they were, the gains of the
peasants and the destruction they wrought would have
amounted merely to one of the countless risings scattered
throughout history except that they became significant through
the political choices implemented by the Londoners.

Another event was in store. The rebels obtained an inter-
view with the king, who took a liberal stance, promising to
eliminate the restrictive taxes, review the tax-collecting proce-
dure, restore certain rights, and oust his ministers. This con-
ciliatory attitude placated the majority of the rebels. The movement was on the verge of disbanding when two of the most
hated officials were murdered. At that moment, the Londoners
believed victory was theirs, whereas the peasants had the king's
word: they no longer had common goals. The bulk of the
peasant mobs (probably those from Essex) left London. But
the rebel leader, Wat Tyler, decided that victory was not yet
won; the process of politicalization had led him to present a
program of total revolution for society. It is also possible that

the king's promise of free pardons to the rebels encouraged
Tyler to stand firm and try to exploit fully the movement's
initial gains. He demanded the annulment of any law not issued
by "Winchester" (in other words, the centralization of legisla-
tive authority in the king's hands); abolition of any other
sovereignty than the king's; the ouster of all bishops; the division of church property among parishioners; and the freeing of
serfs by royal edict. His program was therefore hostile to the
Church and to the expansion of political power. His demands
had an "extremist" tone entirely new to the movement, and they
no longer corresponded (even with respect to the abolition of
serfdom, strange as that may seem) to the desires of the mass
of the peasantry. Tyler tried to make the revolt rebound, to
transform it into a revolution, to systematize it, but he no
longer possessed the armed strength to back his demands. For
some, his program might simply have served to incite violence
and turn the rebellion into civil war: Tyler could have expected the king to retaliate in kind, thus occasioning the return of the peasant mobs. But he did not know that in the
course of revolution, a missed opportunity is a lost one. He
was killed—no one knows just how—apparently without the
king's complicity. Once its leader was gone, the rebellion disintegrated on the spot, Richard II rescinded his grants, and
the army took severe repressive action. That event is altogether typical of revolt that verges on revolution, of the complex causes behind the phenomenon, of the progressive and
then explosive development of the revolutionary plan, and of
the leader's negative rather than positive impact. By the
latter we mean that a revolution, or for that matter a revolt,
does not erupt primarily because a leader or an agitator is
behind it, the creative and provocative role of the leader being
aleatory. It is true that as a movement gathers strength, a
handful of able organizers emerge; but, in any event, the
leader's death (when there is no one to replace him) brings
on the instant collapse of the revolutionary movement, and
that is what is meant by the "negative role" of the leader.

The Tyler rebellion is also typical of the participation of all social "classes" and its reactionary aspect: the rebels lashed out at corrupt officials (a classic demonstration of the people calling for a better-informed king in place of an ill-informed one, as was said of the French monarchy in later years), when, in fact, these officials were "progressive," often liberal in their attitude toward the public, eager to improve financial conditions, to develop administration, and to establish a machinery of state, things the majority of the population cannot abide.

The second example is complementary because it involves a successful revolution of a modern type and illustrates the extraordinary conglomeration of revolutionary elements as well as the combined conservative and progressive nature of the new revolutions. It is the so-called Meiji revolution (1858–77).[46] By dismissing the fantasy that Commodore Perry's landing at Edo instantly exposed Japan to the glow of Western civilization, we uncover a remarkable transformation. It is impossible to summarize that change in view of the extremely complex situation, but certain of its principles may be distilled. In Japan, from at least 1830 onward, a number of pressures existed for trade with the West as well as for industrialization and the application of Western technical developments. Politically, that outlook was represented by the shogun and, generally speaking, his council, the Bakufu. In opposition, the emperor, whose role for centuries had been reduced to a ceremonial one, stood for tradition and the interests of the daimyo or feudal barons (some of whom were also in the Bakufu, while the shogun himself was the greatest feudal lord of all), and for xenophobia. Bitter differences divided the xenophiles and xenophobes and added to the antagonisms between the shogun's supporters and the emperor's allies, between the politicians and the feudalists. However, two elements we normally consider essential appear to have been

---

[46] See Paul Akamatsu's remarkable study, *Meiji 1868*, 1968.

lacking: the economic factor (economic motives did not underlie the revolution, and Japan's economy expanded steadily
from 1800 to 1880 without serious setback) and public participation (generally speaking, the people did not figure in this
whole affair: "at no time did they take an active role or function as a driving force"). Prior to the revolution there was no
popular rebellion, only a scattering of local insurgences
sparked by conditions of impoverishment. The great revolt
of 1831, for example, was not a popular rising but an act of
rich rural merchants and notables who demanded a voice in
political affairs. Only after the revolution, from 1867 onward,
did popular revolts occur, and the significance of that will be
seen shortly.

The emperor prevailed in his war with the shogunate; first
the Bakufu was crushed, then the shogun was forced to capitu-
late. The forces of reaction swept the field. But the daimyo
were not of one mind. Furthermore, between 1866 and 1869
the regime had gradually changed, and during the struggle for
power, the group formerly bound to the emperor had disappeared and the emperor had tried to seize power. But to do so
he was obliged to seek support outside the great feudal clans
and to adopt new and effective tactics—that is, "modern"
and scientific ones. By wooing the xenophobes and the reactionaries, the emperor triumphed in the long run, but at the
price of accepting foreign influence and institutional changes.
For that is what had occurred. It was the emperor who opened
Japan to Western trade and industry; it was he who shattered
the social and political structures far more than the shogun
and the Bakufu had intended or imagined at the start. The
"revolutionary" movement was defeated in respect to its
personalities and its representatives, but it submerged society
in a process that was to be concluded in due time by the
"managers" of revolution. This was an authentic and complete
revolution involving a changed political structure, a change
in the controlling class, a change in ideology, and a change in
the social and economic structures. What more need be said?

During that entire period there was constant and rapid shifting of members of the imperial circle; but as time passed, the opponents of change gradually revealed themselves to be the emperor's initial allies. He was forced to destroy the feudal system that had been his mainstay and that had provoked the revolutionary movement. The great feudal lords were finally overthrown. But this cannot be regarded as a bourgeois-type revolution instituting private capitalism, or a revolution based on class struggle, or the attainment of political power by the economically controlling class. None of those loose interpretations are applicable here. We are dealing with the first specific instance of a "techno-statist" revolution. But what is interesting is to find all the reactionary elements allied with the "leap into history." The xenophobes took the first step. But more than that, the ideology involved the desire to return to the most remote past, to the age (fourteenth century) when the emperor ruled in fact and before the shogunate imposed its dictatorship: the revolutionary legal code of the Meiji thereafter referred constantly to the sources of the monarchy and to the restoration of the past. In short, this was the reactionary framework within which sporadic popular upheavals occurred. The first wave of revolts began in 1863, loosed by xenophobes who tried to incite the people against progressive reforms—and succeeded. Their program called for the expulsion of foreigners, the restoration of imperial power, and the rallying of opinion in the emperor's behalf. But it was short-lived. In contrast, once the revolution was in progress and feudalism under assault, the peasantry rebelled. In 1867 and 1868, entire villages rose in defense of their lords, and *authentic popular revolts* broke out demanding restoration of the old regime (the shogunate) and the preservation of feudalism. The peasants rejected the new administrative system and military service, and the rebellion of 1873 was aimed principally at the latter (300,000 peasants laid waste a whole region in reaction to misconstrued reports).

The period of greatest rebel activity and turmoil occurred

between 1875 and 1877, at the close of the revolutionary period. Protest was then directed against fiscal changes, against "the tyranny of government" and the "cruelty of the (new) officials": *all* of these rebellions were reactionary and were exploited (but not incited) by the moribund feudal clans. The people rebelled to preserve the *status quo* and in defiance of change, which, in itself, frightened them. And when some of the tenant farmers rose in 1873 because of economic conditions, they received no support whatever from the revolutionary intelligentsia, who were in the process of broadening the movement. Yet that was the intellectual group which, after 1830, had initiated reformist and innovative trends within the Bakufu precisely because of the impoverishment of the peasants.

Under pressure of those rebellions, revolution received its constitution by imperial decree in five articles providing: "that all measures be adopted through public debate, and a large assembly established so that the great and the humble may participate actively as one in government; that officials, the military, and the people may implement their own will and pursue their own development; that the imperial task be elevated by invoking the knowledge and skills of civilizations the world over." This was the inauguration of an imperial democracy and state capitalism. The ultimate result of this vast revolution was the founding of a modern, centralized, bureaucratic, and industrial state: once again, the state emerged on the heels of revolution. This state organized a modern national army that helped to overthrow the insurgent feudal clans. In 1869 a complete administrative system was installed. The fiscal structure was stabilized and adapted to the new economy. "Liberalism" came to describe the attitude to foreigners, commercial relations, and religious toleration, but it was a liberalism bound far more closely to statism than that of most Western nations. Capital was basically under government control and was shared with private business at government discretion. The status of property was completely transformed by the abolition of feudalism and its component vassalage. But what replaced it was not a true system of private property: there was private ownership based upon the foundation of state ownership. In the final analysis, the decisive factor was the change in the controlling group: we cannot call it a class because those who rose to power with the emperor were of widely different social origins, and on becoming state officials they formed the nucleus of the new bourgeoisie. They included former members of the nobility (the petty nobility in general), former merchants, and former officials of the abolished feudal system. Their coalescence resulted basically from their educational background and the ideological orientation provided by their schooling and by the intellectual circles in which they moved. The revolution was achieved by those "who gave evidence of an outlook opening onto the past (prior to the shogunal period)—that is to say, who became aware of the historic dimension of their task, manifesting a remarkable capacity to assimilate modern civilization." But what is eminently significant is that the Meiji revolution gave no evidence of a plan, and whereas many "managers" may have been involved in it, they were not conscious of guiding a revolution and did not build upon the gains accumulated in the early revolts. This is an irony of history associated with what impresses me as the typical revolution.

CHAPTER

[2]

REVOLUTION
WITHIN HISTORY

Myth and Model

We have tried to approach the revolt-revolution complex through the data of historical experience, which is the only valid way to explore it intelligently. But within that conceptual framework, what we found was an antihistorical attitude. We realize, however, that everything will begin to shift once we reflect on, envisage, and grasp those phenomena as part of history. Until the eighteenth century, on the rare occasions when the nature of revolution preoccupied men such as Machiavelli, Bodin, and Hobbes, for instance, it was always with the intent of finding ways to prevent popular unrest, to maintain authority, to quell disorder. Revolution was looked upon as a political accident. It was not contemplated, thought about, and studied for its own sake. And it was certainly not desirable. But as intellectuals began to grapple with the problem, revolution emerged from its immediacy. An image of revolution could be perceived, and a completely different purpose: it was less a public explosion than an attempt to apply a theory.

Revolution, perceived globally thereafter, was to be totally
embodied in exceptional revolutionary circumstances, which
were revived, appraised, and analyzed after the fact in order
to enrich the body of human thought. So we shall explore two
relationships with revolution understood and thought of in the
context of history: first, the elaboration of a myth of revolution,
then the attempt to establish a pattern of revolution. It may
lead us directly to the problem, thus far unresolved, of how to
define revolution.

Absolutization: Rational Revolution

Although the entire range of revolutionary movements has
been studied, although Godechot presented a perfectly accurate theory, according to which the French Revolution of
1789 was only an undercurrent in the vast revolutionary mainstream of the years 1770–99, and was ultimately a Western
revolution rather than a French one, 1789 nevertheless has
acquired a unique reputation. It had an unprecedented impact
on the minds of men, not because of any single event—the
king's death, let us say, for many other revolutions sent kings to
their death—not because of its excessive violence and the
severe penalties it imposed—for it was not as bloody as was
said; but because no other revolution had such profound consequences. Hannah Arendt admits this grudgingly.[1] We cannot
overlook the weight of impressions and opinions. It is pointless
to call them errors of historical perspective: even if they were,
the errors are part of history. Human beings licensed the
revolution of 1789–99, and countless factors reinforced it: lofty
principles and the use of propaganda; a challenge to a whole

---

[1] It is certain that the American Revolution, which influenced that of 1789,
had no effect whatever on later revolutionary development. Neither the les-
sons of 1776 nor the doctrine of its "Founding Fathers" had the slightest impact on Europe. It was as if there had never been a revolution in America.
This is indeed what contemporary historians believe! Hannah Arendt, who
holds the American Revolution to be the only genuine one, finds no consola-
tion in the historical "blunder" that made the revolution of 1789 the model
and the catalyst for what followed.

way of life; military successes; the men who made it; the application of new techniques resulting from the industrial revolution; the great variety of organized efforts; imagination and implacability; and the contradictions between pronouncements and actions. It left nothing intact. It was the first global revolution, and one of the few successful revolutions. It had far-reaching consequences. For example, Marx used it as his revolutionary model, analyzed it in depth, and from it—and from it alone, I would add—evolved his concept of class struggle and his theory of revolution. In his usual (and indeed regrettable) manner, he started with a limited historical analysis, then applied it to all of history and went on to construct a universal philosophy of history. The two key concepts in his interpretation of the dialectic of history derive from that revolution. His entire analysis is bound up with the *specificity* of that *single* revolution. The fact alone that it generated the current Marxist movement endows it with special distinction! I have no intention of addressing myself to this point and joining the ranks of writers who have managed to exhaust the subject. I simply wish to emphasize one idea: the revolution of 1789 marked the division between the old pattern of revolution and the new one it was to engender, which took shape solely in the mind of Marx. It highlighted all the characteristics of the relationship between revolt and revolution. More than any previous event, it testified to the significance of the revolutionary doctrine or plan, and, reciprocally, to the role of the administrators and organizers. It inherited the legacy of revolt's libertarian inspiration. Upon it we base our (frequently inflated) affirmations that "liberty is the heartbeat of revolution" and that "liberty is the essence of all revolutions." [2] In his celebrated speech on the tenets of the revolutionary government

---

[2] We cannot accept Hannah Arendt's generality (in *Essay on Revolution,* Chapter I) that the only content of revolution is liberty. In her view, revolutions, civil disturbance, *coups d'état,* and insurrections differ in that revolutions invariably and of necessity introduce liberty; violence is revolutionary only when it attempts to lay a new political foundation for liberty. This strikes me as undoubtedly applicable to America, but without any historical warranty. It is another preconception that allows us to assess the value of historical events when we ought to be observing them directly.

(December 25, 1793), Robespierre stated that "revolution is liberty's war against its enemies," and Saint-Just, once he had exhausted the verbal transports identifying the myth of liberty and began to analyze, contributed his own terrifyingly accurate observations. When the people have tasted victory, they succumb to fear: "fear makes them forget that they were free"; then they become a menace—"it was their passion for liberty." For Saint-Just, liberty is the razor's edge; there is no public freedom if men are not worthy of it: "Search your heart for virtue if you would discover whether you are worthy of liberty." "When souls have lost their marrow and lack the vigor to cherish liberty, they still cling to its name, craving its comfort and protection, forgetful of its virtue."

Thus liberty depends ultimately on the individual. That is the link between the rebel's yearning for liberty and the revolutionary's concept of liberty. But when liberty is won by destroying the oppressor, make no mistake, Saint-Just warns: "Passion is the soul of liberty; in time it withers and fades forever, for we are virtuous only once . . . when a liberated people has established sound laws, its revolution is achieved." But the relationship between virtue and liberty is not simply a word: virtue is self-discipline, and Saint-Just offers a remarkable maxim that defines all revolutionary movements: "Liberty that prevails must become corrupted: I have said all." [3] Thus he depicted at the outset the drama of his and of many other revolutions: the passion for liberty was destined to remove all restraints and, by the same token, to destroy liberty. The perceptiveness alone of such an observation sets that revolution apart, for none prior to it gave comparable evidence of rational thought. But in contrast to the ideas of Saint-Just, which were quickened by the surge of revolution, what rationalizing went on! Condorcet is a typical example: "The word 'revolutionary' can only apply to revolutions whose goal is liberty." A mechanistic attitude and, what is more, a dogmatic state-

---

[3] Saint-Just, *L'Esprit de la Révolution*, 1791.

ment that denies the tragic character of liberty and returns us to the normal course of revolution, wherein, as we have noted, some blurred myth of liberty is always in the background. The revolution of 1789 fostered the traditional myth but could not give it life. That myth remained just as it was, the unattainable vision of a new world without new men, with only new institutions. The revolution shattered the absurd notion that "changing life" was possible without also "changing men," and that it was enough to have proclaimed the Republic and the Constitution. We say therefore that Hannah Arendt's remarkable essay is based entirely on a misconception: she confuses liberty with institutions, free institutions with constitutionality. She regards the evolution of the French constitution, together with its purely classic outlook, as the supreme revolutionary act. She fails to recognize the specificity of the new revolutionary phenomenon and stresses organization, as others have stressed violence. But what is important is to show how the revolution of 1789 relates to traditional upheavals. That revolution, unmistakably a myth of liberty, yet also of a reactionary nature, was largely both conservative and reactionary. We know how conservative the *cahiers* of the States General were. None of them challenged the political system and the king. They dealt with various constitutional alterations and specific changes to the operation of communities; they sought to diminish feudal privileges that had become onerous; many of them were content to rely on the king for reforms; and the most daring among them demanded the abolition of feudalism (already moribund) and of seignorial rights, as well as of the *tailles* and *gabelles*. Nowhere in the *cahiers* was there any hint that revolution was on the way. History had known much graver crises. In short, the *cahiers* made no mention of desired socioeconomic changes or greater commercial flexibility; their restraint revealed their conservative nature.

At first, the revolutionaries were determined only to restore the old order that had been impaired by the abuses of absolute monarchy. The movement leading up to the revolution was not revolutionary "except through inadvertence," as Hannah Arendt aptly puts it. Not the overthrow, but the restoration of the old regime was sought.[4]

Yet there was more behind it: an element of the fundamental doctrine, of the revolutionary plan itself. Couched beneath a more or less misconstrued Rousseauism was the mystique of a *return* to nature, to the primeval age, to the beginning of society, when men were not yet bound by political and social ties. Everything had to start anew because everything had been falsified at the source. Power rested solely upon the sovereign will of the masses, a type of natural and unopposable force that sought to identify the popular will, the expression of which varied according to moods and factions. The return to the past could be discerned on every ideological level during that period. It also took the form of a mythical return to the first ideal moment of the absolute beginning, but instead of being the creation, as in primitive mythology, that *in illo tempore* was the origin of society. It was also a historical return to the great epoch of civil society, beyond monarchy and feudalism, the idyllic age in which men were equal and citizens, in which there was universal sharing of power: the Roman Republic. That explains the reference to Brutuses and Catos, the praenomens, the ceremonious eloquence, the exalting of unfailing civic virtue symbolized by the republican heroes, and the magistrates appointed tribunes and consuls. Like the most traditional revolutions, it sought to renew its ties with the past, to reincarnate itself in something already said, already done, and already seen. It found both mythical and historical roots for itself. It did not attempt to rush headlong into the future, but instead wanted to incarnate a more authentic past. Babeuf, the most inflammatory of the revolutionists, provided the following definition: "What is a political revolution generally? Open warfare between *patricians* and *plebeians*, the rich and the poor. Because the aim of revolution is *to take us back to*

---

4 Tocqueville, *L'Ancien Régime et la Révolution.*

the aim of society, of which we have lost sight, it is also the common welfare." [5] Roman battles were also referred to, recalling history no longer relevant to French society. Taking another view of 1789, and one actually much closer to the thinking of the revolutionaries themselves, Michelet wrote: "I define revolution as the advent of law, the resurrection of human rights, and the revival of justice." [6]

That brief formula contains the two principal themes of the revolution. The advent of law was not simply the valid jurisdiction of a legitimate authority, or the disclaiming of legislation enacted by the old regime, for it heralded the dawn of the social covenant, at which time the reign of law became possible. The specific events of past history were blacked out by the lens of myth. Even the will of the people no longer obtained, but instead, Anglo-Saxon law and ideology, an ideology providing that when the law has ruled, the facts exist and comply with it. The feat of returning to the cradle of society explains the revolutionists' anger and dismay: they were promulgating laws destined to govern the world, and then found that events ran counter to beliefs, that the facts would not yield. The only plausible explanation was lack of virtue, conspiracy, or ill intent. Therefore the facts had to be obliterated in order to uphold the principle that the law reigns supreme, equitably, impartially, and justly over all and everyone. Hence the persecutions, the exclusions, and the penalties, intended simply to eliminate obstacles dividing the facts from the law. Hence the elimination of everyone who represented not primarily conflicting interests or personal antagonisms, but historical strata separating the present from the dawn of society: everyone who stood for accumulated traditions, the nobility and the clergy, customs and habits, privileges (private laws) and pragmatic structures, the flexibility of usage as opposed to the intransigency of dogma, human understanding in contrast to unyielding justice. Those who were condemned were not judged

---

[5] *Le Tribun du peuple,* No. 3.
[6] Michelet, *Histoire de la Révolution française,* Introduction.

offenders but simply the embodiment of obstacles, shadows dimming the crystalline purity of that first dawn of society.

Michelet also speaks of the resurrection of human rights— that is, on an entirely different level, the retracing of history, the return to a time *in history* when a code of rights existed.

The accumulated mass of rules, cavils, jurisdictions, and political artifices had served to obscure the law, to tyrannize over, to stifle, and gradually to destroy it. By rediscovering authentic legality in the past, men could restore it and thus return to an acceptable past. The determination to turn backward in search of justice was common to all revolutions in the immediate circle of that of 1789. Chief among them was the American Revolution, the single goal of which was to correct the abuses of colonial government. Paine wanted only to reclaim the former significance of the word "revolution": the return to an era before men had been dispossessed of their rights and freedoms. This highly conservative attitude gave rise to the opinion that the American Revolution never really occurred! It was made by men who had discussed the issues and taken a joint pledge; in essence, it combined common consent with common deliberation. Yet the very fact that the conspirators escaped revolutionary violence is what enabled them to carry on the old order and to secure, in the state, a new order.

That revolution led to a resolutely aristocratic constitution. Of course, the rebels expelled their enemies and confiscated their property, thereby abolishing feudal obligations. But in the South, the revolution unquestionably benefited the aristocracy by allowing slavery to continue. In certain northern states, many aristocrats stayed on and were warmly welcomed by the revolution. Indentured immigrant labor was maintained, as were certain aspects of the domanial system, offspring of feudalism. These are curious applications of (or should we say deviations from?) the constitution and its guaranteed human rights, but to explain it as class struggle and bourgeois ideology operating behind a mask is oversimplification. Such an interpretation (universal today owing to obsessive Marxism) is quite incomplete and perhaps misleading. We shall have occasion to come back to it. Godechot is infinitely more justified in saying: "The American Revolution sought to establish freedom and democracy by reverting to former institutions. It was revolutionary to the extent that it was conservative." [7] Conservatism also marked the revolutions carried out in Geneva and the Low Countries, which resemble the French Revolution in their turning backward to a distant past.

The Revolution of 1789 is thus very similar to all those we have mentioned. It turned to a mythical or historical past and implied a rejection of probable history, history predictable within the normal course of events. It was a rejection of historical continuity, of the sovereignty of history and the claims it imposed. The most basic opposition to the monarchy gave evidence of that. The revolution involved not a political system, but an attitude toward events. Monarchic policy has always been pragmatic, taking into account facts as well as possibilities, a game with no rules in the thick of events, the object of which is to gain the upper hand in ever-recurring situations. With such mobility, kings took a wide range of postures depending on the potential advantages at hand. Whenever the opportunity arose, they seized upon the legacies of the past. They piled up gains, according to no observable principles or guidelines; they were politicians; that is, they plunged into history, repeated it, and made it respond to them. But we are concerned with a rationality imposed on events, a doctrine that prevails over circumstances. Government as well as the framework of institutions must be rational. Reason rules instead of history; the two are in bitter conflict. History is repudiated on the grounds that reason is mistress of human behavior.

---

[7] Godechot, op. cit., p. 102. We shall not emphasize the American Revolution, which was only a partial revolution. Men living in that period were right to call it instead the War of Independence. We have traced only its broad outline, and for a more detailed treatment, a recent publication will prove more helpful than Hannah Arendt's classic volume. See M. Alden, *A History of the American Revolution*, 1969, the historical detail of which all but destroys the myth of an innovative and liberating revolution.

There is no entering the course of history; instead, men plunge into a beginning, or a fresh beginning, and what follows is not regarded as history either, but as the Apocalypse or entrance into the City of Absolute Good. No chain of consequences was foreseen because such a vision embraced only peace, human welfare, fellowship, and harmony: mediocrity no longer had any claim on events. We are not exploring a revolution in the direction of history, for that was of no interest to any revolutionary of the period 1789–99. We may gauge Marx's error, therefore, in terms of the revolutionary plan of those years.

There is a second point of conflict. It has been said that 1789 "was the first successful revolution, but it was a bourgeois revolution." I do not think we can call it the first successful revolution, for there were those of the medieval communes, the English revolution of 1640, the American Revolution, and many others. All of them had one thing in common: they were achieved by the bourgeoisie. The communes were bourgeois, and even if the word had a different context from the one it acquired later on in the eighteenth and nineteenth centuries, we should recognize the strong economic and social parallels between those groups. Stanislas and Gustavus III made their revolutions with the inspiration of the bourgeoisie and the support of that class. They fulfilled the political and social aspirations of that group. The English revolution, through the agency of Cromwell, was the same as that of the communes: it involved the mercantile, property-owning, and jurist sectors. They opposed the Levelers in the same way that Robespierre opposed the Fanatics and Babeuf. The American Revolution involved primarily the leaders of commerce and the planters, and began for purely commercial reasons. One might almost say that all successful revolutions were, in the final analysis, bourgeois revolutions, led by the bourgeoisie. Does that mean the bourgeoisie was the first revolutionary class in history? The idea is not without validity. The bourgeois is not a rebel. As long as he is not in power, he has the capacity to be a revolutionary,[8] namely, the ability to create the design of future society, the doctrine, which, besides representing his own interests, serves as a tie-line to revolt; and, in addition, his vast managerial talent. He gathers the fruits, sorts them, presses out their juice, and makes the final product. Hence the accepted notion that the bourgeoisie took over the Revolution of 1789, which otherwise was a revolution at the base, of the common people: the artisans who stormed the Bastille (but were not the majority of those artisans of the bourgeoisie?), the *Bras-nus* (the shirtsleeve crowd), and the "stocking-knitters" who gave the revolution its drama. This view seems false to me.

Whether class struggle ultimately played a role in that revolution is still an open question. Was the antagonism between bourgeois and *Bras-nu* so intense that it constituted a class conflict? Guérin holds the view that it was; Soboul rejects it. The answer remains uncertain.

The *Bras-nus* and members of the revolutionary Sections were of course the ones responsible for the spectacular street and prison scenes. But those were instances of mob violence, armed assault, and the exhilarating release of momentary passions, not revolution. Robespierre realized that by crushing the rebel power of the Commune and the Sections he had saved the revolution. For its doctrine, program, and plan were created by the bourgeoisie. It was they who formed, out of the widespread fear and massive outbreaks of revolt, the nucleus of revolutionary institutions, instruments to carry out the revolution, popular societies, and the Committee of Public Safety. Without their impetus, nothing would have been achieved. The rebellion in the Vendée was just as large-scale and popular as that of the *Bras-nus*. And let us not forget that in 1794, nearly two-thirds of the *départements* opposed the revolutionary power. Why, then, was there not another revolution? Because of the lack of a common strategy, the failure to exploit the gains won by violence. The bourgeoisie of the revolution did not expropriate what the populace had achieved by force

---

[8] J. Ellul, *Métamorphose du bourgeois*, 1967.

of arms, for without the bourgeoisie there would have been no progress beyond the stage of revolt, and no revolution at all.

Marx perceived that the bourgeoisie had assumed a revolutionary role. But at some point he had to deal with this perplexing question: Was the bourgeoisie the only group in history capable of achieving a revolution? He answered it by developing his philosophy of the classes and of revolution. The bourgeoisie provided a typical example, and a model, but not the only one. The success of the bourgeoisie could not be traced to its abilities or its intrinsic specificity; otherwise, we would have no general view of history and no hope of another revolution. The bourgeoisie owed its success to its condition alone, its situation in relation to the economic and industrial world. At that point Marx was justified in concluding that any group in similar circumstances at a given moment should be able to carry out a revolution. At the same time, he recognized that, according to this view, the bourgeoisie had not made a revolution in order to return to the past, but that, owing to its task of fulfilling its own condition and exploiting— despite the obstacles represented by certain political and economic structures—the force it embodied, the revolution against those obstacles took the path of history and extended it, regardless of the ideological attitudes of the class in question. Students of Marx admit reluctance to take a stand as to whether Marx was primarily a philosopher who, out of his philosophy, evolved a pattern of history which he then applied to historical reality; or whether his compassion and dismay over the lot of the working class generated his philosophy; or, finally, whether certain historical events he interpreted, particularly the Revolution of 1789, left a deep impression on him, and his interpretation became incorporated in the philosophy he evolved from Hegel. This last aspect is the one to which I would draw attention. Marx was undoubtedly correct in stating that the bourgeoisie, because of its increasing economic influence, needed to reconcile the balance of society with the new economic orientation, and that, in particular, it required the monopoly of political power which normally belongs to the group wielding *de facto* power or, under those circumstances, economic power. That was the very content of the revolution. Marx also indentified accurately the conflicts that divided groups on various social levels, the interests of which differed. Let us call them class conflicts, a term Marx (and many others as well, including Turgot) used in this instance. We know that he proceeded to expand his analysis to cover all revolutionary phenomena. In addition to his error in formulating a general law from a particular instance, he also amputated a part of the phenomenon by considering only the *situation* of the bourgeoisie and not its specific attitude, its essential fitness. The fact that the revolution involved the bourgeoisie is precisely what gave it its dual nature, both old and new.

We have seen how 1789 resembled all prior revolutions, with its rejection of approaching history, its return to the past and to the beginning of things. It was, at the same time, radically new in that it set out toward the future and sought to create a new historical future. Belief in progress was also in evidence. That revolution therefore marked a significant change in the concept of revolution; though it followed the traditional pattern, counter to history, it aspired to advance history toward absolute betterment.

It is amusing to note that Mounier, who failed to discern its truly dual nature, could say that the revolution introduced unwelcome elements—rationalism, ideology, totalitarianism, and individualism—together with very desirable ones: "the threads of our national, monarchic, and Christian tradition." [9] In other words, what was really new and good, the ties with the past, was bad! And R. Labrousse is even more ambiguous: "Men carried out an experiment in behalf of concepts at once reactionary and premature: reactionary because their culture was in essence merely a class culture. . . . Admirers of the literary past . . . seeking to found a nation of citizen laborers and soldiers. . . . Yet that ideology contained a wealth of

---

[9] *Esprit,* 1939.

fruitful intuition, for it envisioned a secular, rational, and homogeneous community, overflowing with fervent self-love, and, in short, totalitarian."[10] Revolution was no longer a repudiation of the predictable future or an acceleration of the pace of history; it was the actual process of creating history. The confusion derives from the inherent nature of the bourgeoisie, which is both conservative and revolutionary. What was the bourgeoisie seeking? Directly or indirectly, the answer to that question marks the trend of history at a given time.

Liberty was only an alibi, a setting, a standard revival of the theme of every revolt. The protagonist was a rational, progressive, and pragmatic class (materialistic in the practical sense of the word). The novelty of that revolution resided in the fact that it was led by a group possessing those qualities. It sought power in order to reconcile political reality with economic reality. And on that, in general, Marx focused his attention. He observed that there was class conflict, and that the class wielding economic power was capable of making a revolution whereby the state would change form and hands. From that he inferred the predominance of economic power and the realignment of political structures after the latter had provided the rising class with every opportunity for development. While the state evolved as the framework of economic activity, the crisis involving that political and social realignment constituted revolution. The design was exquisite, and all the more enticing because it coincided with a particular view of Hegel's philosophy. But it was not the total picture of 1789. The bourgeoisie was a rational class and wanted rationality to prevail in every sector, corresponding to its faith in science (and the advent of scientific development) as well as its theory of progress. The three developed at the same rate. We need not go into the details of Sorel's remarkable analysis of progress,[11] in which he explains its origin and how it constitutes a bourgeois

---

[10] Ibid.
[11] G. Sorel, *Les Illusions du progrès*.

ideology, and Marx's complete espousal of that ideology. The doctrine of progress also typifies the novelty of the revolution, which turned to the future and took its place in history yet to be written, positive history, in which tomorrow could not fail to outshine today, promising endless rewards in every area of existence, and no sacrifices. The phenomenon of revolution is thus but an accelerated phase of progress, or better still, the rerouting onto the track of progress of a train that has gone astray. In that ideological framework, we can see that revolution becomes something quite different from the outcome of revolt or the desperate rejection of a hopeless existence. Though all revolutions prior to 1789 were tragic and, as we have seen, the rebel, like a pirate, knew what fate awaited him, this revolution, because it was made by the bourgeoisie, turned optimistic in spite of the painful execution scenes, the defeats, and the failures. The doctrine of progress was linked with a sense of the revolution's irresistible course; the tide of revolution is such that nothing can withstand it. That theme recurs constantly among the Jacobins, and with Vergniaud as well: a force more powerful than man manifested itself in the revolutionary event. The emergence of the poor, in 1792, as a moving force of revolution reinforced that theme: the flood of poor people gave concrete form to the idea of irresistibility, and certainly must have fostered the notion of a kind of necessity inherent in the course of revolution which later came to be expressed as a historic necessity. Thus the fatalism of the irresistible tide of revolution gave place to the concept of a necessity inherent in the course of history, in which revolution played a part.

Being in the path of progress preceded taking the direction of history. But the rationalism of the bourgeoisie (derived from its economic and financial role, its religious skepticism, its desire for knowledge and participation in scientific development) had many other results, foremost among which was the conceptualizing of ideas. Revolution was a juridical construct that met the demands of reason, but to arrive at it called

for first abstracting its components. Man became the abstract
citizen, and concrete liberty, abstract civil liberty. The
tendency had only just begun; it continued throughout the
rule of the bourgeoisie. It was in the context of that rationality
that the rejection of past history gave place to a theoretical
concept of power. The entire administrative system was based
on abstraction (the structure of the *départements,* for example) as was the judicial one. Abstraction ultimately embraced the homogeneity of the social organism: one man
was the equal of another, whatever the differences in their
social status, their power, or their levels of poverty. But a
social body composed of abstract units required a regulatory
agency. The bourgeoisie envisaged the state itself, apart from
the forms it would assume, as a rationality. The revolutionists
were obviously not familiar with the philosophy of Hegel,
whose ecstatic worship of the state did not reach its zenith
until after the Revolution of 1789. But long before Hegel, and
as an outgrowth of the application of reason to society, they
recognized the desirability of the state: an abstract, rigorous,
perfectly designed, and supreme authority, dispassionate and
impartial, vested neither in perpetually fallible man nor in a
too-remote deity; precise as a scale, yet simple as a squaring
tool; a state that functioned in society as the brain in the
human organism—a recurring image throughout the period.
The bourgeoisie made the revolution to seize power, but also
to institute the supremacy of reason in the state—in order to
achieve at last an ordered state. In the eyes of those masterly
bourgeois administrators and managers, the unpardonable disgrace of monarchic government was its incoherence and in-
effectuality. The common people shouted tyranny; the
bourgeoisie railed against neglect. What shocked the revolutionaries was not the Bastille itself but the fact that anyone
and everyone was imprisoned there haphazardly, without due
process of law, without established rights, without any
systematic examination of charges or penalties. The death
sentence can be imposed indefinitely as long as it is based

upon rational rules and represents a well-ordered system. Fiscal chaos, not excessive taxation, was the chief concern. When the revolutionists finally reorganized the financial system, the burden of taxes became far more severe than it had been ten years earlier, but the system had become coherent, rational, and uncompromising. Bourgeois rationalism required a rational state—that is, the state *per se,* the supreme value, society's crowning achievement. And as a result, revolt and revolution, which strike at the state, serve to fortify it. Tocqueville demonstrated brilliantly that the principal phenomenon of the revolution was unquestionably the development of the state.[12] The monarchy had reached a certain stage of growth and organization and a certain degree of efficient political power, but its long years of service, its unwritten laws, and its traditions immobilized it. The very nature of the monarchy was an obstacle to the harmonious evolution of the state. The bourgeoisie sensed this and experienced it very keenly in numerous small ways, without conceptualizing or being aware of it. They simply felt it was not "normal" for such incoherence and muddle to persist and for government, despite all the devices of tyranny, to remain helpless. Both structural and political changes had occurred in the shift from a feudal to a centralized monarchy, then from a ministerial to an absolute monarchy, but eventually all further movement was blocked. A more radical transformation of the constitution was in order if the state, cramped by the matrix of the monarchy, was to continue to grow and flourish. The bourgeosie was the instrument of this change, both because of its place within the state itself and because of its rational view of society. So the alterations only disguised and facilitated the growth of the core, the rationality, and the finality of the state. With each constitutional reform the revolution fortified the state—additional evidence that it was entirely new and distinct from all other revolutions. We have already seen that

---

[12] Tocqueville, op. cit.; De Jouvenel, *Du Pouvoir,* 1947.

revolution frequently occurred in relation to the state—but against it, and, specifically, against its development and organization. In Russia, England, France, Germany, and China, revolts broke out against the changing aims of political power. And indeed man unfailingly rejects every effort in the direction of efficiency, regulation, tighter organization, and the subdivision of judicial, administrative, and fiscal functions.

In that respect, the Revolution of 1789 was the opposite of all other revolutions. Moreover, until that time liberty had been held to be in direct conflict with power. Liberty within the framework of revolt was violent protest against authority, the *seigneur*, and ultimately (in lieu of the king, who was always removed from such disputes) the state. In practice it was directed against the organ of state rather than against the titular holder of sacred power. The advent of 1789 changed all this, and the state became associated with liberty. The shift in attitude was apparent during the very course of the revolution. Prior to June 1793, Robespierre and Saint-Just regarded the popular societies, clubs, and community action groups as "the pillars of the constitution," "the cornerstones of liberty." But once those men attained power, they were subject to the law of power. It was not opportunism on their part; it was inescapable evidence that when the just cause had triumphed, its law was supreme. Thereafter the popular societies and Commune sections became elements of disorder, of division and treachery, and therefore counterrevolutionary. "The so-called popular societies are rebelling against the popular Great Society of the French people" (Robespierre). The centralized state had become the revolution's masterwork and a liberator.

Through a singular process of transfer, the king, who had been sacred, beyond the reach of rebellion, and unopposed in the struggle for liberty, became a tyrant, and liberty equivalent to the tyrant's death. Conversely, what had been regarded theretofore as the embodiment of oppression, the apparatus of state, its ministries and administrative ranks, became the flagbearer and symbol of liberty. A remarkable relationship grew out of the fact that the state was produced by the revolution. On the one hand, it was the guarantor of liberty—for the first time in history—and power became liberty's champion, guiding, condemning, and doing battle in the name of liberty. On the other hand, liberty became identified with institutions, an innovation that later evolved into liberalism. It was an extension of the American idea that freedom resided in the application of the Constitution. Thus liberty was the victim of both rationalism (the most irrational elements of human nature were incorporated into the most rational of systems) and abstraction. Liberty mediated by the state could not possibly resemble that to which dissident Cossacks, Chinese outlaws, and the *Croquants* gave the same name. It had become abstract in turn, to be divided and redistributed by social power. Liberty interpreted by the state marked the absolutization of the revolution. Prior to the revolution of 1770–89, such an attempt to resolve all manner of social and human problems had never been made. As a result, and concurrently, that revolution was to adopt a new revolutionary banner replacing the traditional one of liberty and signaling the determination to secure the people's welfare. The concern for human welfare grew to such proportions after 1792 that the period could be identified as the great turning point in history. Previously, men had been preoccupied with liberty; afterward, they were preoccupied with social issues, which set the pattern for all future revolutions.[13]

That explains the appearance of the Fanatics, who represented the poor and the yearnings of society. Ever afterward, revolution was involved in a process that marked the era of revolution. Revolt might attain liberty momentarily; revolution transformed it into an institution. But then a social problem intervened: in order to eliminate injustice, the revolution, the supreme act of the poor, was bound to establish increasingly oppressive institutions. No revolution has ever solved "the

---

[13] The central theme of Hannah Arendt's book.

social dilemma," yet all have followed the pattern of the French Revolution in unleashing terrible suffering and deprivation, using those forces to strike at oppression, and then responding to the necessity of instituting even greater oppression. For the pressing imperative to solve the social problem must merge with evidence of the state's perfection. Owing to the event of revolution, the state assumes sole responsibility for securing human welfare, for establishing the reign of virtue, and for implanting a supreme standard of values. That role leaves a distinct mark on revolution, linking it with what has been called the age of suspicion. In 1789, the French Revolution was partly an attack on hypocrisy. It exposed court intrigue, tore the mask from society, and denounced the *real* Marie Antoinette. Soon it took to unmasking the revolutionaries themselves: the raw essence of human beings had to be laid bare. Revolt progressed by accusation; revolution turned to denunciation, and denunciation implied permanent suspicion of everything and everyone. Suspicion was introduced by the Terror and was not invented by philosophers (who are the product of circumstances); it has been the common thread of every revolution until now. But suspicion has only one target: whatever weakens the state; and only one purpose: to make the state the supreme arbiter in all matters. The state thereby acquires a totalitarian function—a great discovery made by that revolution of liberty. A child shall be taken from his parents in order to be educated properly: "The right to stain the most precious hopes of the Republic shall not be yours, and indeed it shall be forcibly denied to fathers if they are so unnatural as to seek to prevent their sons from becoming citizens. . . . The child's total existence belongs to us. . . . In that manner a new people shall be born" (Chazal, 1797). Surely that is the expression of a religious totalitarianism, the high priest of which is the state. The nation is the true religious reality: "Upon the ruins of cast-down superstitions you shall found the sole universal religion that promises peace instead of the sword, that fosters citizens instead of kings or subjects, brothers instead of foes, religion without factions or rites, whose sole doctrine is equality, whose oracles are the laws and whose pontiffs are the magistrates, and whose offerings of incense on behalf of mankind are dedicated only on the altar of the *nation,* the mother and deity of all" (André de Chénier, 1793). Out of this jumble of ideas, we need salvage only the principle of universality, the totality sought by the revolutionists.

The revolution always had a relatively precise, defined, and specific purpose. The verbal transports of the revolutionary orators are well known. Humanity acquired new significance. Nothing was left untouched. The revolution embraced everything, for it succeeded in absorbing even liberty instead of remaining the product of it. But everything absorbed was reshaped and reclaimed through the agency of that supreme achievement, the state. During that period, the absolutization of revolution was bound up with the universalization of the state: one absolute because it led to the state; the other universal because it was the product of the revolution. In that respect, 1789 differed from all prior revolutions. With its new elements, it was to shape the revolutions to come, each of which would lose some of the customary, ancient, and permanent qualities of historical revolutions and gain an increasing number of the innovative elements of 1789. That is also why that revolution is in the tide of history. But for that concept to attain universal credit, Marx had to appear and invest it with his authority. The choice he made was to prove decisive. It involved two alternate directions of history, each prescribed in the revolution: either class conflict, revolution carried out by the subservient class, possessor of the economic power of production and product of the gradual distortion between the forces and relations of production, and reaching prominence when an economic system has exhausted itself and generated intolerable decay in the social structure; or else the growth of the state, which gradually absorbs all sectors of society, each instance of revolution representing merely a crisis in that

growth and the climax of a slow process of transformation.
There was no rational certainty when Marx made his choice.

Myth and Model

Until 1789, revolutions were attempted and occasionally
achieved, but never romanticized. Then the era of the revolutionary epic began. Revolution, in the person of the revolutionaries, started to look at and admire itself, to grimace
and disport in the mirror. The myth of revolution was about to
descend on the modern world. We shall have to define this
elusive word, which is expected to convey any and every shade
of myth. I use it here in the sense it had for Sorel—that is, a
universal system of images capable of evoking instinctively
all the feelings and ideas corresponding to a sociopolitical
movement aimed at mass action; images to which myth gives
intense reality and which arouse intuitive identification between subject and object and among the subjects themselves.
In addition to the fact that it developed differently, the
Revolution of 1789 brought about the rewarding divorce
between "revolution-as-a-means" and "revolution-as-an-end,"
between the objective of revolution and the revolutionary
moment, so perfect intrinsically that it inspired yearnings for
its perpetual presence.

The French Revolution, as has often been observed,
has been the object of many myths. For some, it is the
absolute beginning, the political parousia, the dawn of humanity—the myth Halévy exposed. We know how many
history books regard everything prior to it as merely a prelude,
an introduction, a preamble: civilization did not begin until
1789. For others, it marked the onset of all our troubles, the
emergence of abstract rationalism, political realism, and absolute state power—the myth Mounier exposed. Still another
myth is taking shape, that of the victorious bourgeoisie, of the
domination by the exploiting class that destroys budding

socialism and robs the deserving masses of their rewards and hopes. The elaborate mythology sprung from that event is an indication of its mythical aspirations and its mythically projected self-image: the revolution became an instrument of propaganda because propaganda is what gave it life. Let us bear in mind the vast difference between revolution and everything leading up to it, what we call the plan or aim of revolution which must exist beforehand and has no relationship to the myth *of* revolution. Formerly revolution was fostered by ideology, but not the ideology of revolution itself.

Perhaps a partial answer to Hannah Arendt's thesis lies in the fact that the Revolution of 1789 (but not that of 1771) gained wide repute because it launched and publicized its own epic, in heroic tenor. Although the guillotine's (relatively) few victims became symbols of horror to future generations that viewed the period as an utter blood bath; although the death of Louis XVI attracted far more acclaim than that of the unfortunate Charles I; nevertheless every step of the revolution was extolled, as was each of its personalities, and its laws inspired endless commentary and a dramatic presentation. For the first time, propaganda was used systematically—and very effectively. "Behind the influence of the French, in their character and especially in their language, is a proselytizing force beyond imagination: the entire nation is an inexhaustible source of propaganda," Joseph de Maistre remarked aptly in 1815. The revolution was personified as an object of admiration, to be venerated by the worthy and to inspire terror in the guilty. Behind the image of the nation or of liberty was that of the revolution. Nothing could be allowed to impede its triumphant progress, not because its proposed aims were valid, but because it was valid in itself. The chief concern, at least at the start, was not with institutions or even doctrines; it was with attitudes toward the revolutionary event. Was one for or against it? was the crucial question of those ten years. The revolutionary plan became less important than the fact of revolution, seen as a glorious and dynamic symbol. In former

times an objective might have been advanced *in the interest of*
revolution; now the image of revolution itself was the essential
thing. The old revolutionary plan used to be in the realm of
doctrine, based on revolt; now the plan took the shape of
beliefs and was rooted in revolutionary activity itself.

But here the word "myth" does not imply the mysticism often
present in revolt, which envisioned the fulfillment in some
celestial city of a movement doomed on earth. The two are
vastly different. Mysticism never set revolution as its goal, and
it often served as compensation for visible disaster. In 1789,
revolution inspired its own mystique, in itself an assurance of
success. The revolution became a cult object, claiming men's
unquestioned faith and complete devotion. In other words,
revolution as an entity assumed a positive image in human
consciousness: that is the myth of revolution. Revolution is
the bearer of liberty and justice to oppressed peoples, and
therefore no longer a *means* to obtain one or another result; it
ceases to signify a period of disorder, a crisis, perhaps unavoidable, but to be settled nevertheless by the most rapid and
acceptable means; it is the supreme *moment,* the pivot of
history, that which justifies the movement preceding and
culminating in it exclusively and sends mankind on its journey
of fulfillment. It is the *moment* when man is at last free, an
apotheosis on earth in which all of humanity shares.

But propaganda alone does not explain the occurrence of
myth or the transformation it produces. Propaganda has a lasting effect only on those who are ready to absorb it. A whole
series of contributory phenomena has shaped it; a mental galaxy
has been created which a single word must evoke. Strange as it
may seem, the myth of revolution could not exist until revolution appeared to be a part of history, in the tide of historical
events, so that it was regarded as the very context of history.
As long as it remained a rejection of history, it was some
mysterium tremendum that could never be reasoned—the
final plunge into the unknown, where one encountered God.
Only when it joined the flow of purely human affairs did it

assume the stature of an event, the great event, but a human one. A secular and progressive society had to exist before revolution could acquire the amplitude and vitality of myth for man, who, locked in his own history and denied refuge by his gods, had no other escape than revolution. The shaping of a human and historical attitude toward events did not make them rational, and, in fact, gave rise to the myth of events.

Thus a progressive outlook, a relatively secular society, and the direct experience of individualism had to manifest themselves, culminating in such faith in progress that the act of revolution represented no more than a penstroke eliminating every obstacle to progress. Individualism was freely expressed during the revolutionary period, which produced a wealth of individualists, gave everyone a chance for renown, and immortalized itself through its heroes. We have already noted that the revolution was embodied in the revolutionary hero, all types of which emerged.

It was also a period of tremendous activity. The burst of energy during that brief time obviously had a greater impact on independent thinkers than on others, and to the extent that the revolution struggled to defend individualism, it was indeed triumphant. Related to that was the assurance of control over nature (borne out by elementary scientific probings) and the concept of society as a species of nature with independent laws that had to be recognized and observed as laws were in the physical world, and owing to which society, like nature, could be acted upon through technical means. That correlation between nature and society, between science and politics, seems to me to be the pivotal aspect of the human attitude at the end of the eighteenth century which accounts for the glorification of the revolution, the moment of total, rational, and scientific policy. No earlier government had ever set out to remodel society completely. The most despotic regimes had attempted to bridle dominant groups and to rule by force. But only action on a limited scale, whether oppressive or not, had seemed expedient. Now, however, a refashioning of the entire social organism was in order, and a transformation of all relations and structures to make them responsive to reason. The harmony between politics and science was destined to foster myth by recovering the hope of unity for mankind. The revolution's theme of unity was indeed vital: for a century, strife between philosophy and religion had torn society and divided men's attitudes. Suddenly, the revolution provided a crucible in which all ideas could be blended into the cherished oneness. The religion of the Supreme Being was the promise of that. Another human aspect of the period which explains man's readiness to accept and embrace myth was the waning and devitalization of Christian faith. Of course, its rites and superstitions, its emotional bonds, and its magic continued to operate, but few men continued to believe seriously in the Supreme Dogma, and salvation had little reality and little to offer the men of that period. How, then, did the revolution appear to them? As an exact replica in history, in the present, and man-made, of what Christian doctrine had projected in imagery, in eternity, and in the future: namely, the Last Judgment on the way to paradise. Those were perhaps the last two surviving tenets of a Christian faith in which hell predominated and heaven took care of salvation. To the extent that those beliefs ultimately took the form of imagery in which Christ was absent, they were too vague to remain strictly Christian. But to the extent that the images were innately vital, the firm hold of faith shifted to their projected fulfillment. The revolution did in fact resemble the Last Judgment. It expressed justice that was both transcendent and imminent. What it spoke was absolutely just, but that justice was no longer beyond the realm of events. It was indeed the Last Judgment because no other was ever meant to follow. Tyranny would be abolished and the guilty punished and eliminated. The purging process, aimed at removing the bad from the good, would allow humanity to be regenerated, and society's original sin would not recur. Wherever the revolution touched, the final judgment would establish paradise. Justice and liberty: man reconciled at last with himself and his fellow beings. Thus because the *Christian* Last Judgment and paradise were no longer credible and because those images were firmly rooted in the human consciousness, men were prepared to accept the revolutionary judgment and paradise—that is, to transform revolution into myth. But some sort of collective alchemy is needed to produce a myth, which is never the invention of a single mind or attributable to a particular creator. It seems to me that this myth originated owing to two favorable and concurrent circumstances: the long initial period of theoretical maturation, of ideological preparation, and then the sudden contraction of momentous events. That two-tier movement produced the mythical synthesis consummated in the course of the revolution which made human consciousness accept the myth. Theoretical maturation, the century of enlightenment—we are far removed from the time when revolution was regarded as "the fault of Voltaire, the fault of Rousseau." Historical studies of the last fifty years have persisted in grossly reducing what used to be grossly inflated, and in view of the gulf between the specific ideas of Montesquieu, Rousseau, and the Encyclopedists and what was achieved during the Revolution, have concluded that those philosophers did not affect it at all. Not directly, and perhaps not in regard to the theories and the consciousness of the revolutionaries, but unquestionably they did affect the creation of an ideological climate, the topics of debate, the decline of social structures, and an orientation as well as a disorientation. Finding out *who* actually had read Rousseau or D'Alembert is totally irrelevant, for a trend of opinion may shape itself around the ideas of men whom no one has read. Between 1945 and 1950, the entire French nation turned Existentialist, yet how many people had read Sartre? Marcuse is said to have fathered the Paris riots of 1968, and we know what Cohn-Bendit has said of him. Still, it is perfectly true that those names had a catalytic effect on the ideological trend, though the believers had no knowledge of the ideas or sources involved. The tide of revolution was aided by an exceptionally long, unbroken, and general period of ideological formation, with the result that on the eve of 1789, a body of beliefs existed having a certain intellectual content. In that favorable environment, events would act like so many electric charges (again, I am not *explaining* events in terms of doctrine). If the revolution had been of short duration, if it had assumed only one aspect (constitutional *or* terrorist, for example), or if the outbreaks of violence had been *few* and widely separated, it is probable that no myth *of* the revolution would ever have emerged. The latter had first to acquire a wide range of expressions: peace-loving and aggressive, impartial and despotic, law-abiding and terrorist, virtuous and corrupt, disciplined and chaotic. Time and numerous events had to intervene while the catalyzing process was taking effect. The myth of revolution was born of the very synthesis of various components, for myth involves elements of thought, belief, and imagination, of active participation and of emotion. Even today we are living on that myth.

For us, revolution is always the way out, the possibility, the moment of truth, the end of tyranny, the dawn of the Golden Age. The solid structure of myth has served to foster revolutionary Marxism, anarchism, and National Socialism on the one hand, and the vulgarization of revolution on the other. The propaganda of the Great Revolution is still active among us, having implanted in our consciousness certain images to which we unfailingly respond.

Although we exist on the myth of revolution, still, having recognized that revolution (and not merely revolt) is a phenomenon worthy of observation and interest, we need to understand it and try to define it. Its pattern emerges, as does its myth, when we accept revolution as *a part of* history. Then and there it ceases to be a hypothetical eruption and hopelessly undefinable, the supreme accident that defies understanding. Once we establish revolution as an organic element of human history we can explore its laws and operation and, no matter how odd its appearance, analyze it. Such a flood of historical and analytical literature as poured forth at the close of the Revolution of 1789 had never appeared after any previous revolution. The next step was to discover the constants and to establish a universally valid pattern.

Believers live on myths, intellectuals on patterns. Here we are dealing with reactions to the existence of revolution, not with the activities of revolutionaries. For them, myth is the very core of existence as well as the means of acting upon others. A pattern is a type of strategy; we will take up this point later. For Marx, myth and pattern were closely re- lated, as were intellectual inquiry and objective intervention, the former serving the latter. I shall not reconstruct the revolutionary pattern laid out by Marx, which is all too familiar. In recent years, sociologists seem to have concen- trated on discovering patterns of revolution that can apply to all revolutions. Their efforts appear to follow two main lines of thought. For some, revolutionary movement is seen in socio- logical terms, and therefore entails a multitude of frequently unrelated factors that are inseparable from their historical con- text. If we are searching for a model, it is certainly not a design to fit all situations; the task of abstraction is done but is not carried as far as it can go, and the result is inevitably blurred. A typical example may be found in the work of Decouflé,[14] who sets up a diagrammatic schedule of the revolutionary process (plan/act/counterrevolution) and attempts to differ- entiate between plans according to whether they appear in societies of generalized or of residual poverty. But his exami- nation of "day-to-day revolution" relies heavily on the events of 1789–1871 and largely ignores any number of other revo- lutions. He views the "managers" or "administrators" of

---

[14] Decouflé, *Sociologie des révolutions,* 1968. His analysis, in any event, is far superior to Gallo's *Gauchisme, réformisme et révolution,* 1968, which yields a harvest of historical and sociological misconceptions. We have been unable to utilize Monnerot's excellent *Sociologie de la Révolution,* 1969, as it had not appeared when this manuscript was completed.

revolution somewhat as its gravediggers, whereas we have noted that they are, on the contrary, a characteristic of successfully developing revolutions. What I consider dangerous in such a sociology of revolution is the tendency (typical of nearly the entire sociological field) to identify a phenomenon with a type, to reveal its permanent aspects, and to arrive at a revolutionary identity. I believe that what we may call revolution is not always the same phenomenon, and that no sociological model exists—that, instead, a variety of patterns must be taken into account. Recognizing only one design, Decouflé, for example, proceeds to categorize individual Crusades as revolutions (a very rash assumption when you consider the Crusades in their entirety and not just a single aspect of them), and, conversely, to disregard utterly the fascist and Nazi revolutions, which cannot rightfully be ignored, on the grounds that because revolution represents value, they are not fit to bear that worthy name! It seems to me that revolutions of various types have occurred throughout history and cannot be reduced to a single entity.[15]

Relating (in historically relevant terms) revolution to global society, and a revolutionary plan to totality or historicity, seems to me the right approach to the problem; but it is the field of historical sociology and no longer the precise and binding pattern that Sorokin or Gurvitch tried to establish, and such analyses, unlike those of Marx, are of no material use in either predicting or preparing revolution. They recognize that common data exist and that perhaps a similar movement underlies all revolutions, but they do not take us beyond the descriptive and (relatively) concrete to the abstract and circumstantial. To do that we must go much farther and take a different point of view. In fact, method and point of view are in conflict, for if you evaluate revolution *per se* against the background of all revolutions, as I am doing

---

[15] The hopelessness of that position has led Crane Vinton (*The Anatomy of Revolution,* 1965) and Monnerot (op. cit.) to base their sociology exclusively on the American (1775), French (1789), and Russian (1917) revolutions, a limitation that seems scarcely tenable to me.

here, you cannot possibly reach a broad definition. You must
first observe society as a whole; within that sphere, revolution
then may be isolated and examined. Some historians have
ventured to do that in the hope of discovering a prototype.
I shall mention briefly an article by Cazelles [16] and shall deal
at greater length with one by Janne. Cazelles's detailed examination of an index of a particular period (to wit, the
composition, frequency, and organization of the Royal Council
in France between 1345 and 1360) is the basis for a systematic
correlation of various possible explanations of revolution:
those he mentions are individual or class rivalries, economic
competition, the emergence of ethical or legal standards, the
evolution of a new political philosophy, sociological change,
and dawning nationalism. His general conclusion is that each
global society contains a number of forces in conflict with one
another, each group, latent or open antagonisms—a fact, I
would add, that accounts for the vitality and potential displacement of a group. But an entire society cannot survive
without a system for resolving those conflicts and tensions.
In the period that Cazelles covers, the Royal Council appeared
to fill precisely that function: it was "the monarchy's safety
valve, on which opponents of the regime brought pressure,
and an outlet for the excess 'steam' they discharged periodically; owing to the Council's existence and its diverse jurisdictions and decisions in the midst of the bitter controversies
surrounding it, the king himself was not challenged. . . .
Owing to the Council's existence, revolutions were not too
bloody or too radical, and frequently turned out to be merely
a change in government officials." In other words, the Council
was a sounding board for dissent, an instrument for channeling
the currents of rebellion and for registering pressures, all of
which it absorbed (thus enabling the government to continue
functioning) and also utilized to mold and transform conflicting forces into tools of reform. As long as there is a device

---

[16] Cazelles, "Les Mouvements révolutionnaires du milieu du XVI⁰ siècle et
le cycle de l'action politique," *Revue Historique*, 1962.

for recording grievances, revolution does not occur, and agitation is made to serve a useful purpose. But if that device
becomes unresponsive; if it ceases to detect discord and to
transmit the components of it to the ear of government; if it
adopts one cause over many others; if it fails to provide a
means of negotiation—then the excluded, voiceless, and repressed forces inevitably assume a purely negative character
and revolution will follow. The picture is obviously accurate
and applicable to most revolutionary situations, but the pattern
seems limited and rather bare in contrast to the abundant
variety of revolution.[17] Janne's [18] reduction is much more complex and is closer to the view of T. Parsons. He succeeds in
establishing an authentic model containing what is essential
and meaningful, and eliminating accidental and contingent
factors. Janne starts with a schematic view of society, each
member of which belongs to different groups that interrelate
in various ways. The groups are stratified horizontally, essentially according to social classes, which, for Janne, com-
prise the controlling class, technical cadres, middle classes,
and the masses. There are also vertical stratifications of juxta-
posed groups: political parties, trade unions, churches, major
industry, the army, and the political structure. To determine
a man's social status, all the components must be averaged: in
one column (industry, for example) he may be at the top of
the hierarchy (a member of the cadres), yet elsewhere he may
be at the very bottom (of the political system, for instance, in
which he may be simply a voter and belong to the "masses").
Organizations that are adjuncts of the social structure (divided
into adjacent columns) tend to integrate the entire society.
Each has its own function in the over-all system: when a
change occurs in one column, it affects only the values and

---

[17] It should be noted that in the text of his article Cazelles does not claim to
present a true prototype or to generalize; his is a narrow study of historical
sociology. All the same, the title of the article suggests the intent to establish
a prototype.

[18] H. Janne, "Un modèle théorique du phénomène révolutionnaire," *Annales,
Économies, Sociétés, Civilisations,* 1960.

influence of that group and does not alter the rest of society or the cultural system; for each element of society has its corresponding set of values, a culture or subculture. Thus tension exists between the cultures represented by the horizontal groups and those of the vertical groups. The revolutionary phenomenon therefore has its origin in the pressure exerted by one of the "horizontal" cultures on the vertical or global culture. As long as that pressure does not create a strain in excess of society's resilience, revolution does not occur. When that resilience is overstrained, it triggers the revolutionary phenomenon—but prior to that, society spontaneously gears its entire stabilizing, equalizing, and adaptive apparatus through the agency of the vertical cultures. Political institutions, in particular, become instruments for offsetting "horizontal" stress, but they are less likely to operate in that manner if they are monopolized by the upper stratum (if the culture of the upper stratum alone merges with the culture of the vertical political system). Democracy alleviates the tension, but cannot do so under any and all circumstances. Revolution eventually arrives when pressure from a horizontal source exerts such stress that the monopoly of power retained by the political structure is broken. And if revolutionary power becomes sufficiently organized and integrated to be able to overthrow public power, it thereby is transformed into a new regime bearing a new culture. Apply this pattern and you will understand prerevolutionary situations as well as types and processes of revolution. Janne thus is able to demonstrate that a society in which social stratification is more tightly integrated on the horizontal level (social classes, for example) than in the vertical sense (groups integrated globally) tends toward the revolutionary process. If maximum integration is achieved on the horizontal level of the middle classes, a fascist type of revolution will follow; if it occurs among the masses, a socialist type of revolution. If it is carried out at the level of the peasantry, a *Jacquerie* will result. It should be noted that this scheme does not cover the specific problem of revolt, which is primarily a rural phenomenon. The peasantry has always shown inability to organize in order to acquire the monopoly of power for its own benefit. Accordingly, the normal failure of revolt should not be ascribed to the fact that it is a revolt but to the fact that it is of the peasantry. That is also why peasant risings gradually lose their significance from the nineteenth century onward. Peasant revolution is a sociological problem only for nonindustrial societies. In industrial societies, agriculture becomes a *vertical functional organization,* although the peasantry does not lose all the characteristics of a historically dominant social group. Finally, if maximum integration occurs in a dominated race within a multiracial society, the dominated race either is a majority, in which case revolution is one of decolonization, or it is a minority, and the task of revolution is to integrate the out group with the in group.

The pattern pertains to the revolutionary process, which is set in motion when "the quantum of action of the total negative social relations is greater than the quantum of action of the total positive social relations": what this actually means is that every global society involves elements of integration (positive) and of disintegration (negative). The integrating factors are primarily among the vertical groups, as we have seen, but the hierarchically positioned groups do not necessarily exert a disintegrating force.

The quantitative ratio between positive and negative social relations is therefore the index of integration into the over-all society. "The revolutionary phenomenon is the acute sign of disintegration." Even then, however, the process differs according to where the tension lies or where the divisive force is being exerted. If negative stress permeates society, a condition of general decadence exists, marked by gradual disintegration: it indicates that integration is not functioning properly throughout and not that a revolutionary force is in motion. A void in society is created thereby, inviting the intervention of either a vertical group (the army, for instance) or a horizontal one (a class), and in any case the least disintegrated group. If negative pressure polarizes a vertical group that remains the most closely integrated in society, then a *coup d'état* may occur, but not a revolution, for "the latter implies a new culture that can only emanate from a horizontal organism." If a vertical group attains major status, the global culture is not altered thereby but the standard of values within that culture is. On the other hand, when the polarization of a horizontal group introduces a complete cultural transformation and the group was not the controlling class but now becomes it, a conflict of culture exists among the horizontal groups.

Conversely, if the quantum of action of the total positive social relations is greater than the quantum of action of the total negative social relations, a revolutionary situation does not exist. If conflicts are distributed normally among all group relations, the society is well balanced, stable, and normally integrated in all sectors. If the pressure of negative relations acts primarily on the vertical strata, it indicates a struggle for power among the pressure groups; if it acts upon the horizontal strata, a peaceful (democratic) political struggle is in process among culturally nondominant classes, which tend to merge with political parties (vertical system).

Finally, in order to diminish the rather mechanistic nature of his model, Janne introduces the factor of consciousness. He shows, and rightly so, that emergent consciousness is directly related to the level of integration within each group, which in turn depends upon the relative stress of negative relations. But one must also consider the fact that institutions are incapable of reacting positively (a question with which Cazelles deals): "The self-awareness and the integrating force of a horizontal stratum tending toward revolution rest upon the lag between institutions and their capacity to meet the needs of society. . . . They also have a direct relationship to the degree to which the controlling class abandons its function."

That painstaking analysis is certainly thorough, but somehow unsatisfactory, like the application of mathematics to the study of revolution. For one thing, the pattern is intended to be universal, and, in a certain sense, it obviously is applicable to revolts and revolutions of past centuries. But it is actually rooted in the structure of modern Western societies. Though it may be relevant to other societies, it is based on class concepts, revolution, and the power structure in our own society. Abstraction changes nothing, for pre-established ideas underlie the construction of such a pattern, and all those ideas are bound up with our times and our civilization. In the end, everything hinges on 1789. And in that connection, I find one important element lacking: the diversity of the revolutionary phenomenon, its sources and origins, and its developments, which are too varied for a single pattern of this type to convey. In addition (and I know all too well the criticism this may arouse), revolution is a phenomenon so charged with passion, with suffering, and with yearning, all intensely human and individual as well as collective, that it appears *unnatural* when reduced to a diagram. This is not sheer sentimentality; I say *unnatural* because we are not shown the real phenomenon, but only one aspect of its reality. For if "social circumstances are not things," then reducing factors such as plan, exaltation, and sacrifice to abstractions is not really examining the phenomenon in its sociological specificity. Just as the *Kriegspiel* does not account for war in all its implications, that type of pattern does not tell us what revolution is, even though it helps us to identify a particular situation as revolutionary or to understand a certain power structure. We cannot say the human factor will be added afterward, for if a phenomenon is composed entirely of that human factor, what is left once you reduce it to an abstraction?

In Search of a Definition [19]

The search for an accurate definition was part of the movement that gave rise to the myth of revolution and the con-

---

[19] Outwardly, we are abandoning the nominalist position we took in Chapter 1—namely, accepting as revolutions and revolutionary events those cir-

struction of models. The French Revolution had demonstrated that violence and the overthrow of government did not adequately identify revolutionary situations. Men had ventured much farther: the entire society had been uprooted. The term "class relations" was not yet in use, but it was evident (and served as the basis of myth) that revolution was a beginning and that it brought an era to a close. The critics of 1789 were perhaps the first to try to formulate the content of that movement. Burke's statements are familiar to us, but instead of enumerating all the interpretations that emerged, we shall present only a few significant and modern ones.[20] Evi-

cumstances which men of a particular period commonly referred to as such. We must now consider definitions derived from intellectual analysis performed by intellectuals conscious of the revolutionary phenomenon. It follows that the definitions are necessarily abstract, and we shall examine them not so much to discover what revolution really *is* as to answer this question: What image of revolution has been transmitted to intellectuals by events of Western civilization which have occurred during the past two centuries? That is the aspect of revolution we hope to find in these definitions.

[20] This note is intended simply to demonstrate the confusing definitions that appear in dictionaries and encyclopedias. Littré tells us that revolt is rebellion against established authority and that revolution is sudden and violent change in the political system and government of a state. Those definitions bear the obvious stamp of an era when the virtue of state power went blissfully unchallenged. But what is the difference between the two? Simply *success*. For if rebellion against established authority succeeds, it develops into a sudden change of government, i.e., revolution. Those are oversimplified interpretations that we have already rejected. Robert is more complex and defines revolt as collective and ordinarily violent action by which a group rejects the existing authority and established social standards, and prepares to attack and destroy them. But in respect to revolution (even ignoring what Littré has to say about astronomical and geometrical revolutions), the tendency is to take cover behind a number of possible meanings: *sudden, jolting, and significant* change in the social or ethical system; radical political change, which is actually no different from a *coup d'état* and does not imply a profound transformation of society. Robert's explanation seems to be outmoded. The current view is of a series of historical events occurring within a large community—a nation, for example—when a rebel faction succeeds in taking power and when profound social changes follow. Revolution differs from revolt in its scope and consequences, and from reform in its suddenness and recourse to violence. The meaning is clear, but not the facts. That definition implies the successful seizure of power; it follows that we would have to rule out revolution in connection with the events of 1905 in Russia. We are also told that profound social changes must occur: does that mean the seizure of power without such changes would not constitute revolution? Yet a hundred such events have been called revolutions—among them, the overthrow of Boris Godunov by Pseudo-Demetrius in 1605. And what about revolution brought by power itself? In 1791, for example, when King Stanislas Poniatowski, supported by patriotic Poles among the aristocracy and bourgeoisie, made a democratic revolution by establishing a democratic type of parliament. Or when Gustavus III of Sweden embarked on a vast sociopolitical reorganization between 1789 and 1792, in which the peasants and bourgeoisie acquired equal rights and

dently a standard is needed to deal with these definitions. The concept of the industrial revolution stands out in sharp contrast to the general idea of violence, turmoil, and disorder. Some fifty years ago, when historians abandoned the reporting of history in terms of events, politics, and diplomacy and became captivated by the economic and industrial process, they began speaking of revolution—with a grain of salt—to describe England's industrial expansion in the mid-eighteenth century. Quotation marks always enclosed the word, indicating that it was certainly not to be taken literally: it was a figure of speech. It involved recognition of the fact that the transition from a rural agricultural society to an urban industrial one entailed a profound change in patterns of existence, in customs, and in standards of value, and that it left no segment of society untouched or unaltered. Such a vast and penetrating transformation suggested effects comparable to those of a revolution, and for linguistic convenience, the circumlocution was abbreviated to "industrial revolution," as a metaphor. But the phrase came into common use, the quotation marks disappeared, and the words were taken at their face value: the expression ceased to be a figure of speech and became reality.

Ever since, the majority of historians have sanctioned the

---

the peasantry was emancipated through "a gigantic program for distributing and reallocating land." Those are authentic revolutions brought about by power; if we reject them for that reason, what can we possibly say of China's cultural revolution? But there are more problems ahead. The difference between revolt and revolution is becoming clear, but where does the Commune of 1871 fit in? Bourgeois historians have called it an insurrection; today, however, after much more study, we are inclined to recognize it as a revolution. Yet it had few of the characteristics of revolution. The same holds true of the American Revolution of 1775, though in a different sense, for it did not involve conflict between factions: it was a war, and a national war at that.

Robert mentions *profound* changes, a problem at the start, for how deep must those changes go? The question is crucial. One of the aims of this book is to discover, for our world, how penetrating social changes must be to constitute revolution.

The perplexities are compounded when you try to define revolution in terms of its objectives. "The emancipation of mankind" is Gollwitzer's formula, which simply means liberty and justice and gets us nowhere. Hannah Arendt took liberty as her exclusive criterion, and by eliminating all revolutions that did not have that goal, arrived at some odd conclusions.

term "industrial revolution," and so wholeheartedly that it has assumed priority: revolution is whatever, like the industrial revolution, entails the alteration of economic and social structures through technology and scientific development—the rest is hardly worth a glance!

It is evident that the concept of industrial revolution, which does not touch on turmoil, violence, and conflict of a primarily political nature, embraces phenomena that are not strictly within the domain of revolution. Still, its meaning is accepted. Hauser uses the word to describe economic and social changes during the sixteenth century even though no violence or disorder occurred. The same definition is found in Janne:[21] "Revolution involves the transition from one social structure to another without raising the question of whether the structure itself is either the cause or the effect of the revolutionary phenomenon." It is apparent that the idea of a change in structure is far too broad to define revolution, for not every change in structure applies, and, in any event, I am not certain that we should ignore violence that does not produce change in the social framework. How can you accept a view of the fourteenth and fifteenth centuries such as that of Favier,[22] who does not regard the numerous rebel movements of that period as revolution, but uses that word to describe economic factors behind the revival of agriculture, the developing ties between city and countryside, changes in the human diet, technical advances in production methods, and even financial systems heralding capitalism? No, I maintain that the first bill of exchange was not a revolution! Morineau [23] is justified in decrying those sprawling and shapeless notions of revolution. Have we any right to speak of the "revolution of great discoveries," or, on the subject of Luther, of a "religious revolution"? And of course the arrival of the Spaniards revolutionized Indian history! But that is not what

---

[21] Op. cit.
[22] J. Favier, *De Marco Polo à Christophe Colomb*, 1968.
[23] Morineau, *Le XVIe siècle*, 1969.

is meant by the revolution of great discoveries, although it is
the single revolutionary element in the profound disturbance
within a society. Morineau explains that the revolution in
prices could be traced to the intensification and acceleration
of a phenomenon already present (the components of which
cannot be measured accurately—which immediately casts
doubt on their revolutionary character); that the industrial
revolution in the eighteenth century was an illusion, for the
new economic patterns really resulted from an uninterrupted
series of innovations; and that in every sector, the sixteenth
century appears to have advanced a process of growth that
had already begun. "The word 'revolution' seems out of place."
He is also right to insist on first establishing a precise meaning
for such a word. It is not enough to say that the new century
bore certain marks that distinguished it from the previous one
and that were decisive enough to prevent a return to the past.
In that case, almost every historical movement would warrant
the use of the word, which, in the end, would become useless.
A definition of revolution thus should fall somewhere between
the first interpretation (a sudden and violent thrust culminating in a *coup d'état*) and the too broad concept of a change
in the social structure. Currently, according to Burnham,[24]
we are witnessing a revolution in terms of a fairly rapid
mutation of our society along three lines: a radical change in
social, economic, and political institutions; a change in the
controlling class; and parallel changes in dominant values and
ideologies. That brings us very close to the idea of industrial
revolution, which, in fact, Burnham develops. A new industrial
revolution is in the making, but we know now that social
change alone is no longer sufficient and requires accompanying
changes in political institutions and ideologies. What actually
occurred as a result of the aforesaid industrial revolution has
now been incorporated into its meaning. Although it helps us
to understand the content of the revolution, what Burnham
stresses is the nature of the movement: "The significance is

---

[24] James Burnham, *The Managerial Revolution*, 1942.

not in the change itself but in the rapidity of it. To say that a social revolution is unfolding at this moment is the same as saying that the present is characterized by accelerating social change—that it is a period of transition from one type of society to another." In other words, "transition" in its fullest sense: bridging the inevitably turbulent period between one social system and another as quickly as possible; revolution against free enterprise and capitalism and their ideology. It may or may not entail violence and upheaval.

Carr,[25] whose view coincides with Burnham's, demonstrates that fascist and Nazi revolutions are violent achievements of that transition, which American society is in the process of realizing by democratic means, and just as rapidly. In his opinion, violence is superinduced, and totalitarianism the evidence of hindrances to social progress: society's super-structures remain stable in contrast to the disturbances below, and the obstacles must be removed, but the operation is only superficial because the fundamental conditions remain un-changed and revolutionary, with or without violence.

Mounier,[26] though basically in agreement with that defi-nition, looks at the problem from another angle. "By revo-lution, we mean a combination of rather far-reaching changes intended virtually to erase the real illnesses of a society that has reached an impasse, rapid enough to prevent those terminal illnesses from spreading their poisonous decay throughout the national body, yet slow enough to allow for the growth of whatever requires time to mature. The result is what counts, not how romantic or how restrained the language is. It is enough to know that the operation is a major and vital one, bound to meet violent resistance, which in turn provokes counterviolence." Unlike most definitions, this one involves a strong ethical concept: the real illnesses of society must be erased. The ultimate objective rather than the content of the

---

[25] Carr, *Conditions of Peace,* 1942.
[26] Mounier, "Suite française aux maladies infantiles des révolutions," *Esprit* I, 1944.

phenomenon is significant; that is why Mounier states in his
article that the end justifies the means. For him, however,
revolution must be violent, in order to counter the violence
displayed by the keepers of "established disorder." Mounier
seems to be highly idealistic on this point and seems not to
have grasped the real nature of revolutionary violence, but it is
all to his credit that he has reintroduced it in view of a
tendency on the part of intellectuals to exclude it on the
grounds that it interferes with true understanding of the
revolutionary phenomenon. Ethical concerns dominate two
other aspects of his theory: movement must be rapid so that
the old structures may be uprooted fairly quickly and not be
allowed to blight what is coming into existence. Also, revolutionary speed becomes an imperative: what characterizes it
is not the event that occurs rapidly but the "need for prompt
action in the interest of . . ." Similarly, the movement must
be controlled so as not to become abusive—that is, so that
instead of toppling everything around it, it yields to time in
those areas where haste would induce sterility. Behind the
ethical judgment, then, is a markedly voluntarist and disciplined concept of revolution that postulates a far-reaching
plan (finding a real cure for real illnesses) at odds with the
visionless phenomenon consisting of the blind explosions of
rampaging mobs and the intense and unfamiliar heartbeat of
history in the making. In the end, however, that reassuring
view appears dangerously unrealistic. Although for a time,
notwithstanding communist and fascist revolutions, the
global and profound nature of the phenomenon as well as its
content was emphasized, now, because of universal turbulence
during the past few years, the violent, explosive, and ominous
character of revolution has regained attention. From the
United States comes an abundance of definitions describing
"violent disorder, social rebellion aimed at total change, class
assault,"[27] none of which tell us anything new.

In the long run, two basic attitudes are worth retaining.

[27] Clarence J. Harris, op. cit.; W. Young, *To Be Equal*, 1968.

One, to which Caillois subscribes, holds that a vital conflict exists between the revolutionary process and the violence connected with change. "If we define as revolution the rare crucial cleavages in which the fundamental values of a society, or, shall we say, the constants, hang in the balance simply because revolt was not attempted or even desired by sectors of the population having the most to gain by it, the events of May 1968 perhaps represent a turning-point signaling the end of one process of development and the beginning of another. That surprising word announces a new distribution of forces. It reveals that the old conflicts have lost their edge and new ones are emerging." [28] The foregoing represents a reversal of the traditional attitude toward revolution and projects a different relationship between disorders and significant movement, between event and institution. Revolution is indeed a crucial cleavage in which social constants hang in the balance. The new element is this: insurrection is a necessary component of revolution if it is carried out by those sectors of the population "involved" in the situation to be changed. The relationship is both sociological and vital. If violence is the work of those who have no real stake in it (as was true in May 1968), there is no revolution in the classic sense. But there may be hidden revolution consisting of a new distribution of social forces; in other words, those who were legitimate revolutionaries in the former capitalistic society are no longer so. A new category is emerging, and the real revolution *is* the shift in the revolutionary stratum. For that new revolutionary stratum discloses a fundamental change in the social structures: I would call it the transition from a classic industrial society to a technological society. The latter is coming into being and is not in itself revolution, but it projects new strata into a revolutionary situation. The conjunction of the "spontaneous" deep-rooted movement (sprung from technological mutations in this case) of the entire social framework and the emergence of a kindred controversy, the

---

[28] Caillois, "La Révolution cachée," *Le Monde*, March 1969.

insurgent vigor of which is equivalent to mutation, is precisely the global revolutionary occurrence. That explains the survival of declining, and, in reality, completely outworn, revolutionary forces as well as the reactionary tendency of all revolutions (including the May disorders, which, to the extent that they negated the imperative of a technological society in the name of humanism, were clearly reactionary, despite their verbal bravado and the moral issues they raised).

Two important observations of Bernard de Jouvenel [29] should be added to the outline of our definition. He reminds us that the revolutionary phenomenon is primarily a political event, a fact that has tended to be overlooked in emphasizing socio-economic considerations. Neither Marx nor Lenin made that error; they consistently and correctly regarded revolution as a political occurrence. I agree completely with Jouvenel that: "Subordinate relationships universally and forever pose a political problem. The issue of subordination is more pervasive than that of exploitation, to which Marx tried to limit it." That is certainly true and is in keeping with the record of history: revolution is reaction to, opposition to, assault upon a superior authority that is no longer recognized. It is the refusal to submit to authority. Too simple? Not if we avoid isolating it from the factors we have discussed previously and if we combine it with everything else, for then we surely may conclude that revolution cannot exist without the will to alter the structure of subordination, whatever its form may be. To which Jouvenel adds this conjecture: "If the French Revolution was a revolt against an established *order*, perhaps we should say that the student revolt was directed against an established *movement*." That hardly seems applicable to the May disorders, for, as we have already pointed out, revolt is invariably a rejection of the probable course of history; and if it is directed against an order, that is because the order is self-perpetuating and embodies the image of tomorrow. Revo-

---

[29] Bernard de Jouvenel, "L'Explosion estudiantine," *Analyse et Prévision*, 1968.

lution unfailingly implies movement in opposition to a movement; the May student movement testified to that fact, which
ought to be incorporated in the independent concept of
revolution. In view of the general unwillingness to reflect upon
political order, essential movement, and disorder, Jouvenel's
point enables us to reintegrate those factors in the rational
system of revolution and to revitalize a concept that has
become abstract.

Although this series of approximations brings a global and
complex phenomenon into clearer focus, it tends to blur the
event itself. For revolution as an event rarely fulfills its total
definition. No revolution has revealed itself completely. There
was a threshold, on one side of which it was impossible to
conceive of revolution; then, at a particular time, it became
possible to talk *about* revolution, to try to define it and analyze
its specificity, something unimaginable in prior times. It seems
to me that the conjunction of two conditions produced the
change: awareness of social injustice and the realization that
society was not inviolate. Nowadays, those two data of consciousness appear "natural," obvious, self-evident, and just
what they are: data. Actually, they represent a remarkable
transformation of our mental imagery. The question of injustice did not emerge overnight. Of course man had often
experienced a sense of injustice in terms of the contrast between his own wretchedness and the supposed satisfactions of
the rich, the renowned, and the powerful, and he was dimly
aware of inequality and that people were not treated according to their deserts and that evil brought its own rewards.
But that is quite different from the sense of social injustice
we know today, and it is a mistake to measure the past against
our own image of injustice. For man once endured injustice
as his destiny; it was his "lot." What could he do to change
it? He had no means. The gods, or God, with their own secret
ways and private designs, had cast the dice, resulting in one
man's suffering and another man's reward. All man could do

was to offer prayers to those mysterious powers—and prostrate himself. If the situation became really intolerable, he rebelled, and revolt, precisely because it strikes out against destiny, took on the character we have already discussed: extreme and desperate, self-paralyzing and self-sacrificing when successful, apocalyptic and counter to history. For revolution to detach itself from revolt and cease to be the *tremendum mysterium,* for it to emerge as a rational act, man had to cease enduring suffering and injustice as destiny and to learn that injustice was a "condition," his own, and therefore dependent not on mysterious powers but on the objective and explicable operation of certain sociological factors, human decisions, and political and economic systems. At that stage, the prospect of changing his condition loomed. He was reduced no longer to the necessity of flailing at his gods; neither men nor privileges were sacred, and he saw that he must contend with them. There was hope at last.

This much understanding, however, was not enough. Society had yet to be challenged, to cease to be regarded as a sacred entity. That, too, was not self-evident. Society was looked upon traditionally as something sacred; human beings endured social inequality and injustice (not without protest) because each individual was trapped bodily and spiritually in a social structure, the principle of which was believed, perceived, and experienced as eternal and immutable. Before he could condemn injustice, man first had to sense the injustice of his own situation, which, because it conformed perfectly and visibly to the social framework, was looked upon as just. Experienced through its conventions or ceremonies, the duties it imposed, and the relationships it entailed, society did not appear distinct from individuals; that an individual should oppose the social order was inconceivable, for the solidity of the group and its members disallowed any rupture. A tribal, religious, and cosmic conscience guided personal conduct; at the same time, order was natural, social, and sacred. Under those circumstances, how could there be any concept of revolution? How could anyone imagine society as an infernal machine grinding up humanity, when society was upheld as the source of individual safety, honor, and position? How could that which was sacred be called unjust? Or its Kafkaesque absurdity be revealed when man relied on it for his images and sensations? In reality, humanity's idyll traditionally was contained in the story of Agrippa. Society was imagined as a human body with superior and inferior parts, all of which were equally useful and contributed to the corporate wellbeing. The image was not exclusively medieval; it was shared by nearly all civilizations. A truly severe rupture had to occur before men could be convinced that the system was artificial and subject to change and persuaded to desanctify it by dispelling its myth. Despite markedly deritualistic tendencies, Christianity rarely was able to accomplish that, and then only sporadically, owing to the system's integrating, objective, and subjective power. As long as the system prevailed, revolution was inconceivable because it was not a normal element of society—that is, of history.

Consciousness of injustice; an irreparable breach of relations between man and society: at some point in history, man undoubtedly took upon himself and placed upon his society the burden of his awareness of one or the other of those possibilities—but very rarely the two at once. It was even rarer for society as a whole to give evidence of that understanding. The conjunction of all those factors produced the burgeoning of revolution. The revolution of the Gracchi, for example, seems to have involved (the only instance, to my knowledge, in premodern history) consciousness of social injustice and the vision of a secular society. The Gracchi, along with others, were aware of the inequitable distribution of public land. They recognized that poverty resulted from the organization of society, which could be altered. Tiberius Gracchus, whose political views were of the past, promoted simply the effective enforcement of laws already in existence. Furthermore, he lived in a secular society; Roman society was probably the first of that type before our own. Law was its cornerstone, and therefore the exercise of law could effect infinite change. Tiberius pushed secularization a step further (thereby revealing his awareness of its revolutionary significance) by nullifying, through his own conduct, the sacred character of the tribunate of the people. But despite a favorable climate, the hoped-for revolution did not arrive, less because of political opposition than because of ignorance and indifference on the part of those in whose interests revolution was being promoted. The poor turned their backs on Tiberius the moment reforms took effect, and the new landholders could not wait to sell their property. For one thing, the struggle was led by the aristocracy and the intelligentsia, not by the people, who had not rebelled to impose their will; for another, it was a short-sighted view of change, for instead of launching a process that would transform the entire society, each individual tried to turn his newly acquired benefits into ready cash. As we have said, it appears to be the only example of a sense of social injustice combined with a secular view of society. Every attempt at revolution reveals the presence of one *or* the other; alone, the sense of social injustice leads to desperate violence; the concept of a nonsacred society devoid of the pressure of injustice, to legal reforms. When the two are conjoined, revolution becomes something else: it separates from revolt and is a truly integral part of history, no longer the work of the devil or a Promethean struggle against the gods. It is coherent with history and looms as a concept. It is an instrument that allows man to transform society as well as to control the stormy tide of events. At the same time, it becomes possible to make and to think revolution instead of seeing it made. It can be planned, willed, or specified. The objective conditions essential to revolution do not and cannot come into play until that awareness exists. Apart from man's reflection on injustice and a secular society, the "objective conditions" do not produce a thing. They may all be present and the situation may be "revolutionary," but nothing comes of it because no one has the will or courage or mind for revolution. Thus, only as of 1789 and in the aftermath of that revolution were the two conditions of awareness present simultaneously; that is why it marked the onset of the age of revolution specified as such: revolution distinct from all previous popular movements. It is impossible, therefore, to establish an objective and general pattern of revolution or even an adequate definition applicable to all periods. I believe that it was not by chance that the problem arose in 1785 and that the first attempt was made then to determine a general pattern. The attempt came because revolution was a distinct possibility, not because a different method of reasoning or a broader spectrum of knowledge existed. Today we are more scientific and we make "models" of everything, but that is not why it occurs to us to make a model for revolution: that is an intellectual act involving an intellectual change in our way of looking at things. To conceive of establishing a model for revolution, one must first have had the idea of making a rational, organized, and successful revolution: the two phenomena are linked, and both derive from the same awareness. Then, however, the revolution, a model and an explanation of which we are seeking, is one revolution alone that we now accept as a fact, the image of which we project over all of past history, the traces, premises, warnings, and mutterings of which we look for in every record of revolt, all of which appear identical because we cannot imagine revolution as different from the way we now conceive it. Nothing could be farther from the truth, for history tells us that there is no common ground between what we analyze today and nearly the entire enterprise of social change or rebellion in the past. No longer can we project on former societies the pattern of class struggle, or of conflict between the forces and yields of production, or of a horizontally and vertically structured society. Those images are products of our modern European mentality, which developed them out of the twofold consciousness discussed above, through which revolution became a part of history. No objective general pattern can be distinguished because intellectual and psychic conditions underlie the potential play of structures and objective forces. Revolution can become a global historic event only in relation to a certain type of society, and it is as a global historic event that we define revolution, a pattern for which can be found.

This whole discussion thus strikes me as futile as to its aim, but important and significant in itself. It does not penetrate the reality of revolution; it does indicate, however, the transformation and the changing face of the phenomenon. It teaches us a number of things that were not evident: revolution is now indeed a part of history; it acquired a new image once men saw that it was possible; and today it involves all social groups and all aspects of society. Moreover, only under those conditions can we evaluate the historical records of past revolts and revolutions. From the point of view discussed above, what value have the accounts we use? Some historians feel that popular risings, *coups d'état,* and civil disorders have been chronicled because they were extraordinary and were events in themselves, worthy of being remembered and reported, crucial as well as horrifying. According to others, the majority of those movements were withheld because they were distasteful, the underside of existence, something one never mentions, calling order and sanctity to trial, and only vast movements, of such prolonged duration and implicating such multitudes that it was impossible to conceal them, were transmitted to us. Still others believe the chroniclers did not even trouble themselves to record all the rebellions, peasant risings, and *rebeines* [30] because they were too dull, too commonplace and insignificant to be worth relating and preserving. It is true, unfortunately, that we are unable to visualize those revolutionary phenomena and that revolution only now appears definable and worth reporting for its own sake. In the interim, it had to be conceived of as part of history and to be regarded as a vital thread (not an irregularity) of history.

---

[30] Name given to the sixteenth-century labor revolts in Lyons.

The very discovery of that new meaning revealed a new aspect of revolution. As a valid component of history, and worthy of attention, regard, and even approval, how could it persist in running counter to predictable evolution? Did this not signal the transition from the concept of a revolution within history to that of a revolution in the direction of history? Normalized and become absolute, the object of myth and pattern, revolution could only be conceived of as the creator of history itself. That is exactly what happened.

CHAPTER

[3]

REVOLUTIONS IN
THE DIRECTION
OF HISTORY

Revolution Betrayed

Normalized Revolution

A full explanation of the revolutionary phenomenon had the effect of normalizing it. Revolution ceased to be an unforeseen explosion of anger and despair and became a sketch plan (however complex and intellectually adroit) from the moment it could be shown variously, according first to Hegel, then to Marx, that revolution was a normal, explainable, and relatively predictable phase of history's course. War was already recognized as part of history's pattern, but it was unpredictable. Revolution appeared to be something different, an accident, outside of time and history, a plunge into eternity. It was not really part of history. Then, suddenly, through the intellectual magic of philosophers looking back on the Revolution of 1789, perceiving the great historical changes it had brought, the latent aspirations it had revealed, and the startling mutations it had wrought, the phenomenon of revolution took its place in history through the application of dialectic to history.

In theory, the body of historical thought created by, and then derived from, Hegel is the product of the French Revolution. Hegel evolved the philosophical doctrine of that event, with the result that the ideological relationship between history and revolution was inherent in events themselves. Hegel's "revolutionary" idea was to establish that the philosophical absolute was revealed in the experience of revolution. For does not the dialectic of liberty/necessity, of Master and Slave, reflect for Hegel the direct intellectual apprehension of the apparent necessity underlying the dialectic of revolution/counterrevolution? History does indeed appear to sweep all humanity along in its irresistible tide at the very moment when revolution seeks to establish liberty. However, once it can be demonstrated dialectically that liberty is the product of necessity, then and there the betrayal of revolution takes root. Because revolution is the offspring of that historical dialectic, it is bound to be betrayed.

But what is difficult to explain is the actual transformation of revolutions, for it is true that with the advent of Marx, they changed markedly. It was not a matter of reasoning or philosophic argument; revolution literally changed character in the nineteenth century. Thereafter it was directed toward a practical future, an attempted fusion of the old conflicting forces, and a new synthesis of society. It is sheer imagination, of course, to think that the transformation derived solely from Marx's influence, for we have indicated that the Revolution of 1789 was already headed in that direction. That significant feature of 1789 was to carry forward and develop revolution at the expense of its traditional context (except for the July revolution of 1830, which remains ambiguous). A distinct evolution occurred, related to class divisions and to urban and industrial development. But that alone was not enough, for we have pointed out the important role of beliefs, aims, ideologies, and physical reactions on the individual level. Marx provided a framework for the meaning men gave to their revolutionary act, and a significance that transcended immediate yearnings. The manner in which that body of obscure and complex thought translated itself into the simplest beliefs is in fact astounding; nevertheless it happened. And thereafter revolutionaries were more or less convinced that they were moving in the direction of history, that the essential thing was first to identify that direction in order to take it (success depended on it), and that through revolution they were creating history.[1] Of course, one may say that was not apparent in 1849, in the Latin American revolutions of the nineteenth century, and even in 1871, yet the national revolutions actually had that aim and intention without any specific reference to Marx.

Two principal features of Marxism were gradually absorbed by revolutionary theory. First, the concept of the objective situation: if revolution is a historic moment resulting from the evolution of certain forces, at a given time—the time at which effective action can produce a crisis—the relationship between those forces is particularly advantageous. Conversely, any attempt at revolt is futile if the objective forces have not combined and if the social organism has not reached a certain level of development. The point is not obscure and may be deduced from Marx, for it involves on the one hand the relation between the economic structure and the rest of society, and on the other the class power structure. It follows that revolution is a function of the maturation or the maturity of a society. Revolutionaries can have but one

---

[1] For that matter, any revolution can ultimately take "the direction of history." Ionesco entered the following remark in his *Journal* in 1939: "If history continues to follow the direction of Hitler, nations and ideologies will adopt those ideas [racist metaphysics], which will become dogma and the principles of a new science of man—science can establish and prove anything." Armed force alone is what has altered the metaphysics and anthropology of our times.

goal: not to change various elements within society, but to destroy the class that oppresses them. All this is familiar and needs no elaboration.

The second feature is the partial automation of the revolutionary process. We are all familiar with the debate between the Marxists, who maintain that revolution is produced more or less inevitably by the movement of history itself, and those who believe that man "creates his own history" and, consequently, must achieve revolution. Historical necessity was linked to the poor, whose impoverishment drove them to violence, and who endured necessity as a lifelong condition of existence. "Necessity and violence together made the poor appear invincible, the most powerful force on earth" (Hannah Arendt). Thus the doctrine of revolutionary necessity emerged. Tocqueville explored it and wondered why "the doctrine of fatality . . . has such attraction for historians in a democratic era." He said that in democratic egalitarianism the influence of individuals upon society is overlooked, and that this oversight leads to a belief in the hidden power of history. That was certainly a factor, to the extent that it was reinforced by more important objective forces and supportive ideological beliefs. The beliefs were founded on dialectical reasoning: "Dialectic had created a twofold relationship of continuity and discontinuity between present and past. Capitalism spawns its own gravediggers, shaping the regime that will abolish it, and the future issues from the present, the end from the means, of which it is merely the sum total and the meaning. But can a revolution be born thus? Is it history itself that alters history? Does not revolution as a cleavage first have to reject what preceded it? Does it not create such tensions among men, and even among the proletariat, that political democracy, revolutionary brotherhood, and free speech cannot come until much later, and then as an end and justification in the minds of its leaders rather than as an integral part of the revolutionary movement? Marxism is unwilling to choose between the two faces of dialectics: sometimes it regards revolution as a wave

lifting the Party and the proletariat up and beyond the reach
of all obstacles; sometimes it places revolution beyond existence, in a future that negates the present, at the close of
an infinite process of purification."[2] Whichever position one
adopts, and regardless of the subtleties of Marxist logic, the
fact remains that the roles are determined in advance and
necessity operates. The proletariat is obliged to play the part
clearly assigned by dialectic. It is the bearer of total negation and becomes the engineer of ultimate affirmation. It
cannot fail in its task; once the proletariat has triumphed,
classes cannot reappear, for the proletariat, owing to its utter
despoliation, is also the bearer of the negative absolute, that
is, the virtual positive absolute.[3] It is therefore "the universal
opposed to the particular" (the particular being capitalism).
That is the final phase of the struggle between the universal
and the particular (involving, of course, Hegel's dialectic of
master and slave). Thereafter revolution is all-embracing.
"Philosophy cannot fulfill itself without the disappearance of
the proletariat, and the proletariat cannot free itself without
the fulfillment of philosophy." Similarly, "the proletariat can
exist only on the stage of world history."

That automation (relative as it may be) is the warranty of
success. Marx as much as said that until his time all revolutions had failed. But after history was routed onto tracks and
the power structure was understood scientifically, he was in
a position to assert that revolution was bound to succeed. It
is perfectly evident that if revolution is the locomotive of
history, and if, reciprocally, history is the necessary creator
of revolution, then, in so far as history exists and is correctly
interpreted, revolution cannot fail to succeed. Thus the aim
of revolution was no longer to effect social or political change
but to establish the rule of history: in a simple stroke, the
crisis invested and installed history. What could possibly pre-

---

[2] Merleau-Ponty, *Les Aventures de la Dialectique*, p. 126.
[3] See especially the famous passage on the nature of the proletariat in
Introduction to a Criticism of Hegel's Philosophy of Right.

vent it? Such an achievement, however, requires an enormous leap, which, in fact, is prescribed by dialectic. The problem basically involves the means and level of production, but we are called upon to imagine that in the final stage of production, something resembling a transfiguration occurs resulting in a reconciled society, man reconciled with himself and with nature.[4]

Thus for revolution to prevail, at this stage reason must rule. Irrationality must be barred, and therefore revolt, with its spontaneous and profoundly human character, must be put down. That explains Marx's adamant opposition to Blanquist adventurism as well as to anarchism and syndicalism. All those movements were predicated on human will, on hope and imagination, and were not unlike former revolutions. They were capable of producing only "disruptive and futile action in behalf of a utopia." Embarking on revolution for subjective motives was labeled "petty-bourgeois" reaction, and syndicalism was scorned on grounds that it could effect only "corporative" changes. The focus of Marx's assault in that area did not involve opinion or tactics: his savage purge of the International and his attacks on Bakunin and Proudhon were prompted by the fact that the totality of the revolution was at stake. Once revolution took the direction of history, it either progressed as Marx had foreseen or it did not exist; and, as a matter of course, any other movement had to be counterrevolutionary. The rigidity of Marx's logic anticipated the rigid operation of the regimes it inspired. Was re-

---

[4] Camus and Merleau-Ponty have provided a critical analysis in depth on this subject, which I shall not go into, as it is outside the sphere of this book. I would draw attention simply to one passage in Camus (*The Rebel,* p. 357): "History as a totality could exist only in the eyes of an observer beyond history and the universe. Only for God is there an utmost limit of history. It is impossible, therefore, to act according to plans embracing the totality of universal history. Every historic undertaking can only be an adventure, more or less rational and well founded. It is a risk at the outset. As a risk, it does not warrant any excess or any fixed and immutable posture." As a moralist, Camus rightly condemns the fact that, in implementing its concept of the relationship between revolution and history, Marxism inevitably led to terroristic despotism.

volt to be outlawed? Certainly not, but it would have to be utilized and was acceptable only as something other than itself. The proletariat's beliefs, thoughts, and feelings were inconsequential, for it had a historic role to play, assigned by its historic situation. It must play that role not according to its own inclinations and emotions, but as and when history dictated. That the proletariat must rebel is self-evident, for revolt is the basic element of revolution, but by itself it has no value. Therefore it must operate not when the rebel wishes but when the objective revolutionary moment arrives. And when revolt occurs, it must be taken in hand and guided toward the revolutionary phase. *Battleship Potemkin* illustrates that. Spontaneity in both its forms must be disclaimed—that is, the idea that popular spontaneity reveals the opportune moment for revolt, and the idea that conscious revolutionaries should follow the proletariat instead of leading it. Again, that does not involve tactics but reflects the conflict between the metaphysical rebel and the historical revolutionist, between the will to change the world and mankind and the will to change the social order. Popular spontaneity's value as an initial impetus is recognized, but that is about as far as it goes. All the myths and institutions generated by the tide of revolution are disclaimed: organs of self-guidance and self-defense, including spontaneously created popular committees, are immediately suspect, being incoherent, inefficient, and unaware of history's course. Collective spontaneity is not really capable of devising specific forms of revolutionary organization. Lenin observed that the latter "runs the risk of dissolving into pseudo-intellectual and petty-bourgeois trade unionism." Similarly, Trotsky asserted: "We must become aware of the historic revolutionary mission of the Party. The Party is compelled to maintain its dictatorship and to ignore fluctuations in the spontaneous reactions of the masses as well as momentary hesitations of the working class." It could not be put more succinctly, and it is this problem over which Sartre labors painfully in order to prove that the Party does not deny

the spontaneity of the masses, which in turn attain their fulfillment only through the Party. For the masses become a class
(and hence an effective instrument of revolution) only when
they become integrated in the Party. Recognition of the Party
by the proletariat is not simply recognition of the leadership
and the cadres but has its counterpart in the Party's recognition
of the proletariat—which implies, however, not that the Party
yields to the opinions of proletarians, but that it recognizes the
effects on them of its work to bring them into political life.
"The Party is therefore like a mystery of reason: it is that historical juncture at which the way things must be is understood,
at which concepts acquire life, and any deviation that
would put the relationship of the Party and the class on the
same level as that of the leader and his troops . . . would
constitute an ideology. For then history/science and history/
reality would remain disjunct, and the Party would no longer
be the laboratory of history and the beginning of a true society." [5] On the one hand, the most logical arguments should
not be imposed on the proletariat against its will, for the lack of
agreement indicates that the proletariat is not mature, that the
situation is not objectively revolutionary, and hence that the
theoretically flawless arguments are false. On the other hand, it
is not the proletariat's task to interpret history, to evaluate the
power structure, to understand conjuncture, to present arguments, and to establish political policy. All that need not even
be spelled out to the proletariat. Lenin analyzes at great length
the relationship and the fact that the theorist is always in
the lead, but only one step ahead. The masses should never
be left free to indulge their spontaneity, but neither should
they be regarded as an ordinary tool to be manipulated in
Machiavellian fashion for the sake of some covert political
purpose. "Captive but not manipulated, they set the seal of
truth on Party policies." Truth, revolution, and history are the
real issues at stake in Sartre's confused or else too-transparent
examination of spontaneity. The word has a meaning outside

[5] Merleau-Ponty, op. cit., pp. 76–7.

the sphere of Marxism: what Lenin called "primitivism," the myth of an imminent revolution in economic principles and of worker action confined to that domain. But the word has another significance, essential because it merges with that of the proletarian revolution: the access of the masses to politics, the wedded life of the masses and the Party. Lenin never repudiated the word "spontaneity," or the entity itself, because, "in the final analysis, spontaneity and conscience are not alternatives, and the elimination of spontaneity from Party doctrine would prevent the Party from acting as the conscience of the proletariat." [6] We can see to what extent revolt is deformed, distorted, and dwarfed within this rigorous unity of history and revolution in order to uphold the concept (and practice?) of spontaneity. The rebel is nowhere to be found. Of course, such a doctrinaire attitude toward spontaneity appeals to a purely abstract mind, which is what one may criticize in Sartre, an intellectual, who, unable to grasp reality, replaces it with a philosophical image, and who, when forced to grasp it, explains it in such a manner that it is both fascinating and utterly mystifying. Nothing more mystifying exists on the subject of spontaneity and the Communist Party than the writings of Sartre.[7] Yet the moment you have such a subtle dialectical construction in which the masses/Party relationship is so delicately balanced, you may be sure that it will work out differently in practice. No need to await Stalin and his supposed deformation of Marxism: at the first appearance of French Marxism, the break with other socialist movements occurred over just that issue: the concept of spontancity among the masses, which Lassalle attacked. The masses had to be rigidly officered and guided by the revolutionary elite. Later on, Lenin expressed it in the same way: "Doctrine must subdue spontaneity." Leaders were essential, as were theorists who would not defer to the impatience of the

---

[6] Ibid., p. 169.
[7] Notably: Sartre, "Les Communistes et la paix," *Temps Modernes*, pp. 81, 84.

masses and would force them into submission—by any means.

Regardless of the theories spun around them, rebels are simply a crude mass of manpower, and their rebellion need not be considered on its own merits. We have only to recall Nestor Makno, or the Kronstadt sailors, or the communists' savage annihilation of anarchist organizations during the Spanish Civil War. The repudiation of spontaneity, that disruption of the course of history, was indicative of the reversal soon to follow. We have noted that revolutionary spontaneity is always founded upon revolt and is therefore by nature conservative, or regressive, or utopian. That is also why Marxists, claiming to have the only scientific approach and the key to history and its progress, are correct in terms of their imagery in repudiating revolt and denouncing all spontaneity as reactionary and counterrevolutionary. At the same time they are condemning what is most human and most deeply and genuinely felt: hope and despair, suffering and requital, anger and the rejection of a merciless destiny, all of which they deny. Significantly, in the course of his work Marx gave increasing importance to objective factors [8] and described a growing number of inexorable mechanisms in which man was conspicuously absent. In his last writings, revolution was treated less in terms of the relations between persons (whether classes or not) and more as the interplay of philosophy and socialism; revolution became the product of relations between objective forces in which things and their immanent necessities dominated. Man appeared ultimately as an intruder in the revolutionary plan inscribed in the design of history. Because he had feelings, he was bound to interfere with the majestic advance of the god. Spontaneity had no place as socialism grew more scientific—that is, more dependent on calculation. Although the injection of revolution into systematized history

---

[8] It is also significant that for the past twenty-five years, our intellectuals, in an effort to civilize Marxism and to represent it as overt, flexible, and human, have spotlighted Marx's early writings, especially those of 1844, and have primly curtained off *Capital*, except for its introduction.

appeared to be directed solely against spontaneity, it had the effect of displacing man and his uncertainty.

The entrance of revolution as a normal, natural, and *creative* element of future history into the very heart of intelligible history, the design of which had been rendered rational, resulted in the dismissal of value. Camus went to great lengths to show that the Marxist interpretation of revolution actually eliminated values, which, in his view, had been created forcibly by rebels. He could have reached that conclusion by a less roundabout route, for Marx wrote profusely on the subject. What we call value was, in his eyes, only mystification, which he distrusted utterly. He repeated over and over that revolution had nothing to do with liberty or justice, which were hollow bourgeois images. One passage will suffice to illustrate the point: "I was obliged to include in the preamble (to the text of the Constitution of the International in 1864) two sentences dealing with rights and duties, truth, morality, and justice: I inserted them in such a way as to *avoid offending* anyone." Twenty years later, Engels protested that socialists, basing themselves on Marx, were still talking about liberty and justice. "Marx would reject the political, economic, and social idealism you ascribe to him: a scientist has no ideals. . . . Marxism is not a system of ethics. . . . One must never give way to moral indignation."

It is evident that if history is interpreted scientifically as to its meaning, its orientation, and its intrinsic movement (instead of being merely described by historical science!), and if revolution is inserted therein as a part is inserted in a machine that is both indeterminate and determinate (electronic machines are beginning to display such systems), then there is no need for any kind of value. The concept has nothing in common with value; they are two different and coexistent worlds. Communists who speak of justice, liberty, and democracy are perfectly entitled to do so for propaganda purposes but cease to be Marxists if they take them seriously. In the intellectual sphere of revolution, Marxism implies a purely objective (scientific) attitude, and in the ethical sphere, sheer cynicism. We tend to be shocked by the clan warfare in Marxist nations and the fact that men can condemn their former comrades to death. (Long before Stalin, Lenin's rejection of Rosa Luxemburg and Karl Liebknecht was significant.) But our shock only proves that we do not understand Marxism. Lenin himself described opportunism as (among other things!) the attitude of those who alter the conduct of revolution according to personal feelings of friendship, hate, fear, and personal interests. Reducing everything to the historical process results in the cynicism that allows words to communicate the exact opposite of what they mean (one aspect of the current so-called crisis of language can be laid to the spread of historical cynicism). Qualifying the most extreme dictatorship as liberty no longer poses any problem.[9] When history becomes the master key, the beginning and end of meaning, man is dispossessed of himself more than under the most rigid system of values. In the course of revolution he comes to realize that his last refuge lies in that interpretation of history whose unfolding alone will tell whether it was (in retrospect) correct. Marx expressed it well: "History is the judge; the proletariat carries out the sentence." History is indeed the judge, but the sentence will not be pronounced until *afterward*, for history is deprived of a final orientation, an objective, and a transcendency, and is reduced to a "mechanism" (the word, I know, is irritating to Marxists, who insist, and rightly so, that Marx's ideas are not mechanisms) of the regulations of power. The inner play of those relations must be evaluated and understood, for it alone is meaningful. Current events are the only element of significance; future events (as yet unknown) will prove whether the interpretation was correct or not. Marx is also credited with a remarkable vision of the outcome of history, and Hegel's apt phrase is often cited: "As to the proof, not I, but history at

---

[9] On the theme of historical disintegration, see the remarkable book by A. Robin, *La Fausse Parole*.

its completion will produce it." But such a hypothesis must involve one of two attitudes: either the suspension of judgment until the (final) rendering of proof, or the upholding of whatever in history seems assured of success, primarily power.

Marxists have plainly chosen the latter. But they would question the vagueness of "whatever *seems*," for in their view, to the extent that history's meaning can be interpreted correctly, things do not "seem"—they *are*. An act is bound to succeed if it has been calculated correctly; if it fails, that signals an error in interpretation, a theoretical error, and the failure therefore is proof of the false identity of scientific Marxism. So one is trapped between a system asserted to be flawless and the future, man's last hope of transcendence, for in true utopian fashion, Marx asserted that history would have a moral and rational ending. He did not explain how the change would occur despite the fact that good and evil, integrated in time, never indicate that something is right or wrong, and that only practice determines what is effective and opportune. We are told that everything will be revealed at the end of time. I fail to grasp the nature of that "historical-metahistorical" end of time in contrast to the present, which is so systematized that useful action can be determined scientifically. In that focus, revolution clearly becomes a "thing in itself." It is an indispensable element of history, justified by history, and "the locomotive of history." It can be evaluated only in terms of whether or not it has succeeded. It is valid in itself once it has taken history into a new phase, and not because it has produced a change in personnel or has simply accelerated a movement already begun and sustained. The idea of "revolution acceleration" is decidedly anti-Marxist and is a mediocre and (truly!) petty-bourgeois analysis of the integration of revolution in history. It is neither a matter of shunting history onto new tracks (an anti-Marxist concept) nor one of changing certain factors: we are at the point at which history no longer can channel itself into a void, for the conflicting forces demand a creative explosion, and revolution would introduce a totally new era, completely unlike anything in the past and, at the same time, capable of absorbing the former contradictions and embracing all that existed in every domain (except the mystifications). The result cannot be described simply because it involves a veritable creation of history, a product that is unknowable, an extraordinary "bang" (to use the language of modern physics). The dialectical synthesis is real, not idealistic. In the dialectic of events, the result cannot be predicted, only the certain negation of negation. Because the mutation is so extreme, revolution becomes the final utterance, the single "value." It supersedes the interests of every individual. The reason is clear: without revolution, entry into history is no longer possible, and men, either singly or collectively, would have no history. To preserve mankind's history, revolution must come and must succeed. What does individuality matter anyway, or the loss or gain of a few million lives? Revolution plainly takes precedence over the masses it is intended to save. Stalin and Marx pose no antithesis (except for sentimental Marxists, unwitting disciples of Jaurès!). Because their salvation will be absolute, the oppressed can tolerate a little more oppression; the sacrifice of a few generations is of small consequence if measured against the possibility or impossibility of history. Sacrifice, in any case, and that uncompromising rigidity are the very foundations of successful revolution, for success is not the seizure of power, or the establishment of a just (?) and equitable society, or even the investment of "revolutionary power." Revolution would not be what it is, the maker of history, if it were to fail. Success arrives at the "point of no return." If revolution results in an "unstable organism" such as those produced by chemical reaction, *no revolution whatsoever* has occurred, regardless of the pronouncements made, or the institutions, the men, and the upheavals connected with it. Revolution is not what it is intended to be unless there is no possible turning back—in any sector or in any manner (the doubts plaguing many a communist at the time of the N.E.P. are therefore understandable). Neither intellectual effort, nor mob violence under any circumstances, nor constitutional reform gives access to the point of no return: all those factors can be repossessed, remodeled, and restored by Yesterday. The only irretrievable factor is massacre. The bisecting of time by revolution implies something more than the idyllic elimination of a handful of exploiters which is part of the incredibly perfect evolution described in certain passages of Marx. Here enters a contradiction between Marx's ideas and their inevitable consequences. The crisis is not historically real until physical neutralization is massive enough to prevent society from restoring the past, in respect both to its terrorized and vituperative former masters and to its new masters bent on ridding the revolutionary period of every execrable reminder of the past. Whereas Marx did not project mass killing as a significant factor, or even as a less desirable one, the Revolution of 1789 reached the point of no return via the Terror, and the Revolution of 1917 not until the time of the Bolshevik massacres in November of that year. The accumulated animosities, the overwhelming determination to forget, the unconditional "censures" and collective "complexes," are evidence that revolution has arrived. Only one sign appears: the impossibility of turning back. Revolution must be inexpiable or else it is merely appearance—that is, reformism. That is the inevitable outcome of injecting revolution into history. To repeat, it is not an error of Marxism; it is the fact itself of having placed revolution *in that particular relationship* to history.

Consequences

We have not attempted to present Marx's ideas *on* revolution or *on* history (which may be found in any number of books), but simply to show the novelty of his view of revolution in contrast to the experience of earlier revolutions. The results, warranted by fact and by sociology, confirm that view. With revolt and spontaneity virtually eliminated by systematizing revolution within history, the remaining elements are theory and tactics. Revolutions directed toward history are revolutions of theory and tactics. Although instances of revolt still occur—and, to contradict the foregoing statement, one could cite hundreds of movements based on revolt since 1850— nevertheless the type of revolution that has become "normal" during the past century is the Marxist type, excluding (how and why we have already discussed) the primacy of revolt. When revolt breaks out spontaneously, an immediate effort is made to organize and regulate it, to give it tactical direction, and to enclose it in a Marxist type of revolution (even if it has no trace of Marxism to begin with) if theorists believe, at the moment, that it offers an opportunity to start a revolution in the direction of history; if not, Marxist revolutionaries will seek to crush the revolt.

Moreover, because Marxist revolution is not a conspiracy and entails a popular movement, its aim is to produce, to contrive, and to provoke revolt. That involves tactics and maintaining the appearance of spontaneity. Ideally, the transition to revolution involves visible, but not chaotic, public support; no "public festival of revolution" must occur, only a general manifestation of approval for the revolution under way. The post-1945 revolutions in Czechoslovakia, Hungary, Romania, and Poland are typical. Spontaneity becomes a variable of tactical calculations. At the same time tactics must correspond to circumstance (and therefore to eventual revolt), by means of which the revolutionary stage is reached—or rather, which reveals that the historic moment of revolution has come.

"Doctrine/theory" (the difference is plain in the abstract but difficult to get at) becomes a mainstay. Because revolutionary spontaneity is rejected, the "revolutionary plan"

assumes added importance. Whenever revolt adopts a spontaneous plan, the latter has nothing in common with the
movement of history perceived by Marxism. Although it is a
fact that revolution requires a plan, the plan will be replaced
by doctrine, which in turn becomes the plan.[10] Thereafter
doctrine supplants value, for when revolution is no longer
based on or projected toward values, it must have a certitude.
History allots itself none; doctrine will provide it by replacing
values. Moreover, doctrine becomes pre-eminent because it is
instrumental in revealing and justifying the meaning of
history. Through comparative doctrine and theoretical
analysis, successive situations can be interpreted so as to determine the opportune moment and to grasp the profound
(i.e., potentially revolutionary) reality of experienced events.
Finally, doctrine, owing to its demystifying function, becomes
a major part of revolution itself. If revolution is directed against
the global social organism (as implied by the idea of dialectical movement), it brings with it ideological subversion. In
existing society, ideology is mystification. Only with the aid of
a precise and stringent doctrine can one identify the conscious
or unconscious falsehoods and thus lay the groundwork for a
revolution in depth as well as for the new ideology essential to
its success. It is certain that by every means of perceiving the
phenomenon, doctrine has become the core of the Marxist
revolutionary system. That is perfectly logical (and consistent
with Marx's ideas), and what Marx adds is not the fact that a
doctrine *exists,* but that this doctrine became scientific and
also (as a consequence) became the essence of the revo-

---

[10] Decouflé's analysis (supplemented by several quotations from Marx dealing with the change in human relations, in the entire range of personality, and
in consciousness, which consists in making self-awareness universal) attempts
to demonstrate the overall congruence between the Marxist plan and the
revolutionary plan, and seems inaccurate to me. He does not take into account
the breach, the decisive leap that must be made to advance from emerging
history to millenarianism, which is relatively vague anyway in Marx. The
writings of Marx have to be localized in time: the works in question are early
ones, and some do not even relate to the problem of revolution—in particular,
his well-known study of "consciousness." Decouflé arbitrarily speaks of
"revolutionary consciousness," whereas Marx mentions only consciousness, and
in an entirely different context.

lutionary phenomenon. Lenin described the phenomenon as characterized by "scientific precision," and all the great Marxist theorists, including Plekhanov, Kautsky, and Lukács, have reaffirmed this. It is interesting, therefore, to see what has happened to doctrine and theory in revolutionary practice over the past seventy-five years. I find that four startling transformations have occurred (the nature of which ought to alarm Marxists) which one would not expect of a highly disciplined system of thought and of a scientific method of evolving a theory, and which Althusser was right to point out.

The first transformation involves what may be described as a type of logorrhea. Marxists began to split off in their interpretations of Marx as well as of events (the most celebrated of those disputes pitted Kautsky against Lenin; Lenin proved right in the practical short run, Kautsky in the long run). Ideas were refined and made razor-sharp; the vocabulary became rarefied and abstruse; and a totally hermetic terminology began to graft itself onto that of Marx, which, to begin with, was uncommon and often difficult to grasp because of its ambiguities. Doctrinal controversies raged over the meaning of words and over formulas that were intended to transmit "intellectual/practical" truths, the reality of which grew befogged. The expulsions, excommunications, and fragmentation resulting from interpretations which, to the uninitiated, seem almost to overlap, were extremely damaging. The primacy of doctrine in revolution was destined to, and did, arouse endless dispute over the understanding, the application, and, in short order, the alteration of that doctrine. Discourse took the limelight: everything hinged on the verbal formulation of valid actions, gradually submerging the actions themselves. Soon logorrhea was replaced by logocracy. Reading the best of the Marxist theorists can be a somewhat disconcerting experience to the unconverted, for it brings to mind a particular body of literature: that of the Church Fathers in the third and fourth centuries, at which time fierce debate raged over the word *homoousios* and the unengendered Son of God. In contrast to those infinite subtleties, there was a reciprocal (because it involved reaching the people) tendency to formulate doctrine as catechism, reducing a complex and profound system of thought to excessive simplicity, transforming it into a series of commands. In so doing, doctrine departed from theory and became pure propaganda. The theorists, of course, could distinguish one from the other: on the one hand, the privileged domain of Marxist intellectuals, wherein ideology was at grips with reality and must dictate the course of revolution; and on the other, the popular quarter, which could be reached via slogans summarizing, with varying effectiveness, the necessity for believing something relevant to the current revolutionary phase. Unfortunately, however, it is impossible to keep the two separate. Communication is essential, and the recondite vocabulary merges with the catechisms. Moreover, the theorist is compelled to take account of the ideological transformation affecting the masses, who do not simply swallow catechism whole and model themselves after it, having their own hesitations and spontaneous interpretations. Under the influence of slogans, they become ever so slightly different from what the catechism-makers had anticipated, as if by some process of refraction. A new dimension emerges almost instantly, that of ideology. Ideology is not simply the normal and expected result of revolutionary movement. A veritable transmutation of doctrine (and even of theory) into ideology gradually has taken place, converting into a clutter of arguments, ideas, beliefs, hopes, and hatreds what had been an exact system of understanding phenomena in order to act upon them. For three quarters of a century, a massive influx of "feelings" and subjectivity has invaded that deliberately stringent system. The same cause, if we renew the comparison to early Christian history, accounted for the degradation of Christian faith: the disappearance of the immanence of the Kingdom of God, the indefinite postponement of Parousia—and, in the meantime, man had to exist somehow. That is exactly what transforms precise theory into confused ideology: a breach, ultimately all but total, comes between a "power/being" residing some-where in infinity, and the present, now totally different but requiring justification for the sake of both the utopian future and momentary tactical necessity, the relationship of which to the final outcome is never certain. Not only statements of doctrine were affected, but also dialectics, the very core of the system. Indeed "dialectics plays the precise role of an ideology, helping communism to be different from what it thinks" (Merleau-Ponty). That mutation, which had an immeasurable effect on revolution, was the second avatar of doctrine.

The third transformation was even more alarming. Out of all the dissension and controversy arose the orthodoxy all too familiar to us. It involved two separate elements: a content and a method. Certain factors had to be accepted blindly—namely, the correct method of action and that of interpreting events. That is an inescapable imperative of any revolutionary movement; if such orthodoxy does not emerge on its own, revolution eventually is condemned to defeat or to stagnation. The current opponents of orthodoxy, who condemn Stalinism, for example, have every right *today* to invoke Adorno and Gramsci, but they ought to bear in mind that controversy is a luxury one can afford once success arrives. Without the orthodox rigidity that culminated in Stalin, the Marxist revo-lution would have been crushed, period, and would not be talked about today. Orthodoxy developed gradually as a self-generator for the system—that is, marginally and even in defiance of facts. The question of Marxist opposition to facts is an old one; it was at the heart of the "betrayals" on the part of Jaurès and Bernstein. What should be done when events do not occur as Marx thought they would? When the economic environment is no longer that on which Marx based his reasoning? Marxist revolutionaries knew that revisionism spelled doom for potential revolution, and to guard against it they were compelled to maintain orthodoxy in the face of conflicting facts, either by interpreting facts in such a manner as to render them palatable—supplying them with a meaning different from the obvious one—or, on occasion, by simply denying them. That recalls the last great confrontation over objective and absolute impoverishment which the French Communist Party upheld as dogma in 1954–5. One cannot ignore the strain of such an antithesis between doctrine and facts on a theory claiming to be scientific—that is, a theory operating by strict and accurate examination of facts in order to reach an objective interpretation of a situation. Marx's philosophy hinges on the importance of praxis; yet how can praxis be relied upon when facts are negated, certainly not for the fun of it, but because of the need to sustain doctrine, which is the basis of a correct theoretical interpretation? One is trapped indeed. What is significant about this particular contradiction, one among many, is the fact that it exists also in the sphere of revolutionary events. Marxists have reached the point of denying certain aspects of revolutionary movement.

Let us take two examples. When a mass-supported retaliatory movement is unleashed, one must expect to see it crushed; that is the specific nature of a mass set in motion, which, by its own action, diminishes its initial momentum. In addition, a mass movement cannot be sustained for long on a single theme; if it is to continue, a new and more powerful stimulus must be provided. The spur must cut deeper each time, especially as the mass expands, thus producing a kind of escalation between the mass and the provocation. All his life Lenin struggled with the enigma of facts. His successors tried to simplify the matter by repudiating the fact of revolution and transforming the masses into a well-disciplined, blindly obedient army officered by the Party. That worked out fairly well. But was it still revolution, or had the revolutionary capacity of the masses been sterilized? Let us not label it a Stalinist aberration: it was impossible to *do* otherwise, for the problem was inherent in the doctrine itself.

Another question: in a revolutionary movement, when public opinion begins to shift in that direction, extremist views are bound to prevail. Every revolutionary movement has a threshold at which rational demands are dropped, the initial plan of revolution is abandoned, and any rational course of action dissolves in the passions of the moment. Those are problems involving the myth and celebration of revolution, if you will, but what is evident in all the activity of the past century is the fact that the positions grow increasingly rigid and finally overshadow the primary issue of revolution. That was the case between 1789 and 1795. Kerenskis are invariably defeated, and Ben Bella will always prevail over Ferhat Abbas,[11] Nasser over Naguib, Lumumba over the moderates, and the Black Muslims over Martin Luther King, just as radical factions inevitably take control of a movement as long as that movement relies on mass support and the effects of propaganda. But ultimately there is a breaking-point, in several phases; Brumaire must follow Thermidor. Yet Marxists have sought to bypass that historically tested pattern of movement. In revolutions over the past fifty-odd years they have adopted a tactical posture that negates facts and men. Their prime concern has been to avoid leaning too far to the Left. Maintaining control over a revolutionary movement entails being its most radical element (to prevent a more radical one from taking over) and at the same time guiding its development; the two imperatives are absolutely contradictory. The Party has resolved the problem either by liquidating those who threatened to tip the boat or by simply repudiating them. Unfortunately, what was attainable during a rather brief period is no longer so once revolution becomes a secular affair. Facts cannot be denied forever in the name of theoretical precision. That is what we are seeing today.

The fourth mishap to befall doctrine was that it became so popularized that it was taken for granted. After all the bitter disputes over every inch of it, no one was interested in its

---

[11] In an article in *Le Monde* in 1961, Duverger asserted that Ben Bella could not possibly win out and that Ferhat Abbas was the logical leader of an independent Algeria.

content or in examining it. Althusser's reappraisal of the problem, the only serious attempt in modern times, seems oddly outdated, for the fact that it clings to a theoretical level is both praiseworthy and out of touch with reality. Althusser is the first great theologian of synthetic Marxism and heralds this new stage. It is a foregone conclusion that socialism is good, that we are moving toward socialism, that the only possible goal of revolution is socialism, and that socialism stands for all the aspirations of modern man. But those assumptions are no different from the taking for granted of Christianity by thirteenth-century Western man and are ultimately of no great consequence. Marxism is part of the modern world just as Christianity was part of the feudal one. Embracing it no longer calls for crucial moral awakenings, or great crises, or bitter struggles. Nowadays we inject anything and everything into Marxist socialism. The fact that we speak of Marxism in relation to Mao's writings, to Egyptian, Algerian, African, or even pragmatic (in Nigeria) socialism, and to the proclamations of Fidel Castro is evidence that Marxism no longer has any content. Socialism has become such a vital ingredient of political discourse that today doctrine is all but nonexistent. Fascism and national socialism were in reality forms of socialism and their opposition to Marxism was circumstantial and political rather than doctrinal. Paradoxical as it may seem, national socialism was fundamentally no farther from the ideas of Marx than Maoism now is: each derives from socialism and suggests that all revolutions unfailingly introduce socialism (Marxist at that), as if some "inner mechanism" of revolution (Daniel Guérin) were now operating automatically. What are the modern revolutionists such as Debray and Fanon writing about? Not doctrine. No one appears interested in examining the ideas of Marx or the significance of any aspect of Marxist theory (this is now the province of specialized publications entirely out of touch with reality, and their exquisitely subtle and nonsensical analyses ignore such commonplace evidence). Doctrine has become the assumption that all roads lead to a socialist society—just as Christians have taken for granted the existence of God. At a certain point, a collective belief takes root in a society and the public tires of an unending parade of intellectual refinements. Revolution is the answer, for it will automatically bring socialism (Marxist). Thereafter revolution, not its goal, becomes significant, revolution *per se,* with its own logic and mechanics. Marxism had sought to integrate it in a global concept of history, the universe, and mankind. All that is now taken for granted. But revolution has not come. Doctrine, therefore, is no longer of interest (hence one is no longer a Marxist no matter what one professes); the road to revolution is all that matters. At that point revolution becomes a "fetish," having value in itself and, as we shall see, for itself. The primacy of doctrine is now only immaterial evidence. What is the focus of interest then? Tactics.[12]

Tactics was the other face of Marxism, indissolubly linked, in Marx's mind, to the primary one. Theory and tactics were a fundamental unity corresponding to the core of his philosophy, his praxis. The two were interdependent because, in short, the goal of theory was to discover the direction of history, the aim of tactics to advance history along its own course. Tactics and theory were equally important materially, for, history's judgment being final, the victor was he who made the right choice, and tactics entails determining the most effective means of winning. A rule of action was essential because there was no existing standard to validate action. Marxism would await future vindication of established communism, but in the present, the rule of action was action itself. For it is perfectly true that Marx's outlook was not mechanistic and

---

[12] The mutation of Marxism was well summarized some time ago by Ulmann (*Esprit,* 1933) in one concise sentence: "Therein may be seen the effect of three parallel thrusts on the part of Marxist methodology, Marxist phraseology, and, the most fearful of the three, Marxist tradition." Nowadays, despite the constant reconstruing or overstraining, those three forces have plainly overwhelmed whatever truth Marxism contained.

that he regarded man as the maker of his own history. For that reason, one had to know how to act if the results were to be historical. That concept is vital to the revolutionary moment in view of revolution's function in the revealing of history. The rest is unimportant. Thus Marxists were reduced gradually to the level of revolutionary tacticians involved in three phases: appraisal of the power structure, analysis of the successive stages of a given revolutionary process, and the selection of appropriate methods.[13] The first phase entailed principally the correct application of doctrine. But as it became evident that the complex analysis would not lend itself to generalization, the primary stage of tactics was reduced to a semimechanical application of certain criteria and certain yardsticks. Whereas the analyses of situations put forth by Marx and Lenin are perceptive and closely reasoned, taking into account most factors and arriving at far-reaching conclusions, the post-1944 communist appraisals of events (Togliatti's included) are cursory, simplistic, and rudimentary, or else their utter failure to grasp reality is concealed beneath a haze of words such as characterizes the articles in *Pensée* and *Temps modernes.* The transfer coincided with the establishment of a "revolutionary conformity" signaling the total decline of doctrine and the primacy of its evidence just discussed. Thereafter tactics were all.

Current revolutionary thinking centers on the revolutionary methods of Mao (who is in fact a great strategist) and on the six stages of revolution outlined by Trotsky—to which ought to be added Malaparte's "technique of the *coup d'état*" or Hitler's own very effective system, although neither is much in fashion today. Nevertheless, it is interesting to note that the methods employed by the French students in 1968 were derived directly from the analysis of revolutionary tactics in *Mein Kampf.* The students manifested the important role

---

[13] It is worth noting that this revolutionary technique, whatever the Left may say of it, is not *fundamentally* different from the technique of the *coup d'état* as expounded (and practiced) by Hitler and subsequently formulated by Malaparte and Trinquier.

assigned to tactics; one of their watchwords was: "Action first; action will tell us what we must do." It is the culmination of the importance ascribed to tactics.

Writing about revolution, Mounier reveals himself as influenced by Marxism and also as purveying platitudes when he asserts that the only significant factor is success, and that in the final outcome (without spelling it out) the end justifies the means. "Only one thing matters along the way: the crisis must be settled, and settled as rapidly as possible. . . . If one agrees, everything must be gauged in relation to the outcome. . . . No serious criticism can be pressed to the point of threatening the success of the whole." [14] A consummate apology for dismissing goals and recognizing the primacy of totalizer tactics. That is precisely the way revolutions for freedom fall prey to dire necessity.

Although Lenin's descriptions of revolutionary tactics are altogether the most remarkable ever conceived, they hold to a straight Marxist line because they relate strictly to theory. But tactics rapidly turn into prescriptions. What Stalin formulated was, on a very high level, prescriptions and tactical techniques which any mediocre mind could apply subsequently—and this was, in fact, done successfully. The revolutionary leadership used the right tactics. That was the period when communists were totally preoccupied with spontaneous efficiency and democratic centralism, which provoked bitter opposition, of course, from extremists and dissidents, among others. But Lenin had already pointed out how to deal with them. [15] Tactics, in addition to filling a vital role in revolutionary action and being reduced to formulas, also implied the existence of an executive and radical instrument, the Party, designed to function uniformly like an army. It was the Party, a tactical agent, that ultimately controlled tactics. It brooked no contradiction and no lapse. There again, what

---

[14] *Esprit,* 1944.
[15] For a good analysis of this phenomenon during the 1930's, see R. Leenhardt, "Panorama de l'hérésie révolutionnaire," *Esprit,* No. 40.

may have appeared to be a grotesque deviation from Marxism was a normal derivative of it when one of the elements of that complex system was removed or another given priority. Marx had promoted the Party's absolute control by his fierce efforts to bar his opponents from the International. Later on, however, the major focus shifted from the reality of economic and social facts, or theoretical debates, or the choice of revolution, to the Party line. Inside communism, a mystical self-contemplation developed that made heresy unfathomable and tactics the reverse of what Marx had said. The Party was the "vanguard," "the organized sector" of the proletariat, the consolidating element, and the instrument of the dictatorship of the proletariat; it had to be systematic, antianarchist, centralized, disciplined, unitary, and antifractionist. All those qualifications come directly from Lenin. In 1934, Stalin unblushingly added "bureaucratic" to the description, but at that time the word did not have the unfortunate connotation it now has. The Party became synonymous with *Tactics*, after tactics had become the *All* of Marxism in action. Because the possibility of revolution resides solely in the Party, it *is history*—spontaneous, designed, and achieved. It is the reservoir of all real revolutionary forces, which in turn are recognized as such because they are within the Party. Whatever opposes it is automatically counterrevolutionary. If spontaneous history has any chance of becoming authentic history, it is through the mediation of the Party alone, and within it. The proletariat, which did not *know* what to do but did it as a function of its condition, is now linked to the Party, which provides it with a (single) course of action that serves both the proletariat and the future of mankind. But it is a double-sided image. Without the Party, the proletariat can do nothing and, ultimately, is nothing. Thereafter, it can have no intellectual, ideological, or ethical orientation toward any revolution differing from the one projected and organized in Party tactics. Thus the concentration on tactics finally eliminated everything else, and in order for those tactics to prevail, their most effective instrument also eliminated diversity of opinion about them. But did that necessarily introduce what has been called terrorism? Did such a monocracy lead to Stalinist "excesses"? It seems to me that, on the contrary, communist revolutionary terrorism has been (is) merely a simplistic compensation for the failure of correctly calculated tactics. Marx's ideas about tactics were extremely flexible but profound. I have tried to show how they were gradually impoverished, simplified, and automated. As a system, tactics showed great promise at first, but grew increasingly rigid and inefficient with automation. Although it was the only such system in the political world and consequently far superior to anything bourgeois regimes could devise, still, it had lost its initial aura of genius. It would strive to offset its shortcomings by displaying power. Thus force took its place within that system of political thought and action. What judicious action, designed to follow the course of history, might have accomplished independently, it was tempting to simplify, to avoid calculating sensitively, and instead to execute by force, thus settling but not solving matters. We have already noted that terrorism must play a part in revolution, and it is sheer fantasy to think that the road to socialism is smoothly paved. Every revolutionary period has its violence, but according to the ideas of Marx and also of Lenin, that violence is limited, carefully estimated, and localized so as to obtain a specific and predetermined effect. What occurred, however, was that violence spread in proportion to the decline of tactics owing to the absence of tacticians of the caliber Marx had envisaged, and to the failure to incorporate tactics in a general system. Force became the most expedient way to obtain results, but the results in turn, as we have seen, were taken for granted. The seeds of that development were already present in the controversy between Lenin and Kautsky. It is clear that Kautsky held to a strict Marxist view, for Lenin, despite his penetrating tactical analysis, had veered sharply in the direction of terrorism. Stalin merely took what was handed him and developed it. His successors were left with no theory but with a global presupposition, with no reliable tactics but wedded to terrorism for simplicity's sake. I would say, therefore, that the roots of terrorism are to be found not in Marxist theory or in the primacy of tactics (which goes back to Marx), but in the self-contemplation of the Party and the resulting disregard for reality. Although Marx stipulated that a line of action ought to rest upon knowledge of all the available facts, it is far easier, when in possession of a uniquely powerful instrument such as the Party, to seize everything in reach with one sweeping thrust. Painstaking analysis is a waste of time if the forcible control of affairs will do the trick, and do it much more rapidly.

Mussolini, although a far less gifted tactician than Lenin, was taken by the same lure because he lacked a true grasp of tactics. In any event, the use of violence was still open to interpretation and to a variety of applications within an existing state or in the conquest of power. And it is interesting to see that the Marxist passion for hair-splitting disputes transferred itself to that area. Ardent and tortuous theoretical explorations continued to preoccupy the Party and the satellites, mainly on the subject of how and when to apply force, and were characterized by the extremism and narrow focus of the previous controversies. A significant example is Régis Debray's book, which deals almost exclusively with guerrilla tactics, the Guevarist type earning his highest approval as an effective system and, according to the author, as uniquely revolutionary among the instruments of self-defense and aggressive propaganda. The tone is fiercely assertive; the discussion involves general administrative problems on a national scale. Beyond that the book has little interest, for it does not confront (as Mao does) the real issue of tactics as an integral part of a system expressing a broad doctrine. Everything is highly simplified. The goal of revolution? Not a word about it, although socialism is obviously in mind. The enemy? Debray does not even bother to probe the question; it is simply "American imperialism." After such banalities, the theorist plunges into subtle expositions of logic and method, like an engineer oblivious of the finished product but eager to debate the shape of a turret or the ideal span of a wheel. Although I recognize that such discussions have some value in determining practical action and that the problems warrant careful study, I am appalled by the absurdity of gearing such a vast pseudo-intellectual apparatus in order to justify one or another form of violence. (Concrete estimates are not enough; an ideological cover is supplied so that it may be pulled apart in short order to show what is underneath.) An attempt is even made to relate all that, via Mao, to the great tactical innovation of Marx, the only traces of which are prolixity and a distinctive vocabulary. But the most painful aspect of the book is its title: *Revolution within Revolution.* Without raising the question of the objective or the adversary, and dealing only with the tactics of violence, the author claims to have brought about a revolution within the revolutionary movement (which, to be sure, can only be socialist!). Previously, Bernstein had formulated a revolution within revolution, but the discussion of systematic terrorism strikes me as supremely pretentious when raised to that level—unless one admits to another premise, namely, that revolution is raw force, and that therefore revolution itself is changed by changing the nature and form of that force. But if that is the case, we are dealing with something entirely different, a new version of Blanquism (and orthodox communists are perfectly justified *on this score* to condemn it as adventurism). We may even wonder whether such a book was not inevitable once tactics became the all-absorbing fixation. The vehement tone of the writing conveys the sense of mystical urgency that grips all those who are exasperated by the sluggish and vacillating attitude of South American communist parties. The latter are now permanently at home with the situation. It had been established that revolution could not be achieved overnight and required a whole set of conditions, so it was up to the Party to create them (for a Marxist revolution in the strict sense of the word is inconceivable in Latin America, even under the qualifying circumstances noted by Lenin). Thereafter the Party's revolutionary tactics became a system devoted to its survival and to creating step by step the eventual conditions (taken from Marx) that could make revolution possible. As revolutionary activities grew more and more tortuous, so did the maze of actions and counteractions, and under the banner of tactics the game of revolution could go on indefinitely. Revolution was a long way off, at the end of a road strewn with small skirmishes, small compromises, and small victories, all of which were destined to create the legendary favorable conditions. But finally, with no signs of progress, which generally manifested itself in unexpected ways, one had the feeling of being lost in a virgin socioeconomic forest with no instrument to probe it and no direct path through it. A clutter of minor projects claimed attention before any revolutionary action was possible. Constrained by the delays and obstacles (derived from the doctrine of the objective revolutionary situation), impatient revolutionaries threw themselves eagerly into tactical action, and it is understandable that tactics became their sole object of serious study, all the rest being literature.

In fact, at that time literary men were the ones chiefly concerned with revolutionary tactics. Philosophy professors, not Party members (at least since 1953) but sympathetic, were the pillars of tactical theory. Sartre set the pace. They attempted (by an approach altogether remarkable because it ran counter to that of Marx and Lenin) to reimplant tactics in doctrine. Starting with revolutionary practice (one aspect of it, State terrorism where communist power was established, and subversive activity elsewhere), they tried to explain in detail in terms of global doctrine its decisions, attitudes, and tactical action. The tissue of nonsense spread from there. Moreover, their activism was confined to signing petitions and making speeches. They were the Greek chorus narrating and universalizing the deeds of the protagonists. That is why their literature is just as admirable and just as tiresome as those choral litanies. As for the impatient sector that longed to plunge into the fray, it rejected the earlier analyses of the C.P., accused the Party of overcaution and vacillation, and adopted its own fresh and inspired style. To renew the comparison with Christianity that suggests itself at each stage of development, the Church was established; it had expanded its means of survival and its network of intermediaries between man and God. The faithful then rejected the system and its stability and embarked on spiritual adventure, either in the form of a mystical urge to encounter God directly, or, in the spirit of millenarianism, refusing to wait forever to live the absolute Word of God and beginning to do so then and there, as if to hasten thereby the advent of the Kingdom. But those explosions, even when not repressed by the Church, were inevitably brief and unenduring. Only the Church endured, like the Party.

Where the Course of History Lay

We have seen that revolution, from the moment it began to be perceived as a part of history, a phase of history, could not escape being reduced to a theory as well as to tactics; that it is almost impossible to maintain the unity of those two elements over a relatively long period of time; and, finally, that man, because of his nature, cannot remain forever on the heights enjoying the rarefied air of Marx's total necessity of revolution and is bound to seek compromises, which entail the degradation of theory and tactics along the lines we have indicated. In other words, if revolution must follow the direction of history, one may rely on the fact that it is doomed to betrayal. Revolution is betrayed when it loses its goal, is reduced to a system, and becomes a normal phenomenon *of* history and *in* history. Studies have been made of how the bourgeoisie erred by exploring only the political problem of revolution and neglecting its economic basis,[16] but there is no

---

[16] For one example among many, see Sartre, *Situations II*, pp. 301 *ff.*

evidence of awareness that this explanation contains the seeds of revolution's betrayal. It seems to me that the betrayal has two aspects, both connected with the success of a revolution and both traceable to Lenin. The first aspect derives from the conditions of revolution. For Marx, revolution was the climax of a dialectical system's development, the moment when the two factors reached the requisite point of negating negation. Revolution was thus a phenomenon of maturation and maturity. But it broke out and, through *effective methods,* succeeded in countries which had not reached that level of development—notably Russia. The debate was a classic one and was *seemingly* resolved by Lenin in his *Imperialism: Final Stage of Capitalism.* The same thing occurred afterward in many other countries. Revolution was premature. It had to be explained by going back to Lenin's principles, what I would call the "doctrine of explanations." [17] The facts were there and needed only to be reincorporated in the Marxist system, chiefly by means of a suitable vocabulary. So the law of unequal development was formulated, after which *one* passage in Marx was examined, and the result was the doctrine of Asia's system of production. Both theories may be summarized as follows: the historical lag of a country that has not been developed industrially under the guidance of the bourgeoisie, the absence of an industrial proletariat, the pressures of other capitalist nations on that country, the implanting of a regime that is semi-, para-, post-, or neo-colonial, the sudden emergence of a different type of proletariat (the result of colonization) grafted onto an existing class of the poor—all these factors constituted a set of conditions favoring revolution, which, a priori, could be none other than socialist and Marxist, despite the absence of conditions specified by Marx. Along with the concept of the Asian system of production came the view of an eventual semiprimitive economic structure that

---

[17] This "doctrine of explanations" has become an obsession among Marxist intellectuals—e.g., the literature on the May 1968 disorders, and especially Lefèbvre, *L'Irruption,* 1968.

would allow for the direct transition to socialist collectivism.[18]

Within that framework, one could project the transition to communism without the preliminary interval of industrial capitalism, without the creation of a bourgeoisie or an industrial working class, and without any intermediate phase. By recognizing the concepts of imperialism, of unequal development, and of the Asian system of production, one could bypass the historical phase that Marx considered crucial: that in which the class struggle within a global society [19] became climactic and exclusive and the economic conditions for the establishment of socialism took root. Even a democratic stage could be avoided by leaping directly from feudalism, or even primitive serfdom, straight into socialism. But such explanations of concrete events were extremely far-fetched and, in fact, made it impossible to tell whether a situation was revolutionary or not. That series of doctrinal modifications reached the conclusion (unformulated, of course) that revolution no longer had any objective conditions. To defend that position as a Marxist one was not easy, for Marx had devoted a large part of his work (principally *Capital,* which is grossly neglected) to a detailed analysis of those conditions and to demonstrating that capitalism's internal development prepared the proletariat to fulfill its revolutionary function and accumulated the contradictions that both doomed the capitalist socioeconomic system and gave rise to its own contradiction. Marx never left things to chance; he dealt with facts. By substituting imperialism, Lenin produced a much more superficial and less authoritative work. Above all, he opened the way to later hasty interpretations founded on broad generalities rather than on meaningful analysis. Marx's philosophic

---

[18] Theorists lost sight of the debates that occupied socialists at the end of the nineteenth century and the beginning of the twentieth on the subject of spontaneous communist structures in the Slavic countries—the Mir, for example—and which should have been adaptable to collectivization. Marxists have always maintained that it is impossible to cut short the industrial phase.

[19] To simplify matters even more, the latest theoretical tendency is to claim that there is no longer a global society. (Cf. *L'Homme et la Société,* 1968, No. 8.)

thrust was retained—solely as an inspiration. In the light of those developments, revolution (socialist, it goes without saying) could be made conceivably anywhere and at any time. The poor as a category were substituted baldly for the proletariat (something Marx had always challenged), and even Marx's class struggle was transposed to a conflict between poor and rich nations; all it proved was total ignorance of Marx's concept of class struggle, of its relation to the economic system, and of the ties between the classes themselves. Such a shift cannot be traced to the ideas of Marx; it is merely the expression of the conflict between rich and poor, for a class and a nation do not resemble each other in either function or structure. But if revolution had changed its course completely in terms of Marx's philosophy, could one believe it would have the results he predicted? For the proponents of the law of unequal development, it was all the same: if history skipped from precapitalism to socialism, they agreed it was still socialism (*the* one and only socialism), and this socialism was no different from the socialism which capitalist maturation and decadence were supposed to introduce. The process of development was abridged and the transitions avoided, but the result was identical. That is not easy to accept, for Marx held that socialism absorbed all that capitalism had created and consisted of a transformation of the social structure, participation in the results of development, an administered society, and the reintegration in man's universe of alienated values objectified in the industrial system and by the division of labor. Obviously, if socialism was to assume the task of industrialization (which, for Marx, was incumbent on capitalism), if socialism was to be responsible for division of labor, productivity, industrial bondage, and all the rest, this meant that the socialist stage would witness the development of the proletariat (upon which the industrial structure and not just bourgeois exploitation depends), the subordination of men to things, and, finally, the class struggle. But is there any resemblance between the socialism Marx promised and the socialism established in this

way? They have no common purpose, or function, or inspiration. What is more, revolution has not appeared in the most
advanced nations and seems to confine itself to the least developed ones, so that even Lenin's thesis is questionable, for it
is certain that in explaining why revolution had come to
Russia, Lenin could only have conceived of it as the vanguard
which would trigger revolution in *capitalist* nations. Thus we
have good reason to wonder whether this new model of
"socialist" revolution, instead of being the product of capitalism, is not tied fundamentally to the structure of underdeveloped countries. If that is so, it is not a type of premature
(in contrast to what it should be according to Marx) revolution, but a revolution linked to economic and political lag,
and destined to accelerate the development and modernization
of those countries. A crisis of development, not the promised
future of developed nations. In any event, we are forced to
conclude that the famous theory of the objective revolutionary
situation is false. All the criteria used to determine whether a
situation was or was not favorable to a revolution in the
direction of history were bound up with the theory of class
struggle within a capitalist system.

Nothing remains of the concept that through analysis of
the economic and social development of capitalism in a given
country one may judge whether or not revolution is possible.
Revolution has occurred widely outside that framework. In
fact, the past fifty years have showed that *any* situation may
be regarded, in one way or another, as revolutionary: for
example, the impoverishment of the peasantry, or student
rejection of a particular type of force, or the lag between a
local culture and industrial development. The Havana
Conference in August 1967 actually reached that conclusion.
What is important is that revolution becomes once more a
matter primarily of will. Lenin had taken that view, but then
dropped it in the effort to make his ideas correspond faithfully
to those of Marx, and simply said that revolution is carried
out by competent and courageous revolutionaries. It involves

tactics (an echo of Marx's accent on tactics) and technique on two levels: the general use of force and specific techniques of active revolution. When a good technique is properly applied, revolution almost invariably follows, whatever the circumstances may be. But before being made against an economic system, a certain type of society, or a global structure, that revolution is made against the political system. It becomes political once again. For Marx also, revolution had to be political in that the state was the chief instrument of the dominant class. But the framework, the goal, and the direction of revolution were entirely changed. In that focus, the main objective is to evict the holders of power, to control the machinery of state, and to occupy the seats of authority; the rest will be taken care of subsequently through the intermediary of the state. Revolutionary technique therefore has no need to address itself so directly to a global society or to the latter's profound goals and economic structures, but must be directed instead to a specific state. And the tactical problem becomes the following: the state to be overthrown possesses certain resources, can defend itself in certain sectors, has certain allies, but is vulnerable on certain counts; a different plan of attack is called for from that which will merely meet the thrust of the state. Confronting the state on its own terrain is a lost battle, for power has infinitely superior resources. The correct tactics consist in drawing the revolutionary struggle onto ground where the state cannot make a stand. Every successful revolution during the past fifty years has borne that out. Obviously, such tactics no longer relate to economic appraisals and the question of class relations within the Marxist system. Although attempts are made (occasionally) to validate happenings from a Marxist point of view, such efforts are rather casual and halfhearted. For what difference does it make, now that people share the deep-rooted belief that whatever is connected with revolution has to be socialist and Marxist? The important thing to retain from this discussion is that revolution is now directed against political power and consists in seizing control of it.

. . .

One may find fault with the role and importance given to the dictatorship of the proletariat by Marx. It would appear that his ideas on the subject were never very firm. Lengthy or brief, that dictatorship was meant to be only transitional, and the form of it variable. In his *Communist Manifesto,* Marx was still deeply influenced by the Revolution of 1789, and the power exerted by the victorious proletariat resembled a republic styled after the Constitution of the Year 1. In *The Eighteenth Brumaire of Louis Bonaparte,* Marx had in mind a more authoritarian dictatorship, much stricter, centralized, and destined to achieve the class struggle. In *Civil War in France,* and under the influence of the Commune, he leaned toward a federal and libertarian system. But it is always difficult to tell whether what he described was an ideal situation, or a model, or simply one of several possibilities. Whatever its duration and form, the dictatorship of the proletariat could lead, in the short run, only to the disappearance of the state.[20] That was inherent in the relationship Marx established between the ruling class and political power. If the state was merely an instrument for oppressing the dominated class and had no other function, it had no reason, once the class struggle ended in the victory of the proletariat, to survive, and must of necessity disappear. Revolution meant the end of the state and of government. Although the point cannot be argued, every discussion of communism focuses on it. For the state has been perpetuated in the Soviet Union, in all the people's republics, and in China. When revolutionists take power, they not only fail to destroy it, they reinforce it. And not just temporarily while they dispatch class enemies and bridge the period of transition, but for an apparently limitless duration. Lenin, as we know, was greatly perplexed by that necessity and, once again, sought to justify it, evolving his doctrine of "the state and revolution," a well-known theory dealing with the withering of the state, the administration of things

---

[20] Referring to the "dictatorship of the proletariat," Kautsky said: "That phrase Marx used only once, casually, and haphazardly at that."

supplanting government by men, and the merger of the first act of the proletarian state (seizure of the means of production) with the final specific act of the state. But for Lenin, the state, in addition to its appropriating function and its task of eliminating the remaining bourgeoisie, is relied upon implicitly to bring the peasantry and petty bourgeoisie into the social structure. And why not? For if socialism is not achieved in the manner outlined by Marx and is obliged to do what the bourgeoisie should have done, it must retain the tools to do it—namely, the state. That in turn implies that the state has another substance and another significance and function than those which Marx assigned to it. Moreover, Lenin sees the state as the creator of socialist man, who is not an automatic product of the new economic system. Marx, it seemed, held that the superstructures patterned themselves virtually *ipso facto* after the economic substructure. Well—no! For the molding process depends as much on will as does revolution itself. The political, legal, and cultural structures, as well as human beings, must be shaped. The idea that there might be any element of spontaneity in what is produced after the new economic structure is laid is tantamount to heresy and is labeled "economism." No, the state, through its authority, *must* accomplish that task, and must shape new men through psychological manipulation and propaganda. So here again we find the state assuming a much broader role than Marx intended. Will its power be limited at least to the interval preceding communism? Theoretically, yes. In reality, however, we know that Lenin said it was impossible to predict how long the establishment of communism would take: "We do not, and cannot, know this. . . . We have no data relevant to the problem. . . . What is more, we cannot tell *if* it will happen. It has not occurred to any socialist to pledge that the superior phase of communism will arrive." In other words, the duration of the state is indeterminate, and is likely to be extensive, for in one of his speeches, Lenin, instead of confining the function of the Russian state to establishing a communist society, gave it world-wide scope. "With the aid of this apparatus or club [the state], we will erase exploitation and rid *the earth* of the specter of exploitation. . . . No longer shall some gorge themselves before the very eyes of the starving masses once such things *shall have been made impossible; only then* shall the apparatus be discarded. At such time there shall be neither exploitation nor state." In other words, the state is the sole force capable of achieving the task and the sole structure of Marxist, Leninist, proletarian, and communist action. That is scarcely what Marx had in mind.

Or, for that matter, the first Russian revolutionaries, because the soviets, far from being organs of government, were instruments for dissolving the centralizing state and a confused expression of centrifugal forces as well as of Russian anarchism; normally, they would have evolved into local administrative agencies, but they were destined to disappear with the emergence of the central state. In reality, Lenin was wrong to look to Marx for an explanation of the state's survival, as he had no choice but to reconstitute, reaffirm, and reinforce the state. The perpetuation of the state did not rest upon any tactical error, any lack of determination or courage, or any failure to recognize the potential spontaneity of the masses. To activists (and to non-parlor revolutionaries) it was obvious that the state alone was capable of acting and the instrument best suited to it; at the same time its influence upon society was so pervasive that even if forcibly assaulted, it could not be destroyed or severed from the social body. Thus the organism established by Lenin (with Trotsky's unconditional approval) represented a state of the most rigid type, without any semblance of federalism or revolutionary freedom.

It is important to note how, in certain areas, Lenin was led to do the opposite of what he had advocated. He had pledged a free press, party plurality within the dictatorship of the proletariat, banning of the army and the police, and the abolition of the bureaucracy: all of which he undertook in

October 1917. But by April 1918 he was doing an about-face, and it was he who restored the apparatus of state—which is exactly what it was.[21] Observing the gap between realization and intention is not enough, however, and this "betrayal" must be perceived as inherent in events once Lenin endorsed the state, the existence of which precluded any changes he hoped to bring to it.

In January 1918, at the Third Soviet Congress, Lenin still maintained that the state would wither and applauded the activism of anarchists and the channeling of their ideas into concrete form with encouragement from the Bolsheviks. His reversal began three months later, and the police moved in to suppress anarchism. When *The State and Revolution* appeared in March 1918 and Bukharin proposed reinforcing the theses on the withering of the state, Lenin answered him: "At this moment we favor the State absolutely. . . . To proclaim in advance the state's extinction would be a violation of historical perspective." The phrase "at this moment" revealed the failure to recognize the reality of the state, and the reply sealed the question.

The Red Terror opened in August 1918, and from 1919 onward the various conferences of the soviets, the congresses, and the trade unions were command performances that dealt with narrowly defined issues culminating in prefabricated resolutions. In 1922 Lenin began to outlaw, to arrest, or to exile all leftist elements, branding them idealistic and declaring that the dictatorship he was instituting aimed at "abolishing all the legal constraints imposed on power." [22] The new type of state could survive only through the existence of the Party, forged for the conquest of revolutionary power, the heart and spine of which it represented. All other established organs became no more than a façade and an appearance, as

---

[21] See the excellent summary by Papaoiannou, "Lénine, la Révolution et l'État," *Preuves,* 1967.

[22] Regarding all these facts, which tend to be overlooked nowadays, one should consult the accounts of eyewitnesses such as Victor Serge, as well as the important writings of Pierre Pascal.

Lenin made clear in his essay "Can the Bolsheviks Retain Power?" (1918). In that essay he referred to the soviets as the "new apparatus of State" enabling the Bolsheviks to exercise *their* power and to impose *their* policies. For the Bolsheviks, the soviets served as a façade of legitimacy derived from the reality of power through the intermediary of the Party. When all was done, there was very little difference between the state under Lenin and under Stalin. Stalin simply applied mechanically the principles which Lenin had elabo- rated in a subtle manner. By the beginning of 1921, the entire apparatus of state—dictatorial, and neither proletarian nor popular—was installed. Unquestionably Lenin could not avoid reverting to what he had thought to abandon.

The "betrayal" so often charged against Lenin was nothing more than obedience to necessity. Only a very superficial appraisal (and Marx's certainly did no more than skim the surface) suggests that events might have turned out differ- ently. If Lenin had accepted the risk, the Bolshevik Revolution would have disintegrated. As a result, state power, instead of being reduced whenever possible, was reinforced wherever communism took hold. Moreover, through a series of co- incidences, the state has thrived, not withered, under com- munism. It is not by chance or circumstances that the state has been linked to historical nihilism and totalitarianism, but as a normal result of its transformation into a proletarian communist state. We have noted that general historicism has led to a type of nihilism because revolution in the direction of history negates values instead of creating them.

In the end, this revolution recognizes only one principle: the state. Placing its destiny in the hands of the state, it owes all to, and relies entirely upon, the state. Historical nihilism in turn endows the state with an undreamed-of achievement. Having known no restrictions, the state has no restraints, and because it is inextricably wedded to the state, "revolution, limited only by historical efficacy, signifies unlimited bondage." It was as if part of history's grandeur had faded, the very part that seems most historic. But through its submission to history, revolution rendered another service to the state. Revolution directed against the entire bourgeois society sought to embody total revolution and established a revolutionary totalitarianism in direct proportion to the problems at hand. The revolutionary organs were installed: the Party, the means of regulating every aspect of social life, the concentration and control of all media of communication, and the people's police (shortly to become the secret police). Those measures, in principle, were meant to apply only during the brief period of revolution, but at the close of that period (and Pierre Pascal estimates that the revolutionary *movement* ended in April 1918 with Lenin's famous speech on the urgent necessity of setting to work), the totalitarian organs serving a totalitarian revolution became organs of state and remained totalitarian. That transformation produced the first totalitarian state.[23]

Leninists tried to justify their position by a dogmatic principle: the state, the army, the police, technology, and other factors acquire their character and significance from the global society in which they function, and, pure façades that they are—or, better still, pure malleable matter—change completely according to whether they are part of a capitalist or a socialist society. As a result, capitalist and socialist police forces cannot be equated. But we might counter that statement with the following: Those elements have a structure, a specificity, a pattern of existence and movement, a thrust, and an intrinsic logic that give them authority; because their relations transcend the ideological differences between the regimes or societies in which they exist, they are not altered fundamentally by revolution and a change in regime. In addition, they are the elements that transform new systems and ideologies and produce changes that return the new order to the former one. Trotsky's illusions are manifest in his belief that the Red Army would never have to confront the armed

---

[23] Raymond Aron, *Démocratie et totalitarisme;* and, for a recent analysis, La Loy, *Le Socialisme de Lénine,* 1968.

might of capitalism. And we have come to realize that the Soviet bureaucracy has had the same rank, function, and influence, and has transformed the regime in the same general manner as the Western bureaucracy. That is why H. Lefèbvre's elaborations on the radical novelty of the urban revolution strike me as sheer ideological fantasy negated by our experience of the past fifty years. From the moment when one becomes convinced that in a global society the transition to socialism radically alters all institutions by shifting their orientation one is constrained to depart from reality and embark on theoretical/imaginary constructs—which has led to the betrayal of revolution.

From the time he broke with Stalin, and perhaps even vis-à-vis Lenin, Trotsky (who sealed the fate of the Kronstadt mutineers) denounced Stalin's treason and upheld the doctrine of permanent revolution. His idealism called for revolutionary action that was not solely external and that the masses could experience and comprehend. He rejected any measure threatening to concentrate power in an organization or divide the working class into new ranks of oppressed and oppressors. He urged continuous and genuine self-criticism, knowing how difficult it was to sustain. He realized that although revolution required violence in order to be severely self-critical, the more violence it practiced the less self-critical it became. The need to institutionalize is in strict conformity with the exercise of violence. Trotsky was aware that the Party's monolithism was both inevitable and fatal to the revolution. He perceived that as the revolution became the voluntary creation of an economic mutation, a new relationship evolved between the Party and the proletariat; that the problems were not being *solved* and that new paradoxes constantly emerged. For a long time he appeared to accept the Party and its totalitarianism, its maneuvering, its encroachments, and finally its institutionalization. Although he certainly saw that voluntarism was perverting "the course of history," that course nevertheless seemed assured by revolution. What he did not realize was that once an apparatus of state—whether new or proletarian—began to expand, it produced all the ramifications which he later decried. Experience taught him that it is difficult to accomplish anything political and still retain the flexibility and purity of dialectics, and that as revolution gains ground and becomes established, it loses all desire for self-discipline. In other words, revolution acts *realistically*, like an army over-running the enemy and occupying territory: rather than risk the loss of that territory, it chooses to organize it. Revolution cannot turn upon itself; it makes gains and does not question them. It cannot criticize itself and therefore does not generate dialectical movement. That is what Trotsky seems to have overlooked in condemning Stalin. Yet it is what he experienced directly in helping to repress all opposition to his revolution. Why should he, one of its founders, have sought to prevent the state from being strengthened? Such an attitude must rest upon strict adherence to Marxist principles concerning the nature of power—that is, upon a misconception of the state. Trotsky seems to have persisted in that error.

Whether we like it or not, a type of constant of revolution has existed since 1789. Each successful revolution has left the state enlarged, better organized, more potent, and with wider areas of influence; that has been the pattern even when revo-lution has assaulted and attempted to diminish the state. It is a matter of record which no theory can disprove. The Revo-lution of 1789 introduced the Napoleonic State, and 1848 strengthened that state (and not solely Napoleon III, for the Republic's institutions were already more authoritarian than those of the July Monarchy). The German revolutions between 1848 and 1860 led to Bismarck's type of state. The Revolution of 1917 created the real Russian state (with infinitely greater authority than the czarist one). The Hungarian revolution produced a dictatorship; the 1919–20 revolution of the Italian Left installed Mussolini; and Hitler's revolution introduced an even more absolute state. The same applies to post-1944 revolutions. I stress the fact that in each case dictatorship or the exercise of power by one man is not the important element; it is the institutional transformation, the creation of a more rational, all-embracing, efficient, and systematic state, which, with its far greater sphere of influence, has become the "state/nation" and the "state/organization," whatever its constitutional form or ideology. Mussolini claimed kinship with Sorel and Hegel, and Hitler with Nietzsche. Their state was established on the principle that the universe was senseless and history only the incidental product of force; the results were similar to those effected by liberal or socialist ideologies based on the direction of history and on values. The majority of those revolutions were made in the name of mankind and greater freedom, including that of Hitler, whose speeches echoed Marx's criticism of democracy and liberalism, according to which democratic freedom is formal and artificial. Hitler, too, claimed that the freedom he introduced was genuine and would be reinforced by the omnipotent state—as if a republic must of necessity give rise to the state.[24] Some theorists, such as Maurras and Marxists with oddly related views, have tried to explain the link between revolution and the expansion of the state in terms of a transitional dictatorship. From a theoretical standpoint, that argument prompts the question: how can one reinforce state power by imposing a dictatorship and, at the same time, prepare the way for abolishing it? How, under a dictatorship that suppresses mass development and the expression of public opinion, can a people be encouraged to express or even shape its own will? To believe that dictatorship is a bridge to freedom is to perform an absurd act of faith with no rational, factual, or sociological basis, and is the ideology of pure propaganda. Of course, dictatorship ultimately is transitional, and in each of the examples cited, it came to a halt, leaving the state a

---

[24] A detailed analysis of this point for the years 1914–30 may be found in Barthélemy, *La Crise de la démocratie,* 1931.

stronger, more concentrated, systematized, and absolute institution. It appears less overbearing and arbitrary than dictatorship: a sigh of relief goes up, and freedom seems to be just
around the corner. In reality, state control, now normalized
and rationalized, has never ceased to expand, and although
the situation is heartening, it is all the more dangerous. Just
as a storm churns the seas and destroys dikes, and when it
subsides the sound and fury are gone, but the land inundated
because of the broken dikes remains under water even when
tides return to normal. Nowhere has the state receded since
1789; on the contrary, each crisis or revolution has advanced
it. That is a new feature of revolution. We noted in the first
chapter that former revolutions, which inevitably failed, were
made against the state—that is, not only against a tyrant who
had to be eliminated but against the institutional development
of that organism. Revolutions failed, but at least they did not
lead to the expansion of the state. Conflict broke out between
established power and revolutionists; with their defeat, the
situation was left relatively the same as before. Revolutions
against history were revolutions against the state—and did
not reverse history. Bourgeois revolution, seemingly brought
against the state, actually produced greater efficiency or
greater systematization of that apparatus, in line with the
thinking and aims of the bourgeoisie. Those were revolutions
made in the name of liberty, yet the moment liberty was
proclaimed, it became integrated in power. Liberty was ultimately defined by institutions, which warranted and distributed it. It ceased to be a wild and angry cry for autonomy
raised spontaneously by man, and became a datum, carefully
ordered, embellished, measured, distributed, and, ultimately,
guaranteed by the state. With each surge of human freedom,
the State grew stronger by pledging to secure the very freedom
it absorbed. That was the revolution Marx affirmed and held
to be in history's direction—and so, indeed, it proved to be.
But the very essence of that constant contradiction between
intention and realization compels us to recognize that *revo-*

lution is finally the crisis of the development of the state.
Such an organism and complex of institutions (with all the
human factors it involves) gradually outgrows its structures
and its attire. Those who rebel are certainly defying the state,
not because it interferes with or impedes their movements, but
simply because its irrationality, its harshness, and its replete-
ness have made it oppressive and discreditable. Man becomes
disaffected by the incoherence of an organism that constrains
him by being at once too powerful and too unwieldy. He
makes revolution because the state is all-powerful, with the
result that it becomes more coherent, adaptable, useful, and
serviceable. Then man no longer feels oppressed and cheerfully
accepts that authority now that it has become more rational
and its arbitrary, functional mishaps and blunders are gone
temporarily. Thus the state is left free to resume its growth
and its conquest of society and mankind—until fresh difficulties or failures produce another crisis (for example, failure
to control an economic crisis and to secure the well-being of
citizens).

Today revolution and the state are drawn together by
another common factor: war. Within the framework of expanded state power, it is essential to weigh the relationship
between war and revolution which has been maintained for
the past two centuries. Their mutual dependence has increased steadily. Prior to the thirteenth century, the two were
unrelated: a defeated political power was not threatened by
revolution, and a revolutionary force did not make war. In
our times, this is no longer so; the frenzy of war is the staging
ground of revolution, or else its aftermath, a type of civil war
extending to other nations. The phenomenon has a variety of
causes, but the pre-eminence of the state is the principal one.
Today the aim of all wars is to induce a revolution against a
given political power. A revolution instantly provokes war on
the part of neighboring states that feel threatened, the reason
being that history's course leads back to the growth of the
state, which refuses to be diminished.

If that is indeed the nature of revolution (recognizing its consistent effects for nearly two centuries), then we may have singled out the major orientation of our modern Western society. It would mean that Marx misjudged the nature of the state and the direction of history. Marx unquestionably made a fundamental error in ranking the modern state with political power in all other periods. Here again, as with the social classes, he evolved an unfounded historical generality. Although he grasped the specificity of the modern world in respect to its economic and capitalist structure, he failed to do so in respect to the state. He judged power superficially, attributing to it an unvarying role which always corresponded to the same reality. He repeated what he had done with regard to the classes: analyzing function and direction before observing facts. He built upon the familiar premises of historical dialectics and made the state an instrument of the class struggle, an ally of history. Thus, with tranquil mind, he could say: "The abolition of the state has meaning only for communists, for whom it is a necessary consequence of the elimination of classes, the disappearance of which automatically entails the disappearance of the need for organized power on the part of one class in order to oppress another." Reducing the state to that role rules out any understanding of its sociological reality; furthermore, as we have indicated, in countries headed toward communism, the state shows no tendency whatever to disappear—quite the contrary, in fact. Marx's unquestionable mistake was to regard it as a subordinate or subsidiary organism, the essence of which derived solely from those who occupied its "shell" and used its powers. A very cursory examination informed him only that the tenants of the state were bourgeois in varying degrees and that the state frequently served to repress rebellion and to maintain order. His conclusion was simple—too simple. He failed to recognize that organism's specificity; Marx visualized the state as a protagonist in the very heart of the class struggle, but the latter was incapable of appraising the singular nature of modern state power, or the qualitative difference distinguishing it from traditional political power, or its relative autonomy. The state took vengeance by imposing itself with even greater severity on Marxist revolutionaries. It should have been apparent that with the global society, the state, instead of being subordinate, was superordinate: in relation to the economic and social system it is a superorder, an active organizer, and not a machine, relatively well equipped but completely subject to the social order.

Of course, that was not Marx's sole and unique vision of the state.[25] At the same time, his attitude varied considerably according to the circumstances. In 1871, at the time of the Commune, he recognized the importance of the state and of a revolution against it: "It was a revolution against the state itself, that uncanny and monstrous creation of society; it was the recovery by the people and for the people of its own social existence. It was not a revolution aimed at transferring power from a segment of the ruling class to another class, but a revolution to destroy that hideous apparatus of the class struggle. . . . The Commune is society's recovery of state power. . . ." But a series of retreats was to follow: Marx accepted centralization (in his final version of *Civil War*) and reaffirmed the state's need to organize and to own the means of production, and, finally, in 1891, he reduced the Commune to an accident. He came back to his thesis that the state was simply superstructure and not necessarily the prime target of revolution.

Marx pointed out correctly that on the one hand the state was not a vulnerable superstructure, but played a decisive role in organizing society, and without it the economy could not develop fully; and that on the other hand, revolution had to be political and directed against the state, that great shield of the bourgeoisie, and the only way to penetrate and act upon economic reality was by destroying the state. But despite his recognition of the importance of political power, Marx did not

---

[25] Cf. Rougerie's detailed studies: "Karl Marx, l'État et la Commune," *Preuves*, 1968.

consider it either decisive or superordinate. Our own experience (in contrast to a global philosophy such as Hegel's)
teaches that the state is the prime element in modern societies.
Wherever antistatist movements have sprung up, they have
reinforced its power; wherever no state existed, the initial act
of revolutions as well as of the underdeveloped peoples has
been to create one. Witness the liberated African countries.
And what was Mao's crowning achievement? Wherever he
set foot, the feudal barons and war lords vanished, superseded
by rational order and administration, and by an objectively
equitable system which culminated, despite the specificities
of the regime, in a *Western type* of state. Wherever they might
have established new political structures, communists invariably installed a state system. The economy did not fall in line
automatically, or did so painfully; realistic economic changes
and the beginning of economic development arrived only
through decisions made by central organs. It appears that the
state's role is primary, not secondary. Totally creative, and
not merely the instrument of the class struggle, it manifests
the profound essence of society and makes us realize that the
class conflict is in relation to the state. What is at stake is not
the relationship between two classes within a global society,
but the relationship of that society to the state. Only within
such a conceptual framework can the essence and relative
value of the class struggle be seen and the state's sociological
role in the emergence of classes be understood. The class
struggle does not explain the state, for it is ultimately subordinate to the state. It is not the motor of history. The exercise of
power is at stake, but the real issue is the new structure of
that power: the invasion of society by the state. That is not a
permanent phenomenon in history and does not explain the
development of civilization. It has been a specific fact of our
society for a little over two centuries. However, I believe it is a
mistake to look for a constant, unvarying factor behind civilizations and history itself. Our emphasis on the growth of the
state, its superordination in relation to everything around it,

and its crucial nature, is not confined solely to authoritarian states or dictatorships. Neither its constitutional form nor its system of operation is of prime significance. The state we have in mind may operate liberally or dictatorially: the choice is of great importance to individuals, who naturally prefer not to be arrested and convicted arbitrarily, not to be deported, and to enjoy a semblance of freedom; but in terms of the relationship between society and power, the difference is very slight.

The state can retain its identity by granting concessions, by guaranteeing human rights and freedoms, and by establishing its own rules of the game (civil, criminal, and electoral). It can determine the deconcentration of power even to the point of decentralizing it; to the extent that the actions are its own, the state remains unchanged, for it is always free to alter the methods and form of those actions. In another book [26] I have showed that public opinion, citizen participation, and the efforts of politicians are vain and ineffectual when attempting to defy that structure. The state is perfectly capable of humanizing itself—that is, of adopting a system of human relations—and may even be reduced, like one of its elements, the bureaucracy, to a collection of individuals.[27] That is only a point of view and alters nothing. The human relations in question derive solely from the bureaucratic structure. Weber's analysis still stands, and gives meaning to otherwise meaningless and fragmentary appraisals of administration. In speaking of the state, I thus have three realities in mind: first, the fact that the state gradually assumes responsibility for all the activities of society (this does not involve the state as the provider, but does involve the much larger question of its omnipresence) because no other agency is capable of doing so today in a world as complex and as rapidly changing as ours, where there is a need to mobilize the total resources of a social group. Second, the fact that the state is growing more and more abstract, being the framework of society. Because its

[26] J. Ellul, *The Political Illusion*, 1965 (trans. 1967).
[27] See particularly the works of Crozier.

order and operation are independent of its human components, it acquires the capacity for self-development and a specific organization tied to its inner needs. Finally, although in every society men may protest the unwarranted intervention of power, express their hatred of it, and demand freedom, their hopes and faith reside nevertheless in the state, from which they expect everything. So much so that whenever difficulties occur, they await its decision—and whenever a disturbance arises, bemoan its incompetence. We are not likely to forget François Mitterand's ridiculous speech at the outbreak of the Latin Quarter riots, in which he punctuated his interpellation of M. Pompidou with the refrain: "What have you done with the state?" Modern man's bewilderment at the failure of the state to provide total security is a manifestation of that structure's deep-rootedness. Those three facts characterize the modern state and testify that its development is not about to be challenged and that it is not an accidental phenomenon.

If the state is now the outgrowth of revolution, it is certainly not because of Hegelian philosophy (and my stating this does not imply that I am Hegelian; historical reality is the basis of it), but because all ideological development relates to the state. Ideological development, which is the prime source of revolutionary thought, now has no other conceivable objective than the growth of the state. Those who challenge industrial society also recognize that fact. Galbraith, who holds the state to be society's ultimate champion against the dangers of our consumer society, says that "through the state, society must assert the superiority of esthetic over economic goals, and especially the priority of the urban or natural landscape over its cost. The state must preserve individual freedom of choice. . . ." It is also recognized by those who uphold the supremacy of political action and the conquest of power: the Left unanimously accepts that concept. In view of the general agreement, what else may lie ahead for revolution?

I have often heard it said that fear of the state is like recent history transposed to the plane of the future: past grievances are transferred to the future, and in order to visualize tomorrow's state we must recognize the reality of expanding public activities not necessarily underwritten by the state. I shall return to that view later on, but for the moment let us simply say that any future projection implies a certain historical continuity, that until now the state has not given the slightest indication of decline, and that tomorrow's state, in the perspective of historical evolution, is not so different from today's, except in the sphere of aspirations and hopes. For the state imposes its laws and system on those who wish to use it. That is where Marxists and all those who have tried to turn the apparatus of state into something it is not, have foundered (including Hitler, who, we repeat, launched a major part of his revolution against the bureaucracy and the inhumanity of the state system). To utilize the apparatus, one must learn to observe its laws, just as anyone who gets into a car must respect the laws of its motor if he intends to run it. Of course, the system can be rendered useless and destroyed, but that dazzling prospect, built on the assumption that the state is merely a relatively ineffectual superstructure, becomes a nightmare face to face with the reality of that organism's pervasive presence throughtout the social body, and its cancer-like diffusion, which it is impossible to check without destroying the entire society. One may possibly desire, but should beware of, *that* type of anarchy, for it is not the anarchy advocated by Proudhon and Bakunin: it is the substitution of pure nihilism for a system. The primacy of the state is beginning to be felt now in South and Central America also, reinforced by each revolution. Cuba is a good example. There, as everywhere else, revolutionists seized power and were compelled to adjust themselves to the state, to install order, rationality, and collective administration (backed up by power, of course). As Che Guevara stated: "Revolution becomes speeches, military reviews, parades, committees, political parties, and intrigue, but also plans, administration, and bureaucracy."

As always, we may rely on Bernard de Jouvenel's grasp of reality, and, in fact, everything we have been discussing is summarized by him.[28] He was among the first to discern that, instead of being accidental, the uninterrupted growth of power was the natural course (and neither hypothetical nor yearned for) of history, and that with human efforts, the state exerted an irresistible thrust: "We cherish the cry of liberty that resounds at the outset of every revolution, and we do not realize that there is no liberty without the burden of power. . . . First, we had the rule of Charles I, Louis XVI, and Nicholas II, followed by that of Cromwell, Napoleon, and Stalin. When nations rise to overthrow tyranny, those are the masters they see oppressing them. . . . The Cromwells and Stalins are not casual consequences or accidents arising from social ferment; they are in fact the appointed terminus toward which the turmoil inevitably led: the cycle began with the removal of insufficient power, only to end in the consolidation of absolute power. Revolutions are the liquidation of a weak power and the implanting of a strong one. . . . Revolution resounds with the cursing of tyrants, yet they find no tyrant at the start, but themselves create him in the end. . . . Power is revitalized at its source, imparting unimpeded motion to the nation because the turmoil has swept away obstacles to social progress. Revolution installs tyranny, the severity of which depends on how thoroughly the aristocracy has been uprooted. . . ." Finally, Jouvenel rounds out his remarkable etching with this phrase: "In the last analysis, revolutions are made for power, not for mankind."

Thus the facts bespeak Marx's total error regarding the state, and, consequently, regarding the course of history. History does not hinge upon the conflict between exploiters and exploited, ending in a socialist society, but involves the relationship between the global society and the state, with the latter being constantly strengthened and with the emergence of a new entity that has been termed the "state/nation." The

---

[28] Bernard de Jouvenel, *Du Pouvoir.*

gravity of that error lies in the value and in the actual results of revolution. Marx asserted that revolution had to take the direction of history; that concept was promoted in socialist and proletarian circles, and later revolutionary movements were trained to calculate the course of history in order to enter into it. However, in attempting to create history in the way Marx conceived it, men actually created real history. By challenging "revolution against history," they put revolution to work developing the effective direction of history. But how could such a misconception arise? At first glance, one might think that if Marx erred in assigning to history a predictable direction relative to the class struggle, revolutions based on that principle ought to have failed and Marxism ought to have been degraded by successive failures. However, Marxist revolutions have often succeeded because of two facts that Marx did not perceive. The first relates to the tactical importance he attributed to the seizure of political power, which, in reality, was the whole purpose of the operation and not a matter of tactics—a mere shift of emphasis. If Marx had maintained his earlier belief in the total and immediate destruction of the state through revolution, no Marxist revolution would have succeeded, simply because it would have run counter to the direction of history. The second fact stems from the existing relations between power and the class struggle. When he insisted on the predominance of the latter, Marx did not overlook its influence on power, for in stressing the conflict, he unconsciously stressed the role of the state: giving history *that* direction was inverse recognition of *its own* true direction. The sharpening of the class struggle was bound to affect the stature of the state, and that is exactly what happened. But revolution was no longer the crisis of that struggle; it was the crisis of the state's development. Yet, by the clock of history, the two could coincide; that is, at the height of the class struggle the survival of society was at stake, and social stability could not be restored without transforming the state. Inversely, the progressive growth of the state inevitably manifested itself in the social structure by a sharpening of the class struggle, until the state, unable to expand, was forced to undergo a change that in turn produced a new stratification of society, replacing the old one and creating new classes. But Marx's faulty appraisal of history's course must answer for the betrayal of all revolutions based on his doctrine. It cannot be otherwise, for the betrayal did not stem from deficiencies on the part of any particular Marxists; it was inherent in the initial error and in the insertion of revolution into history's course. In his preface to *Terrorism and Communism*, Kautsky summarized the question before anyone ever mentioned "the betrayal of revolution": "Lenin triumphed because Marxist Socialism failed." But Lenin was not aware that the failure derived from the very essence of the state.

CHAPTER

[4]

VULGARIZED REVOLUTION

As knowledge grew about revolution's development, revolution itself, contained, classified, analyzed, localized within the vast framework of history, and at once objectionable and cherished, became unbearably oppressive. One could outwit it mentally or verbally by seeking new worlds to conquer and thus escape routine reality: that was the beginning of vulgarization.

Revolution has always been a tragic event, the revolutionist thrice unwelcome. Fear was in the prospect of any such upheaval; revolt brought hope to the hopeless and fear to everyone else, though not always the privileged sector. The masses have never endorsed revolution unconditionally and consistently. Revolution, like war, was catastrophic and disastrous, leaving death and ruin in its wake. Worse than war, it was civil war, driving men to kill neighbors and even brothers instead of strangers. With society torn apart, friendship gave place to partisanry and bitter enmity. Revolution inflicted wounds far more grievous and enduring than those of war. That was not the verdict of the possessors, the leaders, and the exploiters; it was the experience of the common people, the endless, bitter experience engraved on its historical memory. And if men were occasionally driven to rebellion, they did not embark on it lightheartedly. The most determined rebels refused to identify themselves as revolutionists; those who consciously accepted the identity embraced revolution with religious solemnity, dedicating themselves to it and staking their lives upon it. But all that has changed, for revolution is now a household word in our society. No nonrevolutionary deserves attention. The least one expects of an artist, an employer, a teacher, a politician, a writer, or a technician is that he be a revolutionary. Advocate reform and you invite abuse, ridicule, and mockery. Reformism is the height of absurdity—if not infamy. Being a revolutionary is no longer tragic; it is the first step to action. Nowadays revolution is not very demanding, and it rarely calls for sacrificing one's life. Debray set out to make a revolution in Bolivia, but a great hue and cry arose when he nearly lost his life. And the May 1968 "revolution" in the Latin Quarter came alive on tiptoe after dark and disappeared with the dawn. The participants slept during the day and took weekends off. Revolution is the daily fare of our affluent consumer society, the minimal requirement of any citizen wishing to share in society. Whoever is not a revolutionist in current French society (and, I venture, throughout the world) is feeble-minded, reactionary, egotistical, and exploitative—damned both morally and intellectually as a worthless idiot. That attitude is not expressed in so many words, but behavior and situations make it evident. Revolution, now perfectly domesticated, is the focus of social conversation, whereas when that was occasionally so in former times, it evoked fear and hatred. Revolutionists were invariably treated like Man in Prévert's *Dîner de têtes*. Things are different now, and revolution is just another timely topic of chatter. Among the ranking bourgeoisie, everybody is a revolutionary, and the Parisian intelligentsia is the vanguard, the flower, and the elite. A rapid breakdown of the first pro-Chinese factions in France shows them to be made up exclusively of prominent members of the middle class, their sons, university graduates with advanced training, and even the bureaucracy. They would meet in chateaux to "chat" about cultural revolution and would resume the discussion later on along the Riviera. It would be interesting to know whether or not the factionalism among those pro-Chinese groups is linked to the factionalism of the middle class. Just as the China sympathizers flock to the latest conversational salons, revolution is on daily display in the headlines—and not just since May 1968. The unquestioned status of revolution does not apply merely to current revolutionary events, as one might assume. The outbreak of a revolution obviously demands press coverage; that in itself is not significant. What is significant, however, is the headlining of meetings between representatives of groups, of statements issued by leaders, of news about parties, of conferences in Havana and elsewhere which realign the delegates of various factions, and the publication of new periodicals—groups, leaders, parties, factions, and periodicals all equally revolutionary. For more than ten years, revolution, latent, planned, institutionalized, organized, reasoned, verbalized, and made explicit, has been our daily news fare. That enormous outlay of information on "revolution" and revolutionists has produced unwittingly a state of mass intoxication. We are made to feel (on the emotional rather than the intellectual plane) that we live in a revolutionary world. Little by little we have come to believe that revolution is besieging every corner of our universe, that it is the permanent reality of life, and that it is everywhere and accounts for everything. Does this mean that we are riding a great wave of revolution? It means just the reverse: that we have reduced revolution to the level of daily news, along with winter sports, the newest automobile models, the latest presidential press conference, the miniskirt, and the Goncourt literary award, and that it ranks equally with all of them. Its unfailing presence in the news has made it customary—a somewhat irrelevant custom that simply inclines us to treat revolution like an old acquaintance whose in-

telligence and culture we take for granted. Is this sector of the
bourgeoisie in for a surprise and likely to discover a Molotov
cocktail in the living room? I doubt it, for the said cocktail is
also part of their routine. They are not oblivious of its effects,
but they know that it is the only way to master reality.
Constant dripping wears away a stone. The most oppressive
dictatorship eventually becomes diluted through habit, and
revolution also; modern man has managed to acquire the habit
beforehand. All the talk of revolution acts as a vaccine and
immunizer: revolution adopts a fictitious cosmos, a pictorial
universe created by the mass media and, in the end, becomes
fiction. The so-called consumer society has assimilated revolution so thoroughly that it, too, is just another item of consumption. "As a concept, revolution . . . will be perpetually
consumable like any other concept. . . . Thus revolution
identifies itself in an assimilative language, in a glossary of
objective terms designating it as complete and 'self-
consuming.' . . . Revolution consumed by the concept of
revolution denotes that revolution is thereby achieved
(formally) and abolished. . . ." [1]

That process is neither willed nor planned nor deliberated.
Nor is it a cunning maneuver on the part of the controlling
classes: it is a reaction of the assimilative power of the
bourgeoisie,[2] which, when threatened by an event or a political
party, discovers spontaneously a way of regaining control.
Young middle-class supporters of a revolutionary movement
should realize (like their brethren of 1792, 1830, and 1848)
that, far from becoming revolutionists by virtue of their inflammatory idiom, dress, and behavior, they are in fact the
logistic vanguard of the bourgeoisie, their very extremism
enabling the bourgeois to establish bridgeheads in the wholly
alien territory of revolution. They have not deserted their
"class"; they are its unconscious representatives.

But vulgarization and routinization are not solely the results

---

[1] Baudrillard, *Le Système des objets*, 1968.
[2] Cf. J. Ellul, *Métamorphose du bourgeois*.

of the bourgeoisie's assimilative capacity; they were abetted—made inevitable, I would say—by the insertion of revolution into the course of history. Once revolution ceased to be the irrational and unpredictable cry of rage, timeless yet historic, of man outdone by destiny, and became a dependable phase within a process, a determinable and determined stage, an appraisal of the power structure, a relationship to a system, and the interpretation of intelligible events, then the vulgarization of the phenomenon was unavoidable. Marx's inclusion of revolution as a knowable event within the sphere of analyzed history could not fail to produce the domestication of revolution which we know today.

On another level, and for different reasons, it is the same process as that involved in the transition from violent strikes to the tiresome and unenthusiastic walkouts of the trade-union bureaucracy. Marx himself, not his interpreters, is responsible. His vision implied, but could not warrant, the shift, which materialized (on both levels) as a result of society's transformation. The change from an industrial society to a technological one made revolution *possible* in terms of Marx's design and, *at the same time*, vulgarized it.

About the Vocabulary

Nowadays the term "revolution" is flagrantly misused to designate anything and everything. It was misemployed initially to denote the industrial transformation during the eighteenth century, which indicates both the extension and degradation of the word's meaning. Moreover, that abuse was already on the way when the arch-conservative Fustel de Coulanges stated: "What I call revolution is not the violent, clamorous events that frequently produce nothing, but a real, effective, and durable change." Revolution was not measured by an event but by lasting results: any deep-rooted transformation of society was tantamount to revolution. The quotation comes from *Leçons à l'Impératrice*, wherein Fustel indicated that the uproar of 1848, and later that of 1871, *did not* constitute revolution, whereas the industrialization and the railroads promised by Napoleon III were a genuine revolution. Fustel, like the Emperor, prided himself on being a revolutionary, although the facts proved otherwise. We must emphasize that industrial progress, no matter how far-reaching, is in no sense a revolution. In 1931, Dandieu rightfully took issue with that use of the word: "Although it [industry] may appear to produce significant changes in customs, these changes stem not from a new spiritual attitude but from an extraordinarily rapid mastery of a particular technical process or apparatus; in reality, it is not a question of revolution but of a steady evolution, which, from the wheelbarrow or the windmill right up to the automobile or the transmission of electricity, progresses at a pace that was formerly slow and is now accelerated, but always continuous. . . . These applications [of scientific discovery] are not revolutionary, whether it be a super *Île-de-France*, TV, or the Dnerprostroi Dam. Spirit, totality, and revolution have but one mode of expression, which effectively unites them: that of explosive and creative violence. . . ." That is indeed a sample of vulgarization: on the one hand the rapidity of the change is noted, and, on the other, its effectiveness in terms of current technological standards. To speak of great speed and efficiency in reference to revolution entails a frightful misuse of words which negates the profound reality of the revolutionary act.

To appreciate the abuse of language fully, we must recognize that technology produces a society that is essentially conservative (though rapidly developing, of course), integrated, and totalizing, at the same time that it introduces far-reaching changes: but these are changes of identity, of a constant relationship to itself. Technology is antirevolutionary yet suggests *total* change because of the "developments" it brings, whereas in reality only forms and methods are altered. It destroys the revolutionary impulse by increasing conformity to its own integrated structure. It brings on a fundamental "implosion" by creating the impression of a liberating explosion, which is purely superficial. The results were soon to be seen, and Dandieu, with his extraordinary discernment, pointed them out: "By forgetting that revolution is inherently spiritual and creative, would-be Leninists marvel only at the colossal factories of Stalin, the results of forced industrialization." This judgment could apply globally to the entire postwar generation, to the hundreds of thousands who became communists and revolutionaries simply because Russia had won the war. If we realize that "between evolution and revolution there is a threshold, that is, a void, a break, a complete change" and that "every revolution constitutes a whole, no part of which may be isolated without altering its revolutionary character,"[3] it becomes apparent why the current concept of industrial revolution indicates that we have lost sight of the meaning of revolution. And this initial example is but one among many.

There is no doubt that present-day art has become revolutionary. When surrealists recognized a particular bond between art and revolution, they had an imposing design in mind. Their view of revolution was not faulty: they had discerned the need to question the very foundations of their society and believed they were attacking its modes of expression. But their understanding of the phenomenon was such that it led ultimately to the noncreation of works of art, and to silence. I would even say that in attempting the impossible, their revolutionary thinking was earnest. Nowadays such self-discipline is foreign to us. We surround ourselves with music, painting, and poetry, and our humblest artists would never dream of not aspiring to the epithet "revolutionary." Revolution, I insist, has become a standard, a philosophic absolute, and, what is more, a guaranteed financial success.

This art is touted as "revolutionary" by art critics, philoso-

---

[3] Aron and Dandieu, *La Révolution nécessaire*, pp. 168 *ff.*

phers, and prominent intellectuals, and modern aestheticians
fling the word about indiscriminately: "Collage is the grand
manner of our century, the most potent ally in the revolt
against pictorialism, serving as an anchor for the dismantled
image of permanent rebellion." Such dilated rhetoric deserves
a private anthology. This effusion of pseudo-intellectual ex-
plicitness merely testifies to the profound miscarriage of
revolution. The most insignificant painting attempts to convey conflict; a play is a revolutionary act; a film is a provocation. All this, moreover, enjoys great success, reaches a vast
public, returns an elegant profit, and promises interesting
commercial possibilities, a future, fame—all accorded by our
existing society, and not by a distant ideal which as yet cannot provide either fame or money. So-called revolutionary art
is probably the peak of vulgarization. A music critic may put
himself out on a limb by asserting that there is evolution rather
than revolution; that there is a kind of logical development in
the musical history of the past fifty years without any formal
break in tradition; that music develops in relation to sociological phenomena (such as the awakening of social consciousness) which are hardly revolutionary at all; and that international exchange has induced acceleration in certain areas but
no permanent changes. Instantly he is branded a reactionary [4]
and earns the violent denunciations of modern music's "cre-
ators," who feel they must be revolutionaries in order to exist.
Thus having progressed beyond serial music and concrete
music despite the revolutionary character which Pierre Henry
and Pierre Schaeffer insist they have, we come to "music in
motion," seeking to divorce itself from tradition and any trace
of the past: the leap into the absolute! The cinema has similar
pretensions, but can disguise them behind its themes and be
provocative through imagery.

With equal glibness, Mr. Sullivan speaks of a "cinema of
insurrection," which he proceeds to illustrate with films of a

---

[4] A series of broadcasts on *France Culture* by Jacques Bourgeois, O.R.T.F.,
April 3, 1968.

patently leftist turn dealing with the misery and absurdity of human existence: one more example of the confusion between propaganda and conscience. In regard to the films he mentions, Mr. Sullivan never once challenges either their sociological significance and the standards created if one takes them seriously, or their presence in a technological society, the spectacle of which they represent. The "insurrectional" nature of these films derives solely from the mental attitude of the viewer. *La Chinoise* and *Dieu noir et Diable blond* have provoked endless debates along these lines, and every aspect of *La Chinoise* has been diagnosed as counterrevolutionary. Let us examine briefly three of those aspects. First, its ambiguity: the merciless climate of Maoist propaganda combined with the grotesque absurdity of youths mouthing catechisms and prefabricated dialogues. The viewer may either go along, trembling with enthusiasm, or else catch a sly wink from the director, who, to avoid being labeled an idiot, pretends to be diverting himself. There is nothing more "demobilizing" than this type of ambiguity. Second, on a more superficial level, you have the nonexistence of any plan. You cannot find any trace of a revolutionary design; you have instead a void—not, unfortunately, the vast emptiness of space confounding our astronauts, but a cerebral vacuum, utterly incapable of expressing any type of revolutionary orientation, and manifesting itself in the placid, cowlike stare of this adorable Chinese woman. Finally, on the most superficial level, you have propaganda. For simple, undiscriminating minds, the film obviously supports the Chinese revolution, exalting Mao and attacking the horrors of American imperialism. Pure propaganda for those who do not catch the wink and discern the void. But propaganda, particularly in the area of promoting "revolution," is, in and by itself, antirevolutionary; even when it sets man in revolt against a command, it has a destructive impact on human nature and turns the armies of rebellion into robots. It suppresses revolt for the sake of a slogan. The very use of propaganda is counterrevolutionary

because it stifles the human spirit and replaces human will
with mechanisms. Lenin himself was a prisoner of the propaganda system he established. Even activist propaganda, arousing the masses and propelling them into the ordeal of
revolution, is in fact antirevolutionary in that it forcibly
"conditions" man, meaning that what he expresses within the
revolutionary movement is no longer himself but someone else
whose watchwords and obsession live within him. I have tried
to indicate that all propaganda, whatever its purpose, is the
epitome of alienation; to employ propaganda in revolution is
to incite revolt among alienated men, alienated in the attempt to draw them into the war against alienation. That is
why the May 1968 disorders did not awaken genuine consciousness. *La Chinoise* is simply bald propaganda. Its maker
may well insist (which, incidentally, he did in contradictory
terms) that he was not trying to create a revolutionary film,
but merely a type of documentary on pro-China groups, their
patrons (bourgeois to the core, as he indicated), and certain
modes of behavior among the youth. I cannot contest his aims,
yet the fact is that the young people took the film for a revolutionary one, and, rather than as an ironic depiction of a
milieu, they experienced it as a hymn to the cultural revolution and evidence that the same thing could be achieved in
France. It is hard to avoid that attitude in the face of those
pronouncements of Mao inscribed in immense red letters, the
calls to revolution, and all the rest; for whatever the film
maker's intention, what counts is how the film was received.
Public understanding has a significant role in the vulgarization of revolution: the fact that so ambiguous and so spuri-
ously revolutionary a film could take hold publicly and be
acclaimed by the majority of the critics (so that anyone who
felt that it was merely a second-rate production did not dare
admit it) is evidence that revolution has become a "pop-
sicle"—something to while away intermission time.

Similarly, "Sigma Week" in Bordeaux may be discounted
as a revolutionary experience, with its living theater, under-

ground films, Marat/Sade, Met' Art group, and "Music in Motion": a week during which every form of excess was rampant. Audiences were spat upon, entire scenes were given over to erotic display, and the nature of revolution was extolled: "raw conflict," "provocation impelling man to change," "a flash of truth," "a stimulating explosion," "a cyclone sweeping down on Bordeaux," "unquestionably something has changed in Bordeaux," "we now know that to experiment is to scandalize, just as Bernanos [poor Bernanos, who would surely have vomited over this whole frightful mess!] spoke of the scandal of truth." I have only touched the surface of those allegedly revolutionary acrobatics, all typically bourgeois (for the bourgeois elite adores this type of display) and lucrative (such revolutionary manifestations are always profitable) in addition to invoking the patronage and blessing of the authorities, notably the mayor of Bordeaux.[5] Some revolution! The most one can ascribe to it is a carnival atmosphere. The carnival as a public entertainment has disappeared, subjected to police and administrative jurisdiction owing to its immoral display, its libertine tendencies, and the traffic tie-ups it caused. Carnivals had an important social function in gratifying the need for a period of total relaxation. "Sigma Week" is merely a very mediocre substitute for a carnival. Why very mediocre? First, because of its aesthetic and intellectual *pretension*, its vanity. One does not join in for amusement's sake, as with the Mardi Gras, but to Participate in the Revolutionary Task of Innovative Art. The grotesque element is no longer in the masks; it is in the participants themselves, conveyed by their ardor and determination. Second, because it is devoid of any spontaneous popular invention in the way of costumes, songs, and jeering outbursts which used to delight the carnival crowds. Instead, we are made painfully aware of a concerted effort on the part of jaded intellectuals, which lacks the slightest vigor or spark. It is mediocre, finally, because public participation, instead of occurring as a spon-

---

[5] Former president of the National Assembly, now prime minister.

taneous outburst, comes as a determined effort, against a chosen background, and for a select audience; it does not spill into the streets and involve the populace. And that is what is taken for revolution! Our forefathers were not so stupid and did not equate carnivals and revolution. The very fact that we can turn a circus parade into a revolutionary act is evidence of the complete vulgarization of the word and the thing itself. Here is the other side of the picture: Imagine (though you know it already) that Soviet art is not revolutionary. This is very important. We deplore the artistic conformity of the socialist world. How can painters, sculptors, film-makers, architects, and writers pour out such fine sentiments and heroic imagery under pressure from the revolution? We cannot forget that *prior to the revolution,* art and literature in Russia were wildly innovative, hence allegedly "revolutionary" in every sense.[6]

Slogans, sects, and "isms" abounded—supremacism, radiantism, Orphism, nonobjectivism—bursting forth between 1900 and 1918. After the revolution came the return to order. What is the answer? That the monstrous Soviet dictators outlawed art? But conformity had set in long before the Idanov report appeared and the doctrine of socialist realism took shape. Blok died under Lenin's regime, observing that "poets die because they can no longer breathe." The problem goes deeper: there was as yet no control of art, and "revolution" in the arts disappeared. Are we to assume that art prepared the way for revolution because of its profoundly subversive character? Or that once revolution arrived it could no longer oppose it? That is the currently accepted notion, which does not appear altogether accurate. In terms of the twentieth century alone, art cannot be said to prepare in any manner for revolution or to contest anything of a profound nature. Art expresses dissent that has no other outlet: it is our

[6] See, among other works, A. Marchais, *Révolution culturelle et expression artistique,* 1967; M. Seuphor, *L'Art abstrait, ses origines, ses premiers maîtres,* 1966.

society's safety valve. Go right ahead and make your infantile revolution in music and painting, make war with your tin soldiers; in the meanwhile society can organize itself calmly, its adult members shouldering the responsibilities. Radicalism on the stage or on the screen serves to absorb tensions and to maintain stability, which also stabilizes society. Revolution knows no preparation; in fact, the more extreme, outlandish, and offensive art is, the more demobilizing are its effects on the real problems of society. Those who might otherwise be seriously concerned with the function of revolution settle for these onanistic ejaculations, for febrile art. Energies are dissipated in wan enterprises, intellectual and emotional dislocation, a sense of guilt, the wild enthusiasm associated with those orgies, and in illusory problems to which attention is diverted: all these are products of revolutionary art, which succeeds in destroying revolutionary consciousness and does not pave the way for a single thing. When a genuine revolution arrives, such as that of 1917, this art has no place and no function (except occasionally a propagandistic one); it must fall back into line and be silent. Blok, a dedicated revolutionist, became aware of that fact and wondered: "Has revolution lost its own way?" (1917) and concluded: "Life has lost its meaning. . . . Fleas have overrun the universe" (1921). What else, indeed, could a lucid artist and determined revolutionary infer?

The criteria applied nowadays to revolutionary art are certainly odd and interesting. These standards have no real or imaginary relationship to sociopolitical revolution: they relate to art itself. Bartók's music is revolutionary in comparison with Chopin's. That is intrinsic revolution, reaching a tiny and specialized sector. The very use of the adjective "revolutionary" to identify any rapid or far-reaching change within a small sphere of communication is indicative of the degree of vulgarization we have attained. We shall return to that question.

One final point remains to be considered. If we examine

what is regarded as a revolutionary project in the field of modern art, we find that it reflects certain specific standards. Three tendencies occur: In some cases, an attempt is made to express occasional mass aspirations by exacerbating them, for we belong to an aging society that requires increasingly potent stimuli to engage its interest. In other cases, art develops in the same fashion as pursuits that condition each other: music and painting illustrate the rule that one must start with the culmination of a musical or pictorial experience in order to advance beyond it—a matter for specialists only —and that if I am familiar with the work of Mr. X, I can appreciate *how* Mr. Y has managed to transcend it. Thus we have increasingly esoteric—that is, counterrevolutionary— arts, their esoteric quality revealed by the abundance of literature devoted to interpreting them. Because art says so little about man's rebellion, the latter must be explained in order to be discerned at all. Painters produce encyclopedic volumes testifying to their aims, their philosophy, and the meaning of their pictures; they work according to a theory of painting or of society which no one (except experts, on a technical level) can decipher, but that does not discourage the enlightened public from acclaiming the latest artistic tours de force. Finally, art is often called revolutionary when it employs new techniques or processes that universal technology makes available to it.

Spray-gun painting is a revolutionary technique; plastic and concrete constructions are a revolutionary art. Yet in a technological society such as ours, it is obvious that making art mirror technical developments or setting out to invent new artistic techniques is the pinnacle of conformity: like choosing the angle of least resistance, which is the most obvious one because it follows the course of our society. The fact that art which is either esoteric (that is, the domain of specialists) or technical can be called revolutionary proves that we are confusing revolution with the global design of our society, and that we have assimilated and vulgarized revolution completely.

. . .

Essentially the same thing applies to literature. The literature of revolution unfortunately tends to be regarded as revolutionary. In spite of Camus's gift for analysis, *The Rebel* illustrates the confusion between literature and reality. He speaks of men without making any distinction between fictional characters and living persons: Ivan Karamazov is as real to him as Nechayev. That immediately places literature within the framework of vulgarized revolution, for the idea that reality can be created simply by speaking and writing about it rests on a curious assumption and a misconception. Camus's misapprehension of reality bolsters his analysis of revolt and also the banal notion that the author and his hero are one; it also encouraged later writers to regard literature as an autonomous act. In examining so-called revolutionary literature—not statements of doctrine, but poetry, novels, and plays—we must separate literary efforts in nonrevolutionary countries from those which have appeared during or after a revolution. We would not question the first category of writings if they made no pretense beyond recording injustice, heralding new truths, and crying liberty; they would stand for what they are: expressions of human suffering in our society. Hamsun and Kierkegaard, Robert Penn Warren and Gorky see themselves for the writers they are, and therefore do not warrant criticism. But then we come to the literature of propaganda, a normal situation, as I see it, in view of the negative relations between propaganda and revolution. Brecht's theater prior to 1944 was truthful despite its propaganda; it stood for what it was and made no pretense of embodying revolution. Thus in a country which had not had a revolution and whose writers managed to be "involved" and still keep their heads, taking themselves for writers and not revolutionaries, the literary scene appeared sound and relatively free of hypocrisy. One must keep in mind the essential point, which bears directly on Sartre, that literature's sole validity relies on its position of independence (relative, to be sure) and of challenge. That is why no genuine literature of dissent and of disclosure in regard to man and society can exist outside societies in which, on the one hand, revolution had not attempted to establish justice, truth, and liberty, and, on the other, literature is generally acknowledged to have no essential function and to be simply literature. Therefore it cannot call itself revolutionary in either sense; it remains merely a witness to the bewilderment of humanity, in which writers themselves share, feeling they have something to say and living in a society which they know will not take their words seriously: then, and only then, the strain, the alarm, and the ambiguity of the situation give rise to an authentic rebellion that is not a spectacle. This is why the only literature of dissent, of revolt, and of challenge, between 1930 and 1960, was American.

But things have changed a good deal in our times. We have literature held to be revolutionary by virtue of its having been produced in nations that have undergone revolutions. In every country, however, the principal trademark of this literature is its conformity and its ignorance of revolution. The least one can say about contemporary Cuban poetry is that it is extremely nonpartisan (in contrast to poetry *before* the revolution, as practiced by Guillén or Rodríguez). Escardo and Jamis write with remarkable subjectivity on "eternal themes." It is neither poetry of revolution nor revolutionary. Literary critics are thoroughly aware of this and assert that "the literary vanguard has fallen behind the political one. . . . The rest of us intellectuals must make up for lost time, surpass ourselves, and become revolutionary intellectuals in the course of revolution." [7]

It is easy enough to maintain that the unifying force of the Cuban revolution has made this poetry possible, but the statement is meaningless. Embarrassed critics speak of the "moral commitment" of those poets to the revolution, asserting that "even when they yield to a *seemingly personal* lyricism, their poems nevertheless embrace revolution." It would take

---

[7] Hernández Retamar, in *Partisans,* 1967.

blind faith to find it! What is true, however, is that they rarely employ the theme of revolution and that their poetry could have been written anywhere men are suffering and lonely, anywhere they love and hate. Apologists for the Cuban revolution recognize that the poets totally reject aesthetic dogma: revolution has not imposed its creed there—which is a good thing. A "revolutionary" literature exists in Latin American countries untouched by revolution (although Cortázar would not agree), but it is practically nonexistent where revolution has been achieved.

As for Chinese literature since the revolution, it is perhaps too soon to judge it; it is only twenty years old. Still, it would seem to have remained on the level of pure destruction. "Fluctuations in the cultural revolution as well as the overwhelming primacy accorded to Maoist thought and its material diffusion have temporarily erased all forms of literary expression deserving of the name. . . . That is why any picture of contemporary Chinese literature seems outdated and brings to mind another period with its discredited or even doomed celebrities. . . . The socialist education movement begun in 1963 and the cultural revolution destroyed nearly everything that preceded them. . . . What now remains as actual literature is basically the critique and condemnation of works tolerated or created prior to 1964." In such an atmosphere of uncertainty it pays to be silent!

The problem of Soviet literature having been dealt with so often, let us examine instead Polish literary development, which is altogether typical.[8] Based on the Soviet model, an orthodox literature of revolution appeared in the beginning, corresponding to the socialist revolution and socialist power. Taking revolution for its theme, it sought to create a literature that was socialist (inevitably propagandistic) and simplistic, as it was destined for mass consumption. "The socialist system and the state took charge of representing revolt." But its

---

[8] In the Polish periodical *Le Mensuel Littéraire*, 1967, see articles by Maciag and Gren.

failure was such that literature gradually lost touch with that mission. The current results are remarkable in that literature is becoming freer. "Literature has almost no means of exerting a constructive influence on reality, and writers tend to feel that literary effort is a completely voluntary act." "A fierce ideological battle is now raging in Poland, but literature is not involved: indeed, our literature depicts no one and is completely indifferent to everything. . . . Literature exists, but only as an applied art; it has become a handicraft. . . . We delude ourselves when we say that our books and discussions reflect the thoughts and desires of our contemporaries; in reality, society's inner life reaches out in an entirely different direction. . . . The significant things are determined beyond or beneath the realm of literature. . . ." These unusually keen observations indicate the true literary situation in modern times, which is in no sense revolutionary.

But that has not discouraged leftist intellectuals from extolling the cause of so-called revolutionary literature under socialism. The resulting vulgarization is tantamount to deceit. Wherever literature has been revived among the socialist nations, it has no relation to revolution. Yet politicians and those with an ax to grind have annexed literature, made it an appendage, and exploited their claims on it, thereby diminishing both literature and revolution.

France seems to have reached the peak of deception in treating literature on a par with reality: if a "revolutionary" theme is involved, a literary work assumes a life of its own and becomes *revolution* in itself. This certainly is related to the growth of structuralism, which nevertheless cannot be blamed for such a startling introversion. It appears that contemporary French authors, vaguely aware that evolution is at an impasse, reject reality and concentrate on their own creative product, to which they assign the value of reality. They have only to speak of revolution and it is there. Just as stage mime conveys a whole story. It is a cross between the earnest conviction of a novelist compelled to inject himself into whatever he writes and a collective psychodrama allowing the audience to interpret and to standardize situations, but not to change them. Jean Genêt's *Les Paravents* convinces the spectator that he has wiped out existing forces and made a revolution: he is less exhausted but far more impressed by revolutionary imperatives than by a day on the barricades— and thoroughly purged of all oppression and injustice. The equivocation is unpardonable. Language is analyzed as if it were a lifeless object and its content of no interest whatsoever, yet this scientific objectivity provides the consistency of reality —the ultimate reality because it serves to explain everything. Similarly, language also endows literary works with solidity and existence, and, by the same token, speech attains its utmost limits, not by scientific means but by psychical amalgamation. J.-P. Faye's *Récit hunique* offers a good example: "To speak of revolution, you must first make it in the very core of the discourse seeking to convey it." Literature no longer fits Sartre's description, does not plunge into extreme difficulty and ambiguity and is not strife-torn: it can remove itself somewhat from history because it has become history, not through realism but through objectivism. For does history not contain revolution? Is revolution not the creator as well as the offspring of history? The parody is complete and banality reaches its summit when those two words become interchangeable. Poets are the wielders of power and the key to revolution!

A fourth aspect of this vulgarization is idealization. The more revolution is talked about, the tamer it becomes. It ceases to be a society's ordeal, the crisis of an ethical and a political system. It is our daily diet: not because we have turned revolutionist but because we have not, and our idealism makes us behave like "regular customers." The present-day attitude to revolution is the same as the former attitude to God. God, whom the Prophets revealed as a terrifying Judge, dissolving mountains in his descent to earth, upon

whom "no one may look . . . and live," was transformed by
the bedbugs infesting the sacristy, by insistent practice and
faithful habit, into a senile Good Shepherd whose beard all
the world might tug, content with form and ritual, satisfied
with barren penitence and hollow charity, and with whom one
usually established a dubious relationship. Today the same
avatar has caught up with revolution. Camus contributed his
small share by declaring: "I rebel, therefore we are": a stun-
ning maxim which, however, contains a slight misconception.
By dint of an otherwise correct philosophic approach and an
intellectual discipline asepticizing whatever it touches, the
real phenomenon has become idealized—that is, relieved of
its unpleasant content. That is philosophy's most common
function. "We are": what a vision! To be born through one's
own creative efforts and to take it all in! It is true that in rebelling I begin to forge myself and to become aware of myself;
it is also true that revolt is the communal link with all of
suffering mankind possessing nothing and aspiring to everything. Agreed up to that point. But can you stop there? Will
you be able to wipe away the blood from the terrifying visage,
the wrath that strikes out blindly, the injustice lashing out to
put an end to still another injustice? "I rebel, therefore we
are"—"Whom shall we kill?" is what Camus should have
added. But that would not have been worthy of humanity and
philosophers.

   In practice, that idealization, initially philosophic, resulted
in merely concealing revolutionary excess and focusing attention on other immoderacies. If revolution is cruel and unjust, compounding all our loves and hatreds, let's not be reminded of it. Let's just gaze on the beautiful, bare-bosomed
maiden Delacroix painted on the barricades. The Jacobins were
condemned ultimately not so much for what they did as for
saying they did it, for announcing, proclaiming, and interpreting it. To declare that counterrevolution would be steeped in
blood, that the people needed a blood bath, and that more and
more heads would have to fall was not the thing to say. Doing

it would have been enough—doing it and concealing it behind an Ideal. But the type of idealization that breeds this familiarity and vulgarization has another facet: the exaltation of revolutionary heroes to compensate for the unacknowledged atrocities. Chapayev illustrates the jovial attitude toward the "comrade machine gun." Enemies are not human; they are silhouettes crumpling in the distance, or else vile and hideous creatures that cannot be dignified as human. The practice of vilifying the foe, for which Hitler is so often taken to task, is a basic ingredient of revolutionary vulgarization. Revolution would not be on every tongue today were it not for that idealistic projection which severely diminishes the bourgeois counterrevolutionary as it glorifies the hero. By the same token, revolution ultimately loses its value and content—its blood content—which must be paid for in countless other ways. Yet how can this be done when you have archangels on one side and objects on the other?

Another phase in the process of vulgarization was that of theorization: revolution lost its element of human uncertainty and was reduced to a meaning and a strategy. Marx, a man with no thirst for blood, achieved the prototype of that process of abstraction. Having established the imperative of a violent revolution and the elimination of capitalists, he did his utmost to disguise the horror of it. Capitalist concentration would be achieved in such a way that only a handful of influential capitalists remained in each country and that the transfer of ownership of the instruments of production would be relatively painless. In the long run (and this is what led many people to believe that Marx's concept of revolution involved no violence) that tiny group, engulfed by the rising tide of the proletariat once the bulk of society (including the army and the bureaucracy) had been proletarianized, would wither of its own accord, would cease to resist, and would resign itself to dispossession. Hence no casualties. In any event, revolution demanded such rigorous intellectual and scientific discipline that violence, unleashed passions, and vengeance were merely undesirable and regrettable accidents instead of being essential factors in revolutionary thinking. Theory screened the human, or inhuman, cruelty of revolution and made it simply a thoroughly aseptic surgical operation, the removal of a troublesome tumor. That mental diagram is extremely helpful in spreading and gaining support for revolutionary ideals. Armchair intellectuals who faint at the sight of a machine gun can become revolutionists under the sway of such principles and of the logic, the inevitability, and the purity of the process. They forget everything but the paper on which it is written. The theorization of revolution was initiated by brilliant scholars and is carried on today by philosophers and sociologists. How comforting the situation appears when we can identify explosive conditions and rationalize the sudden flare-up of violence, when we can point to the conjunction of objective and subjective forces, the causes and reasons underlying revolution, and when we can design plans and techniques. We are at last in the thick of it—terrified at first, but not lost. Once a thing can be explained and reasoned, modern man is quite at home. The wild beast seems tame; statistics and philosophic rationalism (even if it involves irrationalism) provide an appearance of normalcy. But only an appearance. To develop a theory or a sociology of revolution is to conceal its concrete reality, to spread the captivating idea of it by dehumanizing it for both partners—and, by the same token, facilitating it, because anyone can afford to be a revolutionary at no cost in grief and remorse, emotions that never enter the sphere of theory. That is the current position of countless pseudo-intellectuals who today call themselves revolutionaries.

A final and contemporary aspect of this vulgarization through idealization is reflected in the idea of a festival. Revolution is a festival—and we are not the first to say so. Saint-Just's observations on revolution as a festival are well known, but he was honest enough to add: "All I see in France [in 1791] is armed men, tribunals, and sentries—where are all the free men?" And: "The National Assembly has made blunders: public stupidity

so willed it." A far cry from declarations of revolutionary fellowship and its spontaneous, festive display. Sociologists tend to
emphasize that aspect, dwelling on the good-natured and well-
meaning outbursts of public emotion;[9] they go so far as to
distinguish[10] between the era of celebrations initiated by
crowds spilling into the streets and occupying the public domain (joyous public occasions that could last for weeks, as
occurred in Havana when Castro took power in January 1959),
and the era of organized celebrations: the exploitation by revolutionary leadership of this public orientation in order to channel it; the festivals from 1790 to 1794; the festivals of the Commune in March 1871 with their "scenes of exorcism" serving as
a "publicly initiated spectacle and an act of social magic intended to impress the people with the validity of those political
structures in the name of which the revolution was undertaken,
as well as offering them the vision of a community governed by
the will of the majority expressed in its own symbols and linking the participants one to another."[11]

The revolutionary festival, like primitive festivals, stands as
a founding act. That is also the meaning of revolution, as we
have already indicated. It is an ordaining communion—
which usually introduces the rule of hatred and bloodshed. It
is a festival in so far as it requires a focus, a meaningful act,
an invitation to the unreliable mob to partake of eternal
truths—an act establishing the indissoluble bonds men create
among themselves. For example, the oath. An oath confers
sovereignty: the will of each individual dissolves into the
general will at the moment of oath-taking.[12] True enough.

The word "festival" and its image are in constant use. J.-P.
Faye adopts it as the title for the last part of his book on

---

[9] This concept of revolution as a festival first began to shape itself in such
scholarly studies as those on the Sacred, conspicuous consumption, and the
significance of war (with Mauss, Caillois, and Bataille), but subsequently the
comparison was extended arbitrarily to suggest that revolution *is* a festival. At
that point vulgarization enters in.

[10] Lefèbvre, *L'Irruption*, 1968.

[11] Duvignaud, cited by Decouflé, p. 88.

[12] Starobinski, *1789: Les Emblèmes de la raison*, 1968.

revolution, although one is never certain whether it is meant to be synonymous with revolution or with literature on the subject of revolution because the "literary projection" of revolution becomes a thing in itself, something of a "private and endless festival." I am forced to call this a process of mystification. We know for a fact that rebel movements find expression in song, in dance, and in festive gatherings, and that revolutionary governments arrange festivals. But to say that revolution *is* a festival, an outpouring of good-natured fellowship, is something else. *So is war,* which was formerly celebrated as a fresh and joyous event, the celebrants "knowing full well they would die in the course of this festival," as Hugo put it. It is true that public enthusiasm, including that of the working class, greeted the outbreak of the First World War— a great festival that was. And how many speeches have represented war as a festival? In sociological terms, there is no difference between the celebration initiating war and the festivity of revolution. Our leftist intellectuals have transferred their warlike speech to revolution. To regard revolution as a festival is to disregard the grim and bloody festivals of the past. Nero, the artist, singer, and poet, was wont to arrange splendid nocturnal festivals lit by resin-coated slaves flaming like firebrands. And why exclude the stocking-knitters from among those cheerful revolutionary celebrations, for the guillotine had become a spectacle, with seats for sale. Or the Septembrists, for in those days the Paris mobs were also overflowing with good cheer. Mind you, I am not trying to parade the horror of revolution, having no reason to do so or to condemn it. I speak of vulgarization only, and I maintain that to regard revolution as a festival, to commercialize it thus, to tame it and to make it reliable, to diminish it by removing its terror, and to accentuate its joyous side is simply to vulgarize it and to pass it off for something it is not, encouraging people to think of revolution as a great game for boy scouts or a universal fair. Revolution boldly accepted on those terms pays dearly for such false understanding and support. It is no

longer revolution. The rush to rise up and to rebel is the rush to
the fair, the urge to celebrate, and the result is not a revolution
but the enactment of a carnival. Violent occupation of one or
another school, with its threats to those who dissent, culminates
in a banquet to which the dean is invited! Everyone had a
good time and slept with everyone else. Violence and inter-
course always have made good bedfellows. It was a ball.
Similarly, as revolution becomes spontaneous invention, disguise, and relief from routine—that is, festivity, it ceases to
be revolution. The more advocates it attracts, the fewer revolutionaries remain. This image of a festival not only is misleading and a potential source of deceptive propaganda but
also actually prevents the revolutionary act from taking place,
because the latter can only produce a colossal surprise party,
which is precisely what was promised those who attended. The
concept is therefore profoundly demobilizing, for in glorifying
spontaneity (which must never be lost), but uniquely in its
joyous or heroic aspect (which is a lie), it forgets that revolution in our era relies entirely upon calculation, cold foresight,
strategy, structure, and cynical exploitation. The proponents of
this theory of festive revolution, however, are both witnesses
to and agents of vulgarization, of mass consumption, and of
mass distribution.

Let us now examine briefly one last aspect of this vulgarization: the turgid vocabulary. As indicated above, a process
of reduction is at work: "Relax and remember that revolution
is r' ally just a big party." Feel like trying your hand with
Mao? Conversely and simultaneously, the word "revolution" is
used to designate any relatively rapid or important change.
We console ourselves for our inability to make a revolution by
affixing that word to everything in sight. On the most prosaic
level, advertising informs us of a revolution in ball-point pens,
in automobile suspension, or in food-processing—frozen foods
are nothing short of revolutionary. So is any passable method
of rapid reading. And a responsible observer assures us that

Madame Morin's data-processing technique is a revolution. We are told of the "fifteen revolutions in fashion" (G. d'Assailly), of the revolution in Social Security (R. Debray), and, in June 1968, of a revolutionary automated manufacturing system. Such a handy word, a password, a word derived from the intellectual prostitution of our times.

For all the good will behind it, *Robert's* dictionary is plainly out of date. It defines "revolutionary" as "advocating radical change in any area; in current usage are: revolutionary scientific theory, revolutionary technique, process, price. . . ." But the changes are no longer real, and the word is employed so as to suggest that they are. As for the radical nature of the changes, a glance at contemporary writings reveals instead its ridiculous superficiality.

A proposal to change the statute of the University of Paris is greeted as a "revolutionary" program (*Le Monde,* September 17, 1968), and the first signs of cautious attempts to liberalize the regime in Czechoslovakia are extolled as revolutionary—with the essential comment added: "It is a revolution without the usual phenomena of violence and open dissent."

It is indeed significant to find Lefèbvre now saying that revolution is a "series of reforms—with the goal and the global result of dispossessing the ruling class, of denying it the means of production and the administration of the whole society." Social democracy had the same objective, but never approached revolution. The experiment is over; vulgarization has played a part there also. And when a political revolution is the topic, a remarkable vocabulary takes over. In reporting the Moscow-Havana controversy (March 20, 1968), *Le Monde* ran this headline: "*Pravda* does not consider revolution an item for export." A significant illustration of how deeply the word has become rooted in our consumer society: imported and/or exported, it is simply a trade item. Thus habit is involved, and probably the need to express a reality that is in no way revolutionary. Vulgarization thereby sinks to the depths of banality. Yet we still need to know how the custom arose, for a word must respond to a need if advertising uses it constantly. Why this vast movement to generalize and to vulgarize? Three reasons come to mind. The first relates to our relatively stable society, in which we encounter largely familiar, mediocre, and unstimulating experiences. The quest for sensationalism on the part of the press is evidence of twentieth-century Western man's craving for explosive events to enliven his dull existence. A happening must be blown up so that it acquires the significance, the resplendence, the aura of grandeur and inception that we so sorely lack. We need to be persuaded that we live in permanent crisis, in a state of rapture, as witnesses to eternal events. The persuasion is all the more necessary because our existence is gray, boring, meaningless, and redundant. The turgid vocabulary operates within this mediocre reality. Adjectives must be high-sounding in proportion to the flatness of reality.[13] Experimentation must bear the name of revolution, which plunges us into acceleration, brutality, and uncertainty, whereas in reality the changes are technical and orderly. Insignificant things must appear significant, and clever labels enhance the dreariest items. Our ailing souls demand it. Revolution is a desire for revenge upon an excessively ordered universe. That is why ultraconservatives willingly accept immersion in this all-embracing vocabulary of revolution. In return, however, as might be expected, the concept of revolution is drained of its content. The most outstanding of our intellectuals are not above using bloated language, a few recent examples of which follow. Joseph Losey, echoing the general rapture over the May disorders, stated: "The events of the past two months represent the Western world's greatest hope since the World War. But what is now happening [De Gaulle's taking control of the situation] is the greatest danger since Hitler." A molehill magnified to the scale of the Himalayas. Another example: Dean G. Vedal,

---

[13] The fact that bloated language and a dull existence progress hand in hand is not peculiar to our era. It appears to be a historical constant. As Ottoman or Byzantine power began to decline, the titles of the emperor, the nobility, and governing officials waxed altogether grandiloquent and sonorous. A historical fact that ought to be studied in detail.

speaking of a study entitled *Citizens in Power* issued by the
Jean-Moulin Club, termed it a "revolutionary program." The
plan called for, among other things, reducing the number of
French communes, creating large regions, and developing
regional fiscal autonomy. Grass-roots revolution. Bargain-
basement revolution. A hundred years ago such a program
would not have warranted the adjective, but today it does.
Illustrations of this abuse of language are in endless supply.
The second reason is this: we must recognize that revolution
now bears a plus sign in Western eyes. No longer a source of
anxiety and terror, it has become a barnyard animal. So we
proceed to make a value judgment about it: bourgeois man
is implicitly confident that making revolution is *good*. In some
unconscious fashion he has acquired the certainty that he will
survive revolution. Some men will die, of course, but he will
bridge revolution, fearful as it is, and emerge stronger and
more triumphant in a new avatar. Moreover, if revolution has
become a value, that value relates unquestionably to our becoming accustomed to sudden changes produced by science
and technology and to our faith in progress. How can any
advocate of progress be antirevolutionary? Is it not true that
revolution is part of history's course? that it hastens growth?
that 1789 rid France of tyranny, and even 1917 may have had
its assets? that there was good reason to call industrial development a revolution? Thus speaks the voice of progress.
Alongside the desire to cause a stir, to make things happen,
our faith in progress is responsible for the indiscriminate use
of the word "revolution." By lending that imposing image to
petty realities, we persuade ourselves that progress is still on
the march and that the rapidity of change (positive, naturally)
thus implied serves also to accelerate the rate of progress.
Faith in progress has led us, outside this context, to affix a
positive sign to the ever-present Great Agitation.

The third reason is the rationalization of revolution itself—
political or social revolution in its fullest sense. As Camus
rightly observed: "Ideas aimed at enlisting our world in the
cause of revolution have actually become ideologies of consent

rather than of revolt." In the end, it is revolt that the bourgeois fears and would avoid at all costs: brutal rejection, explosive violence, and unleashed passions. But revolution suggests the totally different image of towering beauty, progress, and above all, *established order.* For it is apparent that the instruments of revolution operating initially by trial and error (which must be charged to some untimely vexations best not mentioned) develop into instruments of order, stability, and progress. Think of the utter chaos in Germany: inside of two years, Hitler's revolution brought economic growth, full employment, law and order, stable conditions, and a sharp reduction in crime. And if the revolution of 1917 had been given a fair chance, the story would have been the same. Once the Soviet government installed itself as an instrument of order and progress, people were ready to accept and to justify a few regrettable mass shootings. Revolutionary ideologies became ideologies of consent, for what does modern man want if not to conform and to support? It is the strongest magnetic pole in his mentality. Today revolution is the most powerful force urging adherence, consent, and conformity, resulting in perfect harmony between human expectations and the (realistic) promises of revolutionary power. The latter's attraction is even greater when couched in a vocabulary of violence. The first and third points are not contradictory, for nowadays the average man desires conformity yet speaks of nonconformity. The use of a revolutionary vocabulary resolves this double need. That is why revolution currently oozes the notion of well-being, plays a positive role in our consciousness, and attends to all the menial jobs. Revolution, like a hard-working housemaid, sounds as if she were smashing the fine crystalware when she is simply polishing and arranging it.

Political Vulgarization

The use of the word "revolution," its application to trivial realities, and the belief that art or literature is revolution have ushered in this vulgarization. The same phenomenon has also invaded the political sphere, wherein revolution ought to have retained its stature. Two factors stand out: that the state itself has become revolution, and that the myths of revolution have been reduced to platitudes.

Throughout history the state appeared as the enemy of revolution. Revolution acted against the existing political body. Occasionally the two words became associated, as in Cromwell's revolution, when the resulting state was termed, perhaps for the first time, revolutionary.

Bernard de Jouvenel is undoubtedly correct in asserting that the state is a permanent aggressor in the social order, and that by destroying the structures impeding its growth, the state looms as a permanent revolution in the eyes of a society. The nature of power is to unseat and dispossess social authorities and to ally itself with the common people, the proletariat. It is destined to destroy the social order from which it springs. Jouvenel's brilliant analysis further points out that the state at once "guarantees the *status quo* through its instruments and undermines it through its legislation." "In Essence, it is the champion of privilege; in Development, however, it proves to be the relentless foe of 'the patronate,' a term I use here to embrace all manifestations of social authority." "Not the form of the state but the nature of power is responsible for this tendency." [14] In a sense, therefore, a constant is involved. But the new element here, testifying to the vulgarization, is that whereas the state acknowledges its revolutionary function and the people accept it, only one revolution is possible because the state has acquired a monopoly of revolution, and therefore every political power claims to be leading the political revolution to its completion.

After 1792 the French government was called revolutionary, and Robespierre and Saint-Just developed a rather subtle theory explaining the ties between government and revolution. The explanation was needed to prove the existence of any such

---

[14] Bernard de Jouvenel, *Du Pouvoir*, 1947.

positive relationship, for the opposite view had always prevailed. Robespierre differentiated between "the constitutional structure of power, which respects the law and guarantees public freedom, and the revolutionary structure, which is exceptionally active, observes no set rules, and acts promptly, summoning all its resources to meet danger and necessity. This government is no less legitimate and just. Its aim is to secure the public welfare. The people's sovereignty rather than the nation's is its guide. . . . This government imposes authority and the rule of law. It is not arbitrary but is prescribed by necessity. . . . It is called revolutionary because it operates outside constitutional principles and the Declaration of the Rights of Man, which have been suspended. . . ." That description recognizes the special character of revolutionary government: it is a very temporary institution closely tied to a national situation and to a military threat. Furthermore, its mode of operation rather than its objective is special: it is above the law. That is what makes it revolutionary. It is also the product of revolution. But it has not acquired a "revolutionary essence": the state has no right to claim that distinction. In short, the Convention delegates faced the question honestly: in the course of revolutionary action, the state ceased to observe the law; the rights of man were suspended and abnormal conditions prevailed; hence the unbridled state and the rule of terror. They voiced and acknowledged those facts. Times have changed indeed, for today the revolutionary character of the state is taken for granted. Once we admit that revolution follows the course of history, that it is not achieved overnight, that the transition to communism is not a brief tremor altering capitalist society at the peak of its development, as Marx had led us to expect, but is instead a lengthy process of construction in which the growth of production and the organization of society are products of active political power *after* political revolution but *before* the impending social-economic revolution, then, in terms of this totally changed outlook, the state can claim to be revolutionary—no longer because it is the offspring of revolt or is above the law, but for its own sake. It is revolutionary because it is controlled by the revolutionary class, because its goal is final revolution and there can be no other revolution than the ultimate historic one ushering in communist (or, depending on the options, prehistoric, introducing history) society. That concept of the state as revolutionary and integrated with revolution is a product of Marxism-Leninism. It is a hopeless fiction that has ceased to be fiction and has become universal belief and opinion: its enormous implications are lost. Belief endows an object with reality; at the same time it alters the entire body of knowledge about revolution. Now it is the state that determines the type of revolution and is the instrument of revolution. Castro is entitled to set the standards of true and false revolution: "The difference between true and false revolutionaries is genuine commitment, the determination to act." The state alone has the brains to think revolution, to conduct, to orient, and to provide for it. That in turn confirms the exclusive validity of this single revolutionary instrument: the state sets its seal of approval on everything, on the products that meet its standards, on authorized education, and even on making revolution. The state seal is the only valid one. Moreover, like all states, the revolutionary state incarnates society, whose duty it is to be unswervingly revolutionary. Which brings us to this pearl of wisdom: "Whoever ridicules the flag of a state disgraces himself in the eyes of every civilized citizen and breaks the law. But he who defiles the Red banner . . . expels himself from the community of *honest men*" (proposal issued by the Czechoslovak Communist Party, April 1969). Revolution, guarantor of respectability and conformity. A wondrous avatar, but not a unique pronouncement, as most leftist leaders bear the same message. Again from Castro: "The real dispute is between those who want a revolution and those who seek to curb it." [15] Needless to say, "those who want a

---

[15] This and the following quotations come from Castro's speech at the Havana Conference in August 1967.

revolution" means the Cuban state. It determines the goals and the enemies of that revolution. It rejects flatly any rival orientation, for does not its exclusivity—in this domain as well—free it from parallel action? And from there it launches attacks on so-called Marxist revolutionaries: "Marxists have an idiom that is completely indistinguishable from the Rosary or from the Catholic catechism: they have strait-jacketed revolutionary ideas." The liberator of revolutionary ideas will be, of course, the Cuban state. In the past, fierce ideological battles have engaged Marxists, but primarily the orthodox sector, theorists, party leaders, and those committed to destroying society and the state. Today the same disputes occupy national leaders and direct the machinery of government. The shift from an anti- to a pro-government attitude was nonetheless an outsized pill to swallow—enough to choke on. Stalin managed it, aided by an element of Leninist policy, by divorcing (in strictly associative terms) the machinery of state from that of the Party, which, in the end, had supreme authority and manipulated the façade of government. The Party's secretary general filled the revolutionary function, imparting his blessing to state endeavors, so that the state in turn became revolutionary. This situation is now so common that all these precautions are unnecessary. Some strange things occur as a result. A decision on the part of one "revolutionary" state runs the risk (and this occurs constantly) of causing it to contradict another no less revolutionary state—in short, an intergovernmental affair. We need no reminder of the Russo-Chinese conflict, one side constantly charging the other with being counterrevolutionary. Thus, China asserts this of the U.S.S.R., and vice versa.

The same fact emerged during the Czech crisis of March–September 1968. Revolution is identified solely with the U.S.S.R., the Soviet State, and the Russian Communist League. On August 24, the *Red Star* reported: "Counterrevolution is infiltrating the Czech army." An interesting notion, for who would have thought the army's role was to make revolution?

And because revolution is a sacred cause,[16] *Pravda,* on August 26, spoke of "the iconoclasts of Leninism"—an accurate admission indeed that Leninism has become an icon, a cult object, and a shrine, on a par with the identification of revolution with the state.

We are treated to an endless procession of forces, definitions, and acts, all termed revolutionary and all exactly the opposite. In February 1968, on the heels of mass purges, Castro liquidated the Escalante faction within the Cuban Communist Party. Escalante may have been an abler and more dedicated Marxist than Castro himself, but he lost out and so was branded counterrevolutionary. His pro-Soviet posture, however, made it necessary for Castro to disclaim any intention to offend the U.S.S.R.

A surprising variety of motives related to revolution as well as to necessity determines the posture of the state and, of course, its foreign policy—which is not in the least revolutionary. Castro simply follows the pattern set by his predecessors. The state and revolution are so completely assimilated that whatever opposes one opposes the other. Any infraction of the administrative or the police code, ordinarily a misdemeanor, becomes a political threat to the goddess Revolution, embodied thereafter in the Cop and the Party Secretary. The facts are there. The major charge leveled against the Berlin revolt in 1953, and later the Hungarian revolt, was counterrevolution. Communists and workers, whatever their motives were, sealed their own fate by simply protesting the socialist state. The fact that they may have been earnest Marxists, or trying to improve the political orientation of the socialist state, or upholding the rights of the working class, was of absolutely no importance next to the all-important state. Just as the state sets the limits and the pattern of revolution; just as it decides what is counterrevolutionary; so also it establishes the organs of revolution. We are all too

---

[16] See J. Ellul, *A Critique of the New Commonplaces,* 1966 (trans. 1968).

familiar with the conspicuous confusion dating from 1919 between Russian policy and revolutionary development.

Were the communist parties supporting the Comintern agents of Russian expansionism or strategists of communist revolution? It is easy enough to say they were both. Actually, at times they were one or the other, but invariably they were champions of the primacy of the state, whether it was monarchist, fascist, republican, or communist—never revolutionary in its own right, in any case, regardless of what it claimed to be. The state establishes the instruments of revolution within its own boundaries: in the past, the soviets (which soon became defunct) and now the revolutionary committees in China. Those committees, acting as anchors of the cultural revolution and the framework of a new administration, are spontaneous—theoretically; in fact, the Chinese state institutes them. What a breath-taking spectacle it is to see a state sowing the seeds of revolution across the land! Revolution, tamed and gone limp, obeys every command without raising an eyebrow. But nothing is quite so astonishing as the realization that the state, always the prime target of revolution's hatred, has undergone this remarkable inversion making it now, in its own right, absolute revolution.

Marxism's shining example did not go unheeded, but was assimilated before long by all practitioners of revolution; the state became the universal embodiment of the new truth. Things had changed decidedly since the mid-nineteenth century, when a man brought before the law for inciting revolution was as good as dead. First came the fascist and the Nazi revolutions, each no less authentic than all the others, establishing the new state. In Italy as well as Germany, the crime of opposing revolution—that is, the state—met with deportation and the ax. We should bear in mind that once the assimilation process is complete, the state is self-appointedly revolutionary and brooks no challenge on that score. Communists will call the lie, but on what authority? They them-

selves have set the example. Tito goes so far as to assert that
revolution spreads in proportion to the growth of the state. All
well and good, except that I fail to see a single principle of
that revolutionary state—barring such deceptive phrases as
"peasant and worker state," which are pure verbiage and
vacuous idealism. The state is the sole judge. In June 1967,
from the heights of its revolutionary security, the Chinese
state felt free to announce that the Palestinians in the Israeli
affair represented "the real people and the real democratic
structure; the democratic revolution will be the achievement
of the Palestinians." A feat of sheer abstraction and imagination. The Palestinians democratic and revolutionary? A grim
joke at best. No, they are indeed revolutionary by virtue of
having been so designated by the Chinese state, the warranty
of revolution. Now we know where revolution lies, the only
authentic one. Definitions of this type merely underscore the
fact that the word has been shorn of its meaning and content.
The roots of that degeneration may be traced back to Lenin's
theory of the proletarian reserves, of the objective counterrevolution, and the rest. In the light of this elaborate mystification, we may well ask whether those theories themselves
were not betrayals of revolution, devised with reference to the
needs of the state rather than to the nature of the proletariat.
Let us not be stopped along so favorable a route. Why should
the national revolution be forgotten? After all, Pétain himself
performed a revolutionary act in overturning the Republic.
And when the immense majority in France was against the
state, to proclaim the absolute value of that state—was not
that a revolutionary statement? Anyway, why look for explanations? It is a revolution because the state has said so. And if
another state (Soviet) takes issue, that has no more
significance than if the Soviet state declares China counterrevolutionary. Force alone carries weight. The national revolution continued to operate as long as the Vichy regime held
power. But in 1944 the Vichy state disappeared, and with it
the revolution, which only then could be proved a fraud. The

same holds for Stalin: not until his death was it discovered that he had destroyed the revolution. Yet until 1953 his government was the instrument, the expression, the only possible form of it.

The pattern has spread, with the state engaged principally in being and making revolution. President De Gaulle declared himself the revolutionary premier of France. Revolution is her normal climate. When President Massemba Debat's power was threatened, the first thing he did was to set up a National Revolutionary Council (which, sadly enough, did him little good). In 1968, South Vietnam established a "Government Committee for Revolutionary Development." The Brazilian military took power in 1964 proclaiming the dawn of the *Revolução,* and *Revolución* was the watchword of Argentina's military *coup d'état* in 1966. We end up wondering whether there is any nonrevolutionary state. Constitutionalists ought to revise their appraisal of the state in the light of the fact that today the principal function of *established* political power is to achieve revolution.

The word "revolution" has settled on everything. After the September 1968 referendum, the colonels' regime announced in Athens that "the revolution, which was a historical necessity, was instituted democratically." That admirable explanation unites the major themes of historical necessity and popular legitimacy. It embraces the entire Left. Who would have thought it came from the mouths of fascist colonels? Yet it is nothing new, and when the Mexican government calls its own party the "Institutional Revolutionary Party," in effect it is holding out its hands to the "real" Left. Everyone manages to prove that the word is totally void of meaning.

But how does one explain the now universal relationship between the state and revolution, a relationship verging on assimilation? Within the Marxist-Leninist perspective it is apparent that the state has its function in respect to a particular revolution. Elsewhere, however, any explanation must deal with a decisive change involving revolution itself. We have already noted that the word has acquired a positive sense for the public. What is more, the public has gradually come to accept revolutionary movement as the most profound expression of popular will. The right to vote and even the referendum are but makeshifts; only in the surge of revolution does the populace express itself directly and freely. Now that socialism is banal and the most ordinary commodity in our society (the staunchest reactionaries are compelled to recognize its validity), not only the Revolution of 1789 but that of 1917 as well comes into play. Revolution and the will of the people are one. At the same time we cling to the conviction that a state is valid only in so far as it expresses the popular will: state legitimacy virtually resides in popular sovereignty. As the two trends converge, the state does not appear legitimate unless founded upon an initial revolutionary act. Its legitimacy is all the firmer if its major concern is spreading revolution and acting in the name of revolution. Then there is no discrepancy, no hiatus between the state and its own legitimacy, renewed regularly—not by any election or referendum, which is always contestable and merely transmits the momentary decision of the people, but by an act of the state itself: if revolution is the popular will, the revolution-making state is in permanent accord with its people. A syllogism? On the contrary, it is reality, more concrete than any political theory because it is based on common beliefs, emotional ties, and platitudes. The important point to consider here is that those ideas filtered into the public consciousness along parallel paths, so to speak, without ever merging; once rooted in the individual, they are more persuasive than any demonstration of fact. Thus we reach the point at which governments face the imperious necessity of declaring themselves revolutionary; unless they do so, they cannot hope to appear wholly legitimate to the average citizen. Especially as that citizen, now a firm believer in the excellence of revolution and in its unique power to express the common will, is nevertheless a bit fearful of it—the riots, barricades, and arbitrary executions.

Whereas if the state itself is directing revolution, what a relief! The assurance of order, legality, and planning; revolution's face, no longer hysterical, is simply icy. The man in the street would rather have it thus. And so revolution becomes the very essence of the state. But that identification also bears witness to the appalling lie we are living, and to the dilution, vulgarization, and inversion of revolution. Is it possible for the state to be revolutionary? In order to link two such radically conflicting words, one would have to deny in advance the significance of the state and of the profundity of revolution. "To suggest that government could ever be revolutionary implies a contradiction, for the simple reason that it is government." [17] A simple reason indeed, and one that remains valid today. Who is going to believe that Stalin's dictatorship, Mao's superdictatorship, the current Soviet technocracy, or the authoritarian incoherence of Fidel Castro is revolutionary? Despite Lenin's conclusions, the state is counterrevolutionary, invariably and in its own right, wherever it appears (in a socialist or nonsocialist society), and whatever its origin (revolution or *coup d'état*). It must try to survive, to perpetuate itself at any cost, and to defy challenge—that is, revolution. By inciting revolution elsewhere it is attempting to destroy rival states; it is behaving like a state—regardless of its form. "There are no two types of government, just as there are no two types of religion; government exists by divine right or does not exist at all [true enough, even for Castroism or Maoism],[18] just as religion is either heaven-sent or nonexistent. Democratic government [in its fullest sense, of course] and natural religion are both contradictions unless one chooses to consider them mystifications. . . . In every revolution the people have sought to reform abusive government according to the dictates of their conscience, but their own ideas have betrayed them; in trying to make power serve

---

[17] This and the following quotations are taken from Proudhon, *Idées générales de la révolution au XIXᵉ siècle.*

[18] The bracketed remarks are, of course, my personal comments.

their own interests, in reality they were contending with a foe. Instead of a champion, they dealt themselves a tyrant. . . ." One need not be an anarchist to see the hopeless contradiction. Marx discerned it—and it is not confined to the bourgeois state. Thus the shift in public opinion is a measure of the decadence of revolution.

Political vulgarization of revolution implies degradation of the myth of revolution. The utter discrepancy between revolutionary talk and visible behavior is not enough to explain the change; one must also recognize the construction of a mythical and homely universe, and the misidentification of revolution with just about anything—including the Revolution.

We shall examine three facts. The first and most superficial one relates to certain accepted organs of revolution which, even in their declining phase, persist in mouthing revolution although their actions belie their words. The Confédération Générale du Travail (C.G.T.) is the most flagrant example. For nearly twenty years its policy has been entirely in keeping with the nature of the organization—that is, reformist and bureaucratic. The Confederation's dilemma resembles that of many other organizations: expansion requires reliable cadres, which in turn make a career of trade unionism and develop into bureaucracies. There is no alternative, because the vast membership and intricate operations necessitate a permanent staff. Moreover, unions are now called on to perform increasingly complex economic functions (the Economic Council, and later on the Planning Commission). Without expert representatives they cannot hope to make their influence felt, and their incompetence would bar them from active participation. These experts are obviously not from the work force; their view of economic questions is a trade unionist's view. Nor are they revolutionaries. In other words, the cadres lose both their proletarian character (even if they are proletarian *in origin*) and their revolutionary spirit. That situation of the C.G.T. grows more acute as its role broadens

and it becomes the recognized voice and best-qualified dele-
gate of the working class, and as it enters an unceasing dialogue
with the power structure, gradually participating in the game
known as organized democracy. The C.G.T. thus develops both
structurally and strategically into a purely reform-minded
organization incapable of challenging effectively the social or
political system in which it operates. To disguise this fact,
it deploys the language of revolution and adopts a manifestly
inflexible posture. The C.G.T.'s main support is unquestionably
the extremist wing of the French working class, which demands a distinct style of language, if not of action. The
Confederation is under obligation to attack the capitalist
system persistently, to preach the class struggle, to prophesy a
rhapsodic future, to campaign for the seizure of power by the
proletariat, and to threaten a general strike; otherwise the
bulk of its patrons would desert. It is wedded to that revolutionary jargon because its admirers await with serene
confidence the night of nights. In addition to pressure at the
base, communist dogma sets the tone of its rhetoric. The C.G.T.
is unquestionably communist, and communism still clothes
itself in solid revolutionary intransigence. Principles must
be upheld and a now classic idiom employed; that highly
inflammatory jargon has become meaningless and utterly
stereotyped. Why bother reading official statements of the
Confederation or, for that matter, of the Communist Party,
when you know in advance what they say? You might also
play a little game I took up some time ago: Reread declarations of the C.G.T. every two or three years: they repeat
themselves word for word, rarely mentioning circumstance or
conjuncture (which would be risky, for in the light of fact and
conjuncture the C.G.T.'s record is reformist). Their sole object
is the ritual assertion that the Confederation is revolution, the
agent of the class struggle, and the champion of proletarian
unity. Communist dogma inevitably slips into a stream of
slogans, which in turn meet client demands. . . . The circle
goes round and round. Revolution thus survives in language

214)   VULGARIZED REVOLUTION

that totally contradicts behavior. One last element contributes
to the situation: the factual impotence of the political Left.
To the extent that left-wing political groups are virtually
incapable of action, of making revolution, or even of guaranteeing a political truce because they lack the support, the will
to revolution, the correct approach to situations, and the
strategy, they are weaponless, and their only solace is talk
(not a vice peculiar to the French!). Words build confidence
that something may possibly exist. The growing helplessness
of the political Left is reflected in its rigid posture and its
inflammatory statements. The C.G.T. is closely tied to, and
shares the fate of, the political Left simply because it has
renounced its unionist character—that is, its organization,
objectives, and doctrine. In rejecting independence and becoming a political organ, in challenging anarcho-syndicalism,
it was forced to camp with the political Left and was afflicted
with the latter's impotence. That experience exposed the
C.G.T. to the strange dichotomy between concrete demands
of a restrained and reasonable nature forming a basis of
discussion, and a storm of oratory. It is difficult to contain
specific material objectives within the limits of fixed revolutionary principles for any length of time; events and attitudes
are certain to assert themselves over verbal ritual. In dealing
with the subject of "militant contradiction," D. Mothé speaks
of the breach in the language of trade unions: "Unions are
responsible for directing opposition and retaliation. As administrators, their function differs from that of workers, who
have no administrative responsibilities. Unions are experts in
solving particular problems. . . . In the trade-union world,
communication occurs by allusions barely grazing the surface
of real problems. Unions have on the one hand a language so
riveted to reality that it has produced and continues to produce a vivid and muscular idiom, and on the other hand
speech patterns devoid of reality. Unions are riddled with
contradictions: resisting a class society while collaborating
with it. . . . In modern nations, the aims of trade unionism

are not fundamentally opposed to those of the host society. . . . Even if one holds that raising the standard of living for workers is a mystical slogan inspired by the state . . . it must be recognized that states have become oriented toward that goal. Is it really possible to create an ideology based on a rapid increase in the living standard? Still, the major source of contention between states and trade unions involves that very point." [19] To resolve that impossibility, the ideology is replaced by a vocabulary and a cant to which revolution in its entirety is reduced.

On a somewhat more profound level (where there is also evidence of the phenomenon of adherence, a persistent trust on the part of trade unions in the vapid and unrealistic phraseology we have just discussed), we encounter a kind of pervasive revolutionary mythology that blankets some sectors and produces certain conspicuous attitudes. François Bourricaud has made a detailed study of that imposture operating in Latin America. It is clear and manifest that Latin America is ripe for revolution, rife with revolutionists, and teetering on the brink of revolution—an assumption, fostered by the press and by numerous scholarly publications, which is simply a myth. "The most widespread misconception is that of the conflict between an established nation controlled by a narrow-minded clique, a selfish oligarchy, and an existing country on the verge of rebellion." [20] That belief, that reliance on what is "clear and evident," can only lead to errors and absurd interpretations; for one thing, we are accustomed to consider any peasant rising or student revolt a sign, a prelude, and a beginning of *the* revolution. Because myth contains elements of unshakable belief and universality, it gives rise to interpretation and classification. For those who live and breathe a pervasive myth of revolution, facts are perceived through colored (and sometimes distorting) glass and are

---

[19] D. Mothé, *Militant chez Renault*, pp. 105–38.
[20] François Bourricaud, *Pouvoir et société dans le Pérou contemporain*, 1967.

classified according to the revolutionary design inherent in the myth. Revolutionary circles (for example, the P.S.U. in France, and all the left-wing groups) bear a striking resemblance to religious circles, especially in this area: people live in a myth, as if revolution took care of itself (in the religious quarter, as if God and faith operated automatically). Mind and spirit are so entirely preoccupied with revolution that judgment and logic are suspended. Revolution has become evidence. Formal evidence, to be sure, as the phenomenon is not present, but evidence such that nothing can be external or unrelated to it. Everything is reported or interpreted in terms of revolution, although the latter is not imminent and the revered facts might be relevant to another planet. Gone is the need for proof or for knowledge of reality: myth replaces reality. Dandieu points out that this is invariably the attitude of reformists who cling to the notion "that a reformer or revolutionist may exploit at will, by playing on empiricism or, rather, Hegelian dialectics, certain facets of revolt in order to delude himself as well as others; it does not matter whether he speaks of classes, races, or groups, or whether he recalls imminent conflicts, bloody risings, *coups d'état,* mass destruction or construction: they are merely the stray apparel of revolution in a setting that is not revolutionary. . . ."[21] Indisputable convictions, a pulsating thrill of revolution, and a fixed system of comprehension have nothing in common with a revolutionary attitude, a searching mind, a determination to act, and an approaching revolution. All such efforts to tame revolution are of no avail, for revolution is wild. We are in the realm of myth (political myth, which is quite tame), meaning, in this instance, propaganda, lies, and ultimately delusions. The longer we cling to the illusion of revolution, the more dependent we are on its language and concepts, the closer we come to destroying the real possibility of revolution by vulgarizing it.

· · ·

---

[21] Dandieu, op. cit., p. 169.

In that same context, vulgarization is revealed in the confusion between revolution and many other events. The simplest example in our times is decolonization. It appears supremely evident that decolonization entails, if it is not equivalent to, revolution. At the end of the Resistance period, we took as our watchword: "From resistance to revolution." It suggested a transition, a transformation, a journey: hence a distance. It was not evident that driving out the Germans had to produce a revolution. It simply meant preparing oneself, after the Liberation, to take advantage of the opportunities at hand, of the newly developed political forces, the alliances, organizations, and ideologies forged by common endeavor over a period of three years, in order to attempt a revolution. That hope failed, but the substance of it was valid. The Resistance, a victory over Nazism, was not a revolution. Today, however, decolonization *is* a revolution.

We shall verify that assertion later on. For the moment, let us simply say that this assimilation conveys the extensive vulgarization of the concept of revolution shared by Westerners and other peoples.

The Theology of Revolution [22]

This is the last stage of our inquiry into vulgarization. Christian intellectuals dabble in revolution. Over the past two centuries, they have made a practice in the political, social, and economic spheres, of arriving on the stroke of midnight. They tend to perceive phenomena when the latter are waning. The importance of the working class caught their attention only when it was declining and destined, fairly soon, to be severely

---

[22] The following is a brief bibliography on the subject: *Église et société, l'Éthique sociale chrétienne*, 1966; Rich, *Glaube in Politischer Entscheidung*, 1962; "Théologie de la Révolution," special issue of *Christianisme Social*, 67; "Foi et Révolution," *Frères du Monde*, No. 51, 1968; Gollwitzer, Lochmann, and Shaull, *Une Théologie de la révolution*, 1968; Cardonnel, *Dieu est mort en Jésus-Christ*, 1968. (Reports to the Ecumenical Council on Church and Society, 1966; 4 vols.)

curtailed. Christian intellectuals apprehend that type of fact
when it is manifest, glaring, the object of universal concern,
and, in short, commonplace. Twenty years ago they awoke to
their own ultraconservatism, and two characteristic trends have
developed as a result. First, they try to draw attention to
themselves by assuming one of those supremely banal postures
and taking an extremist view; everyone approves of their latest
discovery, yet they deliver preposterous statements so as not
to be out of step. Soaring from ignorance to rapture, they
completely overlook basic questions. In the second place, they
tend to grab at all forms of experimentation just to make sure
of not missing out on something important. That is why you
find them adopting the most unpredictable and illogical
positions: they want to keep abreast but are mentally un-
equipped to handle such a commitment and fail to understand
it, their reality being a set of whirling mirrors which they
mistake for the sun. Their extremism is therefore only a lame
joke and often blinds them to the presence of vital social
problems. Despite that avant-gardism, they are invariably the
last to see what is happening. The ecumenical conference
Church and Society in 1966 revealed those two tendencies.
When decolonization is a thing of the past, Christian intellectuals become passionate anticolonialists. When a terrorist
minority launches a manifesto, they take it for Marx's *Manifesto* and rush into line. But nobody talks about it three
months later. In other words, when Christian intellectuals are
interested in a problem, that is a sure sign that the problem has
been thoroughly vulgarized. The same applies to revolution.
That has been the burning issue for several years, and recent
demonstrations have confirmed the trend.[23] Today's Christian

---

[23] In reality, a body of Christian thought on revolution emerged well before
our times (e.g., Tommy Fallot, around 1900). And I believe that in 1946 I
was among the first to formulate (in *Présence du monde moderne*) a theology
of revolution—entirely different, however, from the one that is the present
rage. In that same context, it is rather exasperating to find every book on revolution asserting that the Church has always been conservative. That is supreme
ignorance of history, for it is a matter of record that in every revolt and revolution between the fourth century and the eighteenth, the Church took part,

intellectuals are fascinated by revolution, and the churches are flooded with daily reports of revolutionary activities all over the world.

How and why did those Christians become that way? The answer appears to be quite simple. With their customary conformity, Christian intellectuals adopted the pervasive socialist ideology and phraseology. They talk about classes in a familiar way and explain everything in terms of class structure. They too have been infected with the common disease of our society, politicalization. Everything has become political because the state has invaded every corner of life. The issue, as they see it, is not human existence, but the transformation of society. Their main focus is on social ethics and the theological foundations of modern society. "Any solution must be political," asserts the Manifesto of the Priests of the Paris region (May 1968), because the specific function of Christians is to transform existing situations into values and to promote the justification of necessity. That paves the way for some highly impressive statements: "Everything takes place on a political or economic level. . . . [Note the "everything"!] If the historic dimension of man is translated specifically through politics, man's way of expressing God must convey that dimension explicitly. . . . Prayer, theology, and preaching must be political." [24] That is only one among many such statements. Once everything is political (and once that nonsensical platitude is generally accepted), the next step is to define the politics. Our Christian intellectuals are eager to do it and to demonstrate fearlessly that socialism is the only attitude relevant to Christianity (which?). "A Christian must be revolutionary. At our present stage of human discovery and experience, revolution entails the concept of socialism. Modern

either through its clergy, or more rarely through its officials, or still more rarely as a body. Historically, part of the clergy has always supported rebellions of the poor.

[24] R. Domergue, "Dieu et le langage" in *Foi et Révolution,* loc. cit.

Christians must of necessity be socialists." [25] To reach that conclusion, via a remarkably casuistic and unilateral argument, the writer embarked from the premise of socialism, which is in the air we breathe. Further quotations are pointless and would only illustrate the startling conformity that inspires them.

Starting with that sociological adherence to environmental socialism, a network of justifications is built up, as might be expected, derived from the application of Marxist concepts to Christianity (lest we forget that this is the work of clerics!). The Church and Christianity are torn to shreds under the scalpel of a somewhat crude version of Marxism. Some Christians reject revolution because of "reservations of an ideological sort, which, we are told, are theological and, in reality, the manifestations of a sociologically localized Church." [26] Therefore theology (of others, to be sure, for the theology of Christian revolutionaries is a true theology and not the product of environment) is merely an ideology that in turn stems from the sociologism of the Church (reduced at last to human stature). The whole of theology is a bourgeois fabrication. Most of the examples are provided by Père Cardonnel [27]: grace is the theology of an economy of scarcity; addressing God as *Seigneur* is a reflection of bourgeois paternalism; individuals are products of bourgeois individualism; spiritual life is a turning away from the world (ideology of the ruling class); salvation expresses a competitive economy, and so forth. On the other hand, Père Cardonnel does not seem to realize that his pronouncements concerning the True God and his theology of horizontal relations are simply imprints (without any biblical foundation) of environmental sociologism. A third factor contributing to the overpowering

---

[25] M. Blaise, "Une Morale chrétienne pour l'action révolutionnaire," loc. cit. The aforementioned Manifesto adds: "We are determined to join in protesting a world in which human life is sacrificed to profit and money under the capitalist system." Of course, that is the only side he sees.

[26] *Frères du Monde*, No. 51, p. 65.

[27] Cardonnel, "Pas de Révélation sans révolution," loc. cit.

attraction of revolution is the panic of Christians confronted by the curtailment of their role in history. History has assumed such importance that everything relates to it. One is lost if not part of history's course. The answer, therefore, is to plunge into revolutionary action because it alone is certain to make history.

Christian revolutionaries give no evidence of an orientation —except those who have consistently held the view that Christianity, from its very beginning, induced constructive ferment in society, the relations and structures of which it altered. But that group does not concern us here because it regards the transformation achieved (which may be called revolutionary) as the result of faith and God's intervention, a secondary achievement among many, and the culmination of a primary act which is consecration to God. In principle, therefore, that position is not preponderantly revolutionary with respect to the truth revealed or the spiritual life. Nor does it represent a new attitude peculiar to our society. In that context, calling Christianity revolutionary does not contribute to the vulgarization of revolution. There are two main trends among modern Christian revolutionaries.

First, there are the theologians of revolution. Because revolutions do occur and, according to human standards, may appear legitimate, it should be possible to construct a theology of those revolutions and to relate them to Christianity, which need not remain forever wedded to established power. We are not dealing now with a specific Christian will to revolution.[28] Just to be contrary, I shall call it an effort to exonerate Christianity, in the eyes of revolutionary movements, of its timeless conformity, its ties with the state, capitalism, colonization, and all the rest.

---

[28] The theme I treated in *Présence du monde moderne* and which others have studied, e.g., Gerbe (*Christianisme et révolution*, 1963), who shows that the ethics of Jesus are revolutionary, as well as Borovoi (*Rôle de la Théologie dans les révolutions sociales de notre temps*), who sees revolution as intertwined with Repentance and Rebirth and as the concrete manifestation of a spiritual revolution.

The basic elements of this philosophy involve something of a conviction that God is at work in the modern revolutionary movement (a reversal of the time-honored view that historic events are acts of God: *gesta Dei per Francos*). Because we look upon the Earth as the manifestation of sin, "revolution's rejection of that sin-laden reality carries the echo of God's injunction in the social sphere." That also reverses the traditional view according to which curbing vice was a duty of governments and state-instituted order the expression of God's interdiction of disorder and violence. "The faithful are authorized to lead a revolutionary existence and to contribute to the transformation of a world turned revolutionary." As always, the world is dictating behavior to the Christians: because they are part of a society in which revolutionary movement is important, they must support it. They must demonstrate that "the essence of revolution is the irruption of God's sovereignty in the world." This view clearly contradicts the concept of Christianity as a revolutionary force.

Next to Rich, Shaull is the chief exponent of this line of thought. He regards revolution as the most significant fact of our times; the confrontation of groups, races, and classes throughout the world is evidence of the vital issue of social revolution, for our society is extremely malleable, he believes, and technology can promise "justice and security" for everyone. Social structures are losing their stability because the reverence for them is gone, and we are witnessing the birth of messianic movements intended to free man of all that enslaves and dehumanizes him. Shaull considers that, under the circumstances, "revolution is our fate," and we must find new political and social forms. The revolutionary situation also presents "a challenge to the Church." "If we are to preserve the most cherished values of our cultural and religious heritage, we cannot shirk revolutionary combat: there is no responsible attitude apart from that struggle, *whatever its outcome*." Before we go any further, let it be said that Shaull's sociological analysis is weak. His arguments convey anxiety over world problems, a confusion between socialism and revolution, and a sentimental attitude toward the unequal distribution of wealth, rather than a strict appraisal of the situation of a technological society. What is more, I find it dangerous to base a theological revision and a system of ethics on a specious interpretation of facts. To maintain that a Christian standard of ethics should correspond to its sociological context necessitates a correct sociological analysis—it cannot rest on rough "evidence" and approximations. That is all the more important in view of Shaull's assertion that we must participate in revolution (which is *the fact,* as he sees it), whatever the consequences. The transfer is difficult to make, for it implies that revolution becomes a value, and, in a certain sense, an absolute value. In effect, Shaull's argument is shaky and even contradictory. In dealing with theological concepts, he ends up with concrete elements (Christianity is revolutionary, it has a desanctifying effect, it orients us toward an untouched future; messianism on earth should not be discounted; the Kingdom of God is a dynamic reality that judges society). Then he reverts to the primacy of *de facto* revolutions, and instead of deriving a specific revolutionary orientation from his theological argument, he confuses the revolutionary pressure of messianism with *all varieties* of social revolution exploding currently for any number of reasons. In short, because Christian faith has a revolutionary content, involve yourself in all the revolutions taking place outside the sphere of Christianity. Clearly, the common value becomes revolution, and it is the major premise in the syllogism: it is more important to be revolutionary than Christian or non-Christian. Of course, Shaull will protest vehemently that he never said such a thing, but in effect that premise underlies his whole argument. Next he goes on to discover that the idea of humanizing society provides the link with his theological principles. He is certain, on the one hand, that God's mission in Christ is a humanizing one and, on the other hand, that revolution's goal is humanization. Revolution therefore comes under the heading of God's

humanizing activities. From there you can go on to say that
God himself destroys the outworn structures in order to improve human existence. God is the heart of the revolutionary
struggle: that is the essence of revolution! Of course, the
question is never raised as to whether the humanization related to God's work is the same thing as that toward which
revolution moves. The existence of Blok's poem does not seem
to validate the argument. Furthermore, there is not the faintest
suggestion that other forces than God may be at work and
that the "Prince of the Earth" may indeed have a hand in
earthly revolutions. Finally, there is no attempt to distinguish
one revolution from another—communist, nationalist, judicial,
tribal, and Francoist are all the same. Only Marxism has a
privileged status. It should be noted that Shaull has certain
incidental reservations about the results of revolution. He
points out that revolutionists are tempted to believe that they
can create a new world singlehanded and solve all problems,
whereas Christians should recognize that a political struggle
has its limits. But those reservations are minor, and he
dismisses them by asserting that "the new social order established by revolution is a gift." The imperative of accepting
revolution leaves one paralyzed on two accounts. The most
serious discrepancy in Shaull's argument involves revolutionary
tactics. In another study I have tried to point out that current
ideas on Christian ethics focus on tactics. Shaull does not
mention the subject. He merely suggests, in a somewhat
idealistic fashion, the possibility of forming a political guerrilla
army from a cluster of revolutionary cells. The Church, in his
opinion, if prepared to take its vocation (?) seriously, "ought
to constitute the framework within which men could be re-
cruited for that revolutionary commitment." As for violence,
he rejects Wendland's thesis that Christians should participate
only in nonviolent action and offers the following ingenious
solution: "Situations may arise in which the use of violence
alone can initiate the process of transformation; the vital
question is not whether violence is proscribed, but whether its

application, when absolutely imperative, is part of a strategy of relentless struggle for limited changes, or whether it is basic to a design for the total destruction of society." How gracefully he avoids dealing with the tactics of violence, whereas revolutionary violence ought to raise grave problems within his theological perspective. He simply asks the question: "What are the specific elements of God's humanizing activity on earth?" and lists: forgiveness, freedom, justice, and reconciliation. He adds that revolutionary structures cannot serve their purpose unless they give *each social group* an opportunity to participate more fully in determining economic and national community life. He does not seem to realize that the very methods of revolution run counter to those goals and quite frequently include the liquidation of social groups. Silent on the question of means, he is not much more informative as to what Christian ethics might contribute to a definition of ends, falling back on an ethic of situation that permits any finality consistent with society. In the end, we are forced to call this doctrine idealistic, theologically flimsy, and rather remote from reality.

Those ideas were re-explored at the ecumenical council in Upsala in 1968 and were set forth by Mr. Thomas and others. The Council's report contains the same defensive arguments as those previously cited, but attempts to be more subtle: "Faith is not reduced to an ideology of revolution but assumes a dynamic relationship with revolutionary ideologies in order to make revolution more realistic and human. . . ." "Revolution is an attempt to convey within history a hint of the eschatological renewal promised by God; but the true eschatology can shield revolution from false messianism." "The Bible must be experienced as the reconciliation of various strategies operating within revolutionary struggles." Excellent statements, and Mr. Thomas should have confined himself to elaborating only those three. Why did he find it necessary to assert that the return to God is a return to politics, that Christ's mission can be discerned in contemporary revolutions, that

Christianity is meaningless if unable to establish a new
humanism, that failure to support revolution is acceptance of
the conservative ideology, that revolutionary violence is legitimate, and, finally, that the Church has always chosen the side
of power? A tissue of platitudes, prefabricated notions, and
sociological or historical errors that affirm the overwhelming
tide of pressures inciting everyone today—and compelling
every Christian—to call himself a revolutionary.

The second orientation is illustrated by a small group of
people, more influential and extremist, mutually interested in
the magazine *Frères du Monde*. Père Maillard, its editor,
readily admits: "If I thought my faith [Christian, he neglected
to mention] alienated me at all from other people and diminished my revolutionary violence, I would not hesitate to
renounce my faith." A clear statement of the principle underlying Shaull's argument—namely, that revolution is more
fundamental than faith. Are we to believe, with Père Maillard,
that one must choose between Christian faith and revolutionary violence? I think he really means that revolutionary
violence is, in a sense, the only possible outlet for Christian
faith, and that if what I take for faith leads me to curtail that
violence, then my understanding of that faith is faulty and
consequently I ought to abandon it, for by concentrating on
violence I am certain to be on the right Christian path. That
harks back to Père Cardonnel's expression: no revelation without revolution. Before going any further, let us understand
that Père Maillard's impulses are shared by all Christians
alike: opportunities for the poor, solidarity with the Third
World, criticism of capitalist injustice, and that "loving the
Third World means loving *its* revolution, defending its cause,
actively sharing in it with the hope of remaining a nonviolent
participant, and not condemning those who, by killing, place
themselves in mortal danger." Père Maillard takes a nonviolent position in this instance, but elsewhere he says:
"Violence is imposed on us externally: I am forced to confront

it, for refusing to use a gun is the same as allowing injustice to take its course and people to starve. Violent oppression invariably elicits counterviolence from the oppressed; at some point the poor must resort to violence." Not content to merely state the fact (with which I agree entirely), he has to justify it, thus reaching some remarkable conclusions: "We must free ourselves of a purist morality." In other words, he raises the question of tactics, but does not hesitate to accept the worst of them: "*Anyone who makes the decision to commit himself* warrants our respect"; the commitment, not his fellow man, is now the important factor. As to fellowship, revolutionary action takes precedence over common faith. "I no longer care about Christians for their own sake, only about men whose concern for their fellow beings is of a universal nature. If they really intend to preserve mankind, united we shall solve the problem of methods." We wonder whether the Community of Saints has any meaning today, for, according to Père Maillard's theology, revolutionaries, not saints, are sanctified in Christ. His acknowledgment of Che Guevara as a genuine martyr indicates that position. As for love, his concept of it and Paul's in Chapter 13 of First Corinthians have nothing in common. "We may be shocked by certain forms of repression mounted against the opponents of national policy.[29] Do not condemn those people too hastily; they are wise men. . . . We must not allow our scruples to hold back the global revolution of our brothers. There is a real choice to be made. Charitable love should be repudiated as too idyllic; true love must withstand political, economic, and sociological scrutiny.[30] Man should be loved according to his social rank." I am all for protesting the petty and shabby mediocrity of the Christian concept of love, but I do not believe we can combat error and falsehood by compounding them.

---

[29] Note that once again we have a justification of dictatorship (but what type?) and a distinctly rapid assimilation of the revolutionary party with the "nation."

[30] I must confess that the political and sociological scrutiny of the *Cahiers des Frères du Monde,* from which these quotations come, seems sorely lacking.

That attitude is shared by Père Cardonnel, who maintains that the sole means of expression for Christians is revolution, which voices Faith,[31] Charity, Hope, and the Resurrection. Relying on a combination of puns and punditics to defend his view, the author reveals his extremely confused thinking and utter ignorance of political and social conditions. Of course, it can be said that spreading the Gospel is awakening the poor to knowledge of their latent power and launching them into the class struggle, that man's revolution to conquer alienation is proof of Christ's resurrection, and that loving the possessors denotes dispossessing them (agreed—but let's admit that their guts may go flying in the bargain!). "Instead of being tempered, revolutionary action must be pursued relentlessly out of the love for our foes which inspires us to destroy their privileged status. . . ." That worthy opinion reminds me of countless World War I sermons exhorting Christians to love their enemies by blasting them to shreds. M. Cardonnel belongs to the grand tradition of the auto-da-fé. His reasoning is overrun with trite remarks, platitudes (the modern sort), and conformity. He believes in the equality symbolized by God, in violence that prepares the way for nonviolence, in rhapsodic tomorrows after the wretched capitalists have been destroyed, in the democratic character of Cuba's revolution; he also believes that a revolutionary leader is "the voice of the mass conscience, prodding a people into nationhood and acting as their interpreter" (which is literally what the *Führerprinzip* was), that revolutionaries (non-Christian) are the fulfillment of divine love; indeed he believes everything—except, of course, that God is transcendent or that our salvation resides in divine grace. Père Cardonnel is truly a pillar of medieval Catholicism!

The story continues with Père Maillard's dismissal of the possibility of reintegrating violence and Christian love or of

---

[31] Faith or belief? It is hard to tell, for having asserted that keeping the faith is degrading and that we have to trust somebody, he proceeds to make ample use of the word he has rejected.

establishing a relationship between Christianity and revolution. Now we encounter the most interesting side of his philosophy: Christian premises, he asserts, cannot serve as a point of departure for demonstrating the revolutionary element or force inherent in Christianity's message. He also denies that we should engage in revolution as evidence of our submission to Christ. We ought to embrace revolution solely as human beings because it has value for its own sake. Why that exclusivity and that gulf between Christianity and revolution when, as we know, everyone else is bent on uniting the two and finding a motive for revolution in Christianity? That view, according to Père Maillard, represents the Christian urge to "repossess" revolution; whereas others have begun it and are now sustaining it, along come Christians and incorporate that human act into their system, ascribing a value to it, which is an improper thing. One should not steal the fruits of another man's labor. Christians have nothing to contribute to revolution; what they are trying to do, either by seeking a revolutionary concept in the Bible or by establishing a theology of revolution, is to expropriate revolution and to parade falsely the rights and titles of others. They are thus perverting the course and the meaning of revolution. In any event, some elements of the Bible—Love, for example—will surely mitigate revolution, impair it, and dull its edge. Christians would be wise, therefore, to suspend their Christianity and embrace revolution simply as human beings, on a human plane and without reference to Christian principles. That extremist view is at least honest and free of the Christian passion for "justifying" events. But it raises the question: What is the point, then, of engaging in revolution?

Père Maillard's *implicit* answer is that revolution ultimately has value for its own sake. The best of us are committed to it and the promise of human liberty resides in it; therefore it is the only path a man can take. Revolution assumes absolute value and is no longer contingent on human motives. Moreover, such a commitment will reveal a basic answer to Christians. Note the reversal that occurs here: a man should engage in revolution not because he is a Christian, but, if he does commit himself, as a Christian he will get an immense satisfaction, that of encountering the essence of otherness. For that single meaningful encounter requires total and unqualified commitment. Only by committing himself to revolution (absolute necessity, which, by demanding the total subjective commitment of individuals, engages them in a total encounter), and only by doing so without regard for any Christian scruples can a Christian encounter otherness. At that moment he also encounters God.

By retracing the two principal trends among the theologies of revolution, we can see that vulgarization has reached a peak: all the previously noted elements are present, in profusion. Thus what is significant is not just the fact that Christians have begun to take an interest in the subject, but also the way they go about it.

Revolution has been transformed into value, a standard of good, and now of faith. In the process, revolution emerges as a substitute for faith and hope. In these times we are fools to cling to faith and hope against the background of what is called a myth (God, for example), whereas if we can relate them to some concrete and contemporary reality we can restore hope and faith and maintain a semblance of Christianity. That possibility rests on the emerging image of revolution as the expression of Christian love, which, according to the Scriptures, transcends both hope and faith.

An utterly vapid use of words to convey either sociological or theological meaning. Verbiage quite as vacuous as that of the C.G.T. and totally meaningless. It is particularly interesting to see how the distinct vocabulary of theology can be distorted by a psychoanalytic, a Marxist, or a sociological critique (I ought to say pseudo-Freudian, pseudo-Marxist, and pseudo-sociological) until it becomes irrelevant and applicable to a hundred other things.

The tyranny of events: whereas revolution ought to be rooted in solid reasoning, enabling us to apprehend the event, we are provided with a series of pale theological rationalizations dictated by the need to keep abreast of so-called popular trends and shedding no light either on revelation or on society. Such a theology of revolution reveals merely the emotional fluctuations of disoriented Christians confronted by the most concrete of realities, which they are incapable of assessing or absorbing, but which they embrace with all the zeal and innocence of neophytes.[32]

Such a theology takes its greatest toll by misleading people, as, for example, Latin American Christians, who are now obsessed by *this* revolution, the two main thrusts of which have been identified by Shaull[33]: that of Christian Democracy in Chile, led by President Frei—which, however, did not progress beyond an institutional phase and remained a Christian movement—and that of the "New Christian Left" in Brazil, Marxist-oriented and a protest against widespread poverty.

Far be it from me to suggest that Christians should abandon their concern with human poverty. The question is to identify the true source of that poverty, to know where the path of meaningful revolution lies—revolution more profound than socialism—and to discern the unique prophetic calling of Christians. Such a theology of revolution merely shunts them onto a sidetrack.

The least one may do to combat such ideas is to upset one of their basic premises by asking whether that theology of revolution is not simply an ideology *per se* which fashions revolution into a kind of universal law governing both Religion and Revelation. R. Shinn raised that very question at the conference on *Church and Society.* West, too, has understandable reservations (about the validity of a theology of

---

[32] That was particularly apparent in the discussions held in the celebrated permanent Amphitheater of the Centre Saint-Yves in May–June 1968, during which a recurring charge was the inapplicability of Church doctrine to the pressures of modern existence.

[33] Shaull, "Église et révolution" in *Une Théologie de la révolution.*

forgiveness and of reconciliation) indicating that, in the long run, there is probably no valid theology (in the proper sense of the word) of revolution.[34] Let us go a step further.

To know the full impact of vulgarization, we have only to look at the forms of protest Christian revolutionaries adopt. The most earnest among them gravitate toward parties or movements that they regard as revolutionary; others join guerrilla forces (but there again, as in the case of Camilo Torrès, the same ambiguities shape the Christian decision to enter into such a commitment). That decision is an extremely conformist one that requires little forethought and does not reveal any distinctly Christian attitude, but it deserves respect in terms of the risk involved. And what do the rest do? They attempt to occupy a church, or lead a protest march complete with placards during Mass, or steal a file from the office of a right-wing religious news organ—shabby jokes, good for a laugh if the participants were not deathly serious, convinced that they are working at revolution, putting the Church and society to the torch, displaying breath-taking audacity, and giving proof of a new Christian faith. The only thing they prove is that Christians adapt admirably to the impulses of society, and that revolution has become the most banal, puerile, and meaningless word in an endless stream of discourse.

---

[34] West, loc. cit.

CHAPTER

[5]

NECESSARY
REVOLUTION

Is There a Necessary Revolution?

Let us first find a definition. "Necessary" may involve necessity, that which occurs through the operation of laws or mechanisms outside the sphere of human control.[1] Revolution thus would arrive automatically as a result of the interplay of social forces and historical events. The view of revolution within the tide of history, which I have already discussed, tends to project that idea. It is not what I mean here by "necessary revolution." The word "necessary" has other connotations, more elusive and indeterminate—such as, for example, desirable, or even probable—but they do not concern us particularly. For us, "necessary" denotes a moral imperative, revolution that *must* be made. Not because circumstances favor it, or because it is fashionable to talk revolution, or because more or less revolutionary doctrines exist. The necessity must be experienced

---

[1] That is how I used the word in *Le Vouloir et le faire* (1963).

as an ethical command, but a hypothetical one, and it requires us to ask whether the "necessary" exists.

Yet look at the spectacular progress we have made, the superb and even harmonious development, with science and technology outracing man and promising him ever-increasing security, knowledge, contentment, and mastery; universal equality is around the corner despite residual inequalities, which will disappear gradually as rapid economic expansion overtakes us; order is spreading, and with it, justice; culture reaches out in ever-broadening circles, educating and informing the whole planet, making the pursuit of leisure a reality; the conquest of disease goes on; moral consciousness is taking hold. Modern man is more concerned with the plight of the poor, more readily shocked by injustice, more determined to have peace; never before in history has he armed himself so purposefully against evil and war or acquired greater freedom than by divorcing himself from archaic religions and sexual taboos. Finally, never before have men created such great works of art, raising every area of creativity and of aesthetic exploration to its peak. How, then, could we ever conceive of revolution as a necessity? Undeniable and unfailing progress takes care of everything. Instead, we ought to look on revolution as a deplorable accident, its confusion and disorder as a threat to the steady development of society. Let us therefore reject the imperative of revolution.

Of course, we have not considered the simple and basic motives driving men to explode literally in anger and retaliation. But then don't we live in a world of growing injustice? The gulf between rich and poor has widened. We know that the most affluent nation is host to an impoverished minority of Blacks, Puerto Ricans, and even whites whose subsistence level is below $1000. Not to mention the inequality between possessor and nonpossessor nations. We cannot deny that those are intimately experienced factors driving men to revolution. The unbalanced distribution of wealth and of power are absolutely intolerable; so are racism and the spiritual dis-

possession of humanity, its options dictated by invisible, unknown, and hostile forces acting for obscure reasons, the
effects of which alone are felt while the oppressor's identity
and purpose remain a mystery. Let's pin the blame somewhere
—on the Cheka, the S.S., the C.I.A., the National Security
Force, or whatever it happens to be called, on colonialists,
imperialists, "the Two Hundred Families," the C.P., the Jews,
or the K.K.K.—let's point to that anonymous force replacing
me and God in deciding my destiny. Those are basic, un-
adorned feelings rooted in experience, real or perhaps
imaginary, but always rejected. There we find a source of
revolt and maybe of revolution. For a destitute urban dweller,
the ubiquitous displays of material abundance make revolution
an obvious necessity. For a starving citizen of the Third
World who knows that in some distant places the docks are
piled high with goods; for the humiliated and offended person
whose color forces him to walk in the gutter and to go to inferior schools and movie houses; for a man compelled to join
the army and go to war though he refuses to bear arms and
wishes to love his brothers—for all such people the impulse to
revolution is experienced directly, and necessity manifests
itself viscerally.

I will not contest the statistics: whether one quarter of
humanity is starving or the three quarters so readily cited
makes no difference: a single human being dying of hunger
would suffice. Three billion human beings have no greater
value than one. Nor do I deny that the American Indians were
exploited by American industry. But we have to control our
indignation, which is not a tool for revolution; if anything, it
is an instrument of propaganda. We may take an objective and
informed attitude toward such matters, protesting Injustice,
Inequality, and Exploitation raised to the absolute power by
Capital Letters—and we might as well have said nothing, for
the protest is valid for every society, every group, and every
era; it is mere talk, well-intentioned of course, but unavoidably
continuous and insignificant. Generalizations destroy meaning.

Or we react to the shock directly, profoundly, and within the framework of our own existence because the situations are *real* and we understand the justification for opposing and rejecting "all that." But I must warn that "all that" amounts to very little in terms of necessary revolution—that is, revolution that must be made in order to change effectively the destiny of modern man. We face an insoluble dilemma today: things that are perceived as motives for revolt, as tremors of revolution, and that relate to the concrete reality experienced by living persons, have no bearing on necessary revolution, which has a totally different context. Even if we were able to erase imperialism and colonialism, to eliminate hunger, to satisfy human needs for knowledge, to level conditions at the top, we still would not have come a step nearer to necessary revolution, because it lies elsewhere. Far be it from me to say we should disregard "all that," or children dying of hunger, or insane and futile wars; of course we must struggle, but that has nothing to do with revolution.

Mounier's statement (in 1944) is no longer applicable: "We know the main outline of the inevitable revolution: the expulsion of moneyed power, the elimination of the proletariat, the founding of a workers' republic, the training and accession of the new popular élites." That "revolution" was eminently avoidable, as we have noted, and despite the changes it brought, the problem of a revolution-in-the-making remained unsolved, for it was not the crucial one. Because Mounier did not press his analysis beyond the need for economic revolution, he included The Revolution in that category: "a revolution born of economic crisis has to be materialist at the outset. Can we deny the necessity of it?" True indeed, but he was using "necessity" in the sense of "fatality": "A vast revolution is in operation, dictated with no concern for human desires by some obscure impulse of history." How could we even attempt to escape it? Yes, but that fact alone tells us it was not the revolution men had to *make;* it was self-generated revolution. As a cry of human agony and the response to its plea, it was (and still is) indispensable, but it is no longer the choice we must make in the face of new demands upon us; in other words, the struggle against things we perceive as the source of our agony is no longer revolution in any sense. To combat the causes of unequally shared wealth is not at all revolutionary, for the problem of revolution lies elsewhere at present, and its necessity is not the same. All of us are now aware of the issues and the injustice, the whole story, and the elimination of those problems is at hand because technology is helping us to meet them and because thousands of people are determined to solve them. The present crisis is less distinct and has less impact on us, for man's condition no longer hinges on feeding himself.

As Ulmann rightly observed: "If material revolution is the prime value and, so to speak, revolution at any price, in any form . . . then we need only appeal to our discontent. Long-smoldering resentment will spark the conflict. . . . But we suffer from something other than disaffection, however grievous and even mutilating it may be. Our task, as we see it, is not to reconcile the disaffected. Instead of pouring our efforts into cultivating a revolutionary situation, the time has come for us to choose our allies. . . . To achieve the task of revolution is unquestionably important. . . . But it is not enough to unite the disaffected or even the amputees of capitalism: they must be chosen according to the source and the nature of their rebellion. Only on a clear signal identifying the *reasons* for our revolt and for our refusal to live in the artificial world of capitalism, only with the technological means to pierce our suffocating shell, will our revolutionary unity be forged" (*Esprit,* 1933). Even today that is the necessary revolution.

The problem involves much more than social structures. You may institute new socialist, capitalist, or constitutional systems and you will not have solved it; you have merely gone round in circles. For the essence of humanity is at stake, threatened by outer forces, and the problem is that man is not aware of it at first. The threat does not visit pangs of hunger on him. Just as every aspect of our society has grown more abstract, the threat to human existence has become mysterious, and the phenomenon's seeming reality often turns out to be mere appearance. During the Middle Ages, the plague's mark was the bubo; the swelling required treatment and was lanced in the hope of curing it. But in doing that, the physician encountered a totally different condition. Marxist efforts to explain human misery in terms of economic structures also took the direct route from effect to cause. Once again, however, our society has changed markedly, and, curiously enough, in so far as revolution is concerned there is now a choice of roads. While all areas of modern existence have become increasingly abstract in respect to their complexity as well as to their symbolism, revolution seems to have regressed and grown more tangible: it is present wherever color creates social barriers, or masters exploit their workers, or famines occur. We have reverted to medieval logic. Yet *that* now represents the necessity of revolution. And in adopting a theory or doctrine of revolution, we reason invariably according to those elementary data and recognizable experiences.

The contradiction between society's over-all movement toward abstraction and the basically concrete foundations of current revolutionary doctrine (Sartre's above all) is proof that we have taken the wrong turning. Such a philosophy of revolution does not relate to existing society, but only to outworn stereotypes superimposed on tragic and inhuman situations, which in themselves are not revolutionary. Revolutionary necessity lies elsewhere. And because necessity is involved, it cannot be elaborated artificially or arbitrarily, but must be rooted in reality and direct experience. Its impact on us may be less dramatic once we get to the heart of it.

For *revolution* to be *necessary*, two conditions are requisite: first, man must sense to some degree that he cannot endure life as it is, even though he may not be able to explain why;

secondly, the basic social structures must be blocked, that is, incapable of acting to satisfy express needs or of providing access to that satisfaction. Make no mistake: as long as there is still a way to alter society by easing the conflicts and tensions, the forces of control will eventually find it—through trial and error and even revolt—but settling the conflicts without recourse to revolution remains a possibility, and then revolution will not occur, man being no more eager for it than for war. He may be thrust into it; he may also rush to the festival, but he really does not want to. Ordinarily he is more attracted to stirring and superficial revolts that respond to his exasperation, his emotional fires, or a provocative occurrence, but he is not engaging in revolution—much less essential revolution. The aforementioned pervasive malaise of our times thus can produce extensive disorder but does not lead to necessary revolution because the underlying global structures are not blocked; as a matter of fact, they are extremely active. All are now oriented toward erasing social injustice, satisfying world hunger, and curbing imperialism: their evolution is not only possible but indeed is polarized by those universally acknowledged goals. The depth of our concern cannot alter the fact that the second essential of revolution does not exist.

On the other hand, several more vital and deep-rooted structures do appear soundly blocked—not paralyzed, but simply developing at their own independent pace, unaffected by outside factors, allowing no more humane or generous objective to alter their course, and obedient only to their own inner logic. I refer to technology and the state. Those structures conform perfectly to the second requisite of necessary revolution. But is the first one also present? Although from time to time man protests them, one can scarcely say that he rejects statism, or bureaucracies, or a repressive consumer society, or the inhumanity of technology. The issues are not vital, for they do not appear to represent the overwhelming experience of the human community, which, on the contrary, is only too happy to go on consuming, to make further claims on the state in every domain, and to vaunt its pride in scientific progress. Yet a vague anxiety prevails, suggesting that perhaps the idea of revolution as a necessity is still alive and might compel some of us to attempt it. That anxiety seems to converge at two points: man senses (but does not understand) the insignificance of our whole society; he senses that one road to survival, but not to life, is open, for he is aware collectively of an antinomy between growth and development.

As man accumulates knowledge and resources, the significance of his past and present seems to fade. Once religion and the sacred cornerstones of his existence were gone, he was at the mercy of infinite anxiety that no amount of knowledge could allay. In fact, that anxiety grew in proportion to his increasing security and well-being. Each time he set about solving a problem, expecting to banish all his uncertainties, the outcome was like a plaything in the hands of a spoiled child: having set his heart on possessing a bluebird, and a particular one, he got it, only to find it was a common sparrow, and lifeless. The vast adventure that has absorbed us for the past two centuries has left each of us in his own fashion more frustrated than triumphant, whether because we admit the futility of our occupations, or because of the paltry quality of our satisfactions and our leisure, or the questionable values and way of life we pursue. More than anyone, Western man has the impression he is wasting his life, perhaps because he no longer has concrete, attainable goals to depend on and with the assurance that everything will be different once they are achieved, perhaps because there is no sacred standard to give meaning to his existence. I have no doubt that our malaise derives from the absence of meaningfulness and value to a much greater extent than from a lack of material things.[2] Current demands for a share in responsibilities and decisions and for self-direction are but the by-products of that sense of

---

[2] Ricoeur and Castelli have published basic works on this subject (e.g., *Le Temps harcelant* and *L'Enquête quotidienne*).

meaninglessness. Except for rare ascetics, man cannot exist in a void. The concerted effort to replace the significance of life with the significance of history has failed despite all the attendant propaganda. At present, and probably for a long time to come, knowing that the human odyssey advances by compass is small compensation for the lack of direction in one's personal odyssey. Is this petit-bourgeois sentimentalism? Factually rather than metaphysically speaking, the feeling is almost universal in the West and represents the core of man's spiritual development as he becomes more individualized in the course of history. It also appears to be the tendency of the African and South American peoples. We cannot dismiss, therefore, the anguish, the fears, the moral incertitude, or the passionate aspirations characteristic of contemporary existence. Nor can we suppress the problem by saying that man has only to give direction to his life or to his actions. That might be possible if it were within every man's power of individual invention alone, in which case the psychiatric wards would stretch to infinity. The meaning of life does not reside in our imaginations but in a common purpose and common beliefs; if it is to be reliable, it must be communicable. It is a product of common sense.[3] It cannot be decreed arbitrarily. Man cannot live without purpose, yet the individual is unable to provide himself with a stabilizing and satisfying one. Except for certain artists, ascetics, and the Cheval factor!

Our civilization is battering its head against that enormous obstacle. For those who still aspire to exist as individuals, society arouses no desire to go on living, and life is completely insipid despite the abundant diversions, gadgets, and leisure time. With society so organized and man what he is, divested of his privileges and his illusions, it is impossible to *superimpose* meaning and value on existence within that particular

---

[3] Castelli. Common sense is the opposite of the commonplaces that I have criticized (in *A Critique of the New Commonplaces,* 1966 [trans. 1968]), which are characterized by absence of meaning.

society. Meaning and value merely would dust a shiny film onto the surface of technological reality and would vanish at the slightest human stir.

Viewed collectively, the problem is slightly different. Let us examine two complementary aspects of it. On the one hand, the vast apparatus of mass production-consumption-communication into which society pours all its efforts and resources has not achieved its purpose: "No quantitative reduction of [the proletariat's] poverty, no illusion of hierarchical integration is a permanent cure for its discontent." "Now it is capitalist affluence that has failed." [4] The situationists have the most acceptable approach here. They observe that developing the production-consumption cycle, improving the standard of living, and combatting poverty through increased consumption represent what they term organized "survival." Before industry developed, man was to some degree under the death sentence (physically). Industrial production reprieved him. But at what price? Perhaps the condemned man of former times enjoyed a fuller life than does modern man. Subsequent efforts of American capitalism, syndicalism, and Soviet socialism to resolve man's pivotal problem by increased production simply improved and organized his chances of survival. Nothing more. Yet the crucial question is life, and because industrial output does not overcome or remove or confront it, we say therefore that capitalist affluence has failed.

Revolution, then, is knowing where, how, and when the people of that society shall come into full life. It requires a drastic reassessment: we must abandon the unscientific and unfounded notion of a kind of identity or continuity linking economic growth, development, and progress. The obvious solution for those who talk about underdeveloped nations is growth, and growth leads of necessity to development. Progress usually is added for its splendid ring. There is hopeless con-

---

[4] Debord, *La Société du Spectacle*, Nos. 114–15, 1967.

fusion as to the proper use of the words. At one extreme, writers equate growth and progress (recognizing only one type of progress: economic) and measure progress by productivity, whereas social progress pertains merely to abundant satisfactions, and hence to rising incomes on a broader scale.[5] It is pointless to elaborate that view, which is so damaging to our society and discloses a basically faulty grasp of the problem. The dominance of such thinking makes revolution imperative. According to F. Perroux, growth denotes a quantitative upward trend in an economic setting, unaccompanied by proportional or structural changes. In underdeveloped countries, the economic life of which is ruled by international monopolies, the latter may augment production; there will be growth, and the national income will increase. But neither economic power nor, for instance, agricultural output will be altered as a result: development would occur if a rising volume of production were reinforced by nationalized agriculture, diversified production, and modernized agricultural techniques. All that is relegated to the sphere of economics, as if a country's development depended solely on the economic factor. It is astounding to realize how far non-Marxist economists have gone in accepting the supposedly Marxist concept of economic primacy and extending it to everything else. It seems to me that, on the contrary, it is essential to observe the gap, and perhaps the conflict, dividing the three.

Economic growth is pure economics. National development, however, is a global cultural fact, and "progress" (in its positive sense) is a human fact, individual as well as collective, as Sorel rightly noted. Let us take the example of Sardinia, an extensive study of which has been made by Le Lannou. He speaks of the "mixed blessings lavished on the island from abroad": economic "advantages" of every sort translated partly in terms of growth, partly of development as

---

[5] Dayre's *Productivité mesure du progrès* (1961) is a typical example of this approach.

Perroux construes the word—that is, structural changes resulting from a massive industrial effort over a period of fifty
years, expansion of intensive methods of sheep-raising which
displaced farming, and other factors. Structures are transformed. Expanding production and "development" produce
"total assymmetry" in the Sardinian economy, enabling Le
Lannou to assert: "Those are the manifest conditions of
Sardinia's (real) underdevelopment." "As for the needs of
society, the island itself has had to provide for them, but the
institutions it established bear the negative stamp of defense
mechanisms." [6] There we see the contradiction between
economic growth and factual underdevelopment that is both
social and human, the underdevelopment being actually a
product of that growth. Elsewhere I have attempted to trace
the declining condition of the working class and the attendant
regression of Western society resulting from industrial growth.

The Third World's apostles of economic development would
do well to reflect on those examples. In reality, I believe we
should be talking about contradiction, not continuity. That is
Lantz's [7] point in censuring sociologists (he ought to have
included economists and the general public) for confusing
change, growth, and progress. We are at the stage of "recon-
ciling social conservatism, economic expansion, and industrial
progress." If we confine our sphere of reference to economic
growth alone, we are closing our eyes to social stagnation and,
what is worse, to human regression. "We are faced with
economic growth often equated with preserving the existing
structures. . . . We need only observe how each social stratum
adapts to the growth, idealizing it and mistaking it for
progress. . . . [Everything is predicated] on an ideology of
growth promoting *ipso facto* moral evolution. The organic
solidarity evoked by that development dissolves indi-

---

[6] Le Lannou, *Le Déménagement du territoire*, pp. 149 *ff*. in the series *Pâtres
et paysans de la Sardaigne*.
[7] P. Lantz, "Le Temps des sociologues," in *L'Homme et la Société*, No. 3,
1967. The same approach is found in C. W. Mills, *The Sociological Imagination*.

vidualism." Lantz's detailed and well-grounded analysis traces the manner in which alterations conceived of as growth or even development ultimately reinforce a society's self-image, never challenging it and inducing further conformity because that society clings to *the self-image it projects,* including its illusions of structural change, which always follow a pattern of exclusive quantitative growth. "The concept of growth is dangerous in that it confuses the idea with the reality and ends up being taken for one or the other." As I see it, that is precisely why revolution is indispensable and necessary: we must get off the standard (and unexplored) one-way street that starts with growth. That is necessity.

If the human condition and the existing social pressures indicate the necessity of revolution, we have yet to determine what kind of revolution, for that is something sociologists like to recommend, arguing that because man lags behind society and its institutions, he must change in order to adapt and to realize his full potential. Duvignaud [8] and others share that view, as well as the host of social critics who say that man must manage somehow to adjust himself psychologically to his environment.[9] In both cases the manifest excellence of technical progress and of the new society is the basic premise, from which it follows that man has fallen behind. Amid his jumbled inheritance of threadbare ideas and emotional ties to belief, to reason, and to morality, he is up to the level of the marvels of science and technology. The central problem of revolution, therefore, is to revolutionize man and force him to change in accord with his environment. A choice is forced upon us. We must decide between the accumulation, perfection, and primacy of material things, and that ambiguous, doubt-ridden, and uncelebrated (except for his learning) creature known as man. For in fact, as has already been noted, the two are irreconcilable. Yet the seemingly illogical choice I

---

[8] Duvignaud, *Pour entrer dans le XXᵉ siècle.*
[9] That is the thrust of "human relations," for example, and Burnier advances the same idea, though more indirectly, in *Tendances et volontés de la société française,* 1967, p. 439.

make is man with all his imperfections. I reject out of hand
the notion of human backwardness measured against the
brilliant achievements of science to which man ought to adapt.
In making that wager I am not quite certain whom I am
acting for or what standard governs my choice. Obviously it
is not traditional humanism, or the meaningless concept of
making technology man's servant.[10] It is a revolutionary attitude in that we are wagering on uncertainty against the overwhelming evidence of society's predictable course. It is our
only alternative to that foreseeable development.

On one side stands everything that technology (based on
science and every branch of knowledge, including human
skills—which today would appear vital) is preparing and unquestionably will achieve, and that we can project to some
extent; on the other stands man with all his inadequacies, his
dilemmas, and his unpredictability. That is the choice we
must make, knowing that no conciliation is possible. That is
the essence of the revolutionary decision. It can have no other
content in our times. The decision is necessitated by the
absence of meaning and by the antithesis between growth and
progress. But the choice we make may be entirely conformist,
driving man even deeper into a rut, habituating him to a
purposeless existence, and, in the end, assimilating growth
and progress—or it may be sparked by the existing conflict
and hence become revolutionary.

That brings us back to the view of revolution as an essential
part of the human personality: "Human society is based on the
creative violence which has engendered individual consciousness as well as social order. In that sense, revolution is man
himself." "Revolution is the emancipation of human *personality*." [11] Camus's position (which I criticized earlier from
another standpoint) is the same when he says: "I rebel, therefore we are." Revolution is man himself. I believe that man
comes into being through his revolutionary acts. By radically

[10] I have made lengthy critiques of humanism in *Métamorphose du bourgeois* and of the question of making technology subservient to man in *The
Technological Society*, 1952 (trans. 1964).
[11] Aron and Dandieu, op. cit., pp. 9–14.

challenging the totality of his environment down to its structures and values, he enters upon a new existence and changes in the process of changing his environment. Today the human environment is technological. That does not mean that man naturally possesses an inner revolutionary quality acting as a *vis dormitiva,* or that revolution is instinctive, the response to a need: he engages in revolution by a decision, a wager, an absurd gesture of revolt and rejection in the face of his in-human condition. His choice is absurd because its chances of success or effectiveness are minimal. But only through this decision to try to find some meaning in meaninglessness, to give meaning to an absurd act involving him completely, does man exist. Revolution in our times is indeed necessitated by the new human situation (two elements of which we have noted), but it is not a human impulse driving us to revolution in order "to be." In that respect we are never sure of the decision; it is an objective necessity, but there is no guarantee that an individual will take that path or assume that vocation today, though he is called on to do so. The attitude is not one of withdrawal or individual retreat, but has to be revolutionary by the single fact of our immersion in a collective society from which we cannot divorce ourselves as individuals; and because we are all caught in the tide of vital human concerns, we have no right to dissociate ourselves from it, for the destiny of our era is our own destiny.

But that destiny is not revolution, as they who degrade it seem to think: it is counterrevolution or integration. We are all bound, whether or not we like it, to a community; but we can refuse to put up with it. And here is the necessity of which I speak: we must will, not this destiny, but the struggle against it.

The Characteristics of Necessary Revolution

These characteristics must combine the features of revolution which we have already found recurring throughout history and which we recognize as the basic structures of our times. A major question immediately arises: must revolution take the direction of history? To talk of revolution outside history simply would plunge us into the metaphysics of revolution, a sorely overworked subject these days, or else into some variety of utopianism. We must deal with revolution within history. That is self-evident. We cannot assert that revolution must oppose unmade history because we do not know what that history will be and because revolution, whether it fails or succeeds, is part of history, will help to make it, and will belong to it. Let us avoid the current tendency, a by-product of distorted Marxism, to look back at a revolution made, achieved, and over with and to conclude that because of its influence on history, it took the course of history. Those who undertook and achieved it had no warranty that it was history in the making. Marxist reckoning on that score is entirely false. We are in a position to judge only the probable and predictable course that events will take if unimpeded.

The tide of human affairs conveys an element of necessity, a sense of fatality, a significance revealed by the projection of events and the lines of force within the existing society. With that in mind, we must judge whether or not present-day revolution is directed toward that necessity and is simply the acceleration of history's seemingly normal movement. To the extent that it always has been and always has intended to be the expression of human freedom on the humblest and most immediate level of experience, or the loftiest and most idealized, it cannot reinforce fate or act merely as a spur in the flanks of history. It is a fundamental error to try to integrate man's wild cry for freedom into the necessary course of events—this is Marxism's unpardonable deception—and to promote the concept that man can rebel and attain freedom by submitting to the mechanism of history, which he would supposedly be creating while it unfolded.

If we reject the view of global and inexorable historical movement, then we must proceed from specific phenomena in present society. Various tendencies in evidence there are bound to elicit value judgments from revolutionaries, for revolution and revolutionary thinking are founded on value judgments. Revolutionary action implies an ethical choice based on a particular image of man. Every revolutionary movement is a response to the question: What is good for man? To deny that, to believe that revolutionary doctrine can be strictly scientific and revolutionary action purely objective is the fallacy of scientism and a negation of the passion inherent in revolution. Marx himself is a prime example. The merit of revolutionary thinking derives from its reliance on a strict, flawless, profound, and lucid investigation of contemporary human reality and environment in order to make that ethical choice. Some of the expected changes appear desirable, others do not. Among the former (decolonization and socialization, for example), is revolutionary action required to bring about transformations which, as we have said, now entail a strong probability factor? Indeed, the very fact that they appear certain to be realized in the decades ahead makes them certainties in the eyes of present-day revolutionaries. A great many people are fascinated by the question and maintain that the changes will come about without the need for revolutionaries to spend their mental and physical energies promoting them. Once an objective has gained wide public support and political and economic conditions have begun to materialize, once a mass movement is under way, let things take their course: the objective is as good as won. A faceless crowd will do the job. Revolutionaries must turn their attention elsewhere. Equally probable developments such as bureaucracies, centralization, and a consumer society, are much less desirable. Here revolutionary action, instead of seeking to accelerate the movement and reinforce its historic thrust, appears to aim at arresting, combatting, blocking, or deviating those tendencies.

Necessary revolution, like all authentic revolutions in that respect, is thus revolution against the predictable course of history. At the same time it is the real force of history because it releases history. That has been the function of every revolution. In regard to 1789, Madaule said: "What they hoped to accomplish and whether or not the results met their expectations is immaterial; the fact is that they released history. Out of an exhausted nation they drew fresh, undreamed-of strength that no one had thought possible. That in itself is perhaps a revolution: virtue reborn, a palingenesis, rather than a permanent and painless relocation in the Promised Land or the return to an earthly paradise. Revolutionaries are sorcerers. They strike barren rock and waters gush forth." [12] That corresponds precisely to the requisite of revolution we discussed earlier: it can only occur within a blocked society, the structures of which no longer can contain or control irrupting conflicts. The current insistence on placing revolution in the framework of socialism, colonization, imperialism, and their company does its part to aid the gradual blockage of those structures, to fix the attention of live forces on outdated problems, and to curb the movement of history. What is called for is an estimation of the likely evolution (for an obstructed society, I repeat, is not immobilized: it evolves according to its own logic, increasingly hostile to all manifestations of creativity and independence) and awareness of the fact that necessary revolution can be brought only against that necessity, precisely because it is necessity, obstruction, and therefore in itself the negation of freedom.

The second characteristic derives evidently from the first. Revolution is necessarily an act of negation and opposition, a cleavage: it is "anti." I am well aware that revolution evokes values, which surely should apply in judging revolutionary action; and if I mention "freedom," it immediately elicits a value (although it is something else, in my opinion, and greater than that). We are looking at a way of judging actions rather than at a fixed objective or a moral achievement. In

---

[12] Madaule, "La Révolution ramenée aux limites de l'histoire," *Esprit*, 1939.

other words, when revolutionists speak of justice, for example, it does not necessarily mean that they believe they will attain it or will create a just society. They must hold up their own acts to the light of justice, and justice may appear in the process. As for the objective, it has to be concrete, practical, and unidealized. Justice, if it enters in, will be conveyed perhaps by just tactics, but certainly will not be integrated into the fabric of a projected utopia. Utopias are supremely counterrevolutionary, and it is perfectly evident why our French pseudorevolutionaries, ex- or neo-Marxist, chastened by their vain efforts to deliver a revolution that was nowhere in sight, have suddenly discovered the delights of utopia and adopted Fourier as their fairy godfather. Revolution cannot be made in the name of values or for the purpose of replacing one social-economic-political system with a more efficient and nearly perfect one. It can only operate "counter." That is not merely a fact; it is a necessity, I believe, for revolution to be negative and destructive. Its role is to challenge, and only as it begins to focus its defiance and rejection can it shape itself and assume value. "Positive" revolution, for the sake of a more nearly perfect order, *never* materializes: it is idealistic, dissolving into dreams, or, at the utmost, emerging as reformism. It cannot do otherwise. Revolution purporting to be positive in terms of either history or values, operates by the spread of ideas or by a democratic process and gradual change: it is not revolution. It is rapidly absorbed by the social system it sought to destroy. That was the fate of social democracy and of Yugoslav-style democratic communism. Only a revolution against humanity's unpardonable condition is revolution, rooted in rebellion and carried out willfully at a given historic moment. Revolution "against" returns to the source of revolt, without which there can be no revolution. Revolution "for" never does that. Rebellion is not triggered by the prospect of some splendid value or the need to overcome some minor obstacle on an otherwise clear public highway. The historical relationship between revolt and revolution, which we discussed earlier, also applies to necessary revolution. It, too, must avoid idealism and concentrate on the root cause of man's present turmoil, suffering, and despair—and, I repeat, neither hunger nor war is the real enemy. They are mere specters of still more unmerciful foes against which the tide of human rebellion suddenly may surge from the depths of its habitually repressed, but perhaps explosive, anguish. Revolt firmly anchored in an existing implosion may cause revolution to explode, providing the theoretical analysis of the objective is adequate and permits a clear understanding of what is being fought against.

The third feature: though revolution must be "anti," it has to be designed in terms of the current social framework. Two factors enter in. First, revolution must strike at structures, transcending circumstance, spectacle, routine, and current affairs. Recognizing this, Marx sought the roots of phenomena, a more comprehensive explanation of appearances, the realities behind the shifting political scene, and came up with a diagrammatic representation of the entire political, democratic, and social panorama, the economic key to which was, for him, the class struggle. That was as far as he could go in his day, primarily because the new social framework was not yet shaped. The work has to be done all over again. A serious desire for revolution is incompatible with such superficialities as attacking Gaullism or police brutality. Today that fact is harder than ever to face because of our society's reliance on spectacle and instant communication. Waves of information bombard us relentlessly, and our poor heads, reduced to sieves, cannot retain anything substantial or articulate anything solid (except, of course, in the realm of philosophy!). In the light of our subjection to a perpetual spectacle, the endless array of images comprising our universe, it is extremely painful to admit that the whole performance is simply shadow play, and that no matter how absorbed we are by university reform, regionalization, Saint-Gobain, labor developments, the disintegration of N.A.T.O., the Palestine conflict, the presence of Russian warships in the Atlantic, moon landings, or the development of an artificial heart, all that, strictly speaking, is unimportant. Revolution cannot reach out in any of those directions: behind the phantasmagoria (which are real enough, but made phantasmagorial by the magic of mass media) we must try to isolate the structures that flashing images ultimately hide (by their powerful attraction) and reveal (in their fragmented reality). Revolution must reserve its main thrust for those structures. What is the sense of wasting your brains and energy on a muleta when the matador waving his television screen under your nose can take an even worse jab at you. To my great sorrow, I see *all* modern revolutionary movements making their final agonized lunge at television screens.

If the social edifice is to come under attack, let us make sure it is the one *in our midst, of our society*. We have already noted that planning, in all historic revolutions worthy of the name, has been equal to the task. By exploring the basic realities of the *existing* environment, we are almost certain to discover guidelines for action. The essential point is to stop mulling over societies that exist only in the past or pluperfect tense. It is not easy. To take a single example, the revolutionary classifications established by Marx applied precisely to the society of 1850. But to pretend now that the needed attack on our present social structures defines the class struggle (exploitative production, unequal distribution owing to the surplus value factor, alienation in the marketplace) is simply a dream of revolution which began for some when they fell asleep in 1871, and for others in 1917. They toss and turn, fighting nightmarish battles and dreaming of rapturous tomorrows. But the sun is not up, friend, and you are still in the total darkness of theory. The disastrous state of current revolutionary thought comes of its stubborn adherence to century-old social analyses and to a model for revolution valid fifty years ago.

. . .

The problem of the Third World, of needy nations, and of hunger thus has continued to cloud our reason; it is indeed a human problem, at once essential and tragic, but it has nothing to do with revolution. Neither factual revolution nor a socialist system will deal satisfactorily with the desperate situation. Vital economic and technological changes are occurring, but they will not lead inevitably to socialism (unless the word is used loosely), and revolutionary action, except in a few instances, can do little to improve matters. Blaming American imperialism for Latin America's poverty is simplistic logic, adequate for revolutionary agitation, but for nothing else. Checking and destroying that imperialism will not *settle* a single thing, any more than did the elimination of colonialism in Africa. For the underdeveloped nations, the answer lies partly in eliminating the privileged minorities that have risen to power in those newly independent countries. But that is not genuine revolution, much less the necessary revolution confronting us today. Yves Lacoste rightly calls it a fallacy to judge events by the yardstick of past developments in the U.S.S.R. and says that launching a massive program of industrialization in the Third World would be disastrous.[13] He describes the needed changes, which, in most cases, are well within reach, concluding that some form of *coup d'état* probably will be necessary to introduce agrarian reform, but that improving health standards, controlling the birth rate, and raising public purchasing power do not demand a revolution (any more than does the subdivision of large landholdings). In other words, those issues are irrelevant to revolution viewed as a necessity. So is the notion of dividing the world into proletarian and imperialist nations in place of class divisions. To imagine the nonpossessor nations and the Third World playing the same role in present society as that of the proletariat in the capitalist society of 1900 is a fatal illusion, for the

---

[13] On these questions, cf. Dumont, *L'Afrique noire est mal partie*, 1965; Yves Lacoste, *Géographie du sous-développement*, 1966; Rullière, *La Réforme agraire en Amérique Latine*, 1968.

relations, the social structures, and the aims are not the same. To expect them to revive a play that ended its season long ago is to condemn them to a false revolution (for the majority of them) and to immobility (in respect to their own needs). It is asking today's cast of actors to repeat the performance on a darkened stage, behind closed curtains, in an empty theater. The economically advanced nations need not even attempt revolutionary action because the problems vital to the Third World are already known and acknowledged—just as the problems of the working class are *virtually* solved. I do not say they *are solved,* only that their urgent importance is little short of an accepted fact. Everyone agrees that the Third World must be helped to help itself. Everyone agrees to make sacrifices and try to find a workable solution. Everyone agrees to accept changes within his own system for the sake of that solution. Of course, certain difficulties remain to be ironed out in the way of political or capitalist self-interest, private interests in conflict with those aims, lack of agreement as to tactics, capitalist or socialist institutions that controvert the will to aid those countries, and technical shortcomings. But historical experience makes it perfectly clear that the obstacles will give way rapidly once the public is convinced of and pledged to the necessity of overcoming the problems.

When a mainstream of opinion gathers, there is no need to reinforce it by talking of revolution; it will shatter the dikes and set its own course. Imperialism is no longer the central issue, for in order to preserve its privileges and profits, imperialism must find a positive answer to the Third World's dilemma just as the owners of industry were (and still are) obliged, without revolution, to alter both the economic system and working conditions in order to survive as owners. Therefore the problem of revolution cannot be considered on that level or in terms of those aims or factors. By clinging to an obsolete pattern, we are simply inviting endless repetitions of a revolution now impossible because its objective does not exist. More than thirty years ago, Dandieu pointed out, on a different yet related subject: "Once the iron law of wages ceases to apply, revolution is no longer a class question. . . . A fact that the most determined, or at least lucid, revolutionaries find it hard to reconcile because it entails a new religion and a new posture. The iron law that has ceased to shape social relations still exerts its powerful influence and prestige on human minds. We long for it, especially the working class, the essence of whose oppression it defined." [14]

Let us now examine another feature of revolution *against* the *structures* of the *existing* society: the ties between revolution and revolt. Rebellion has always been the outlet for the excluded sector of society, the small minority of outsiders subjected to the fiercest exploitation and suffering. Marx's theory of the exploiting class and the exploited class depicts that situation. The exploited class alone can rebel, and therefore alone can become revolutionary. The greater the exploitation, the broader, more intense, and radical the struggle. Revolution relies on the diametrical opposition of the power to be attacked and destroyed. However, that essentially valid analysis could apply only, as Marx noted, to a society divided into a number of conflicting groups, to a social framework unable to withstand the sporadic inner shocks that ordinarily do not penetrate the social fortress. In that respect our society has undergone a profound change over the past fifty years. It has become global, not in the sense that sociologists term a society "global" (a global nation, class, or society as opposed to the family, a partial society), but actively so: all-absorbing and vigorously assimilative. It absorbs and assimilates the most seemingly disparate forces. It has become collective and collectivizing, abstract, rigid, more highly structured, its pillars invisible yet firmly embedded. Under those circumstances (which we shall explore), revolution no longer can remain a struggle between an exploiting and an exploited class: the struggle itself reinforces the totalizing tendency of society

---

[14] Aron and Dandieu, op. cit., p. 48.

and advances it. Yet because revolution must always emanate from the diametrical opposite of the organism under attack, if that organism is truly totalitarian its sole antithesis is the individual.

A global, all-absorbing society tending to be so structured that all its parts are highly co-ordinate, each one reinforcing yet dependent on the others, cannot be divided. Marx recognized that fact, but as his society had not yet become global, a good many of his observations on the subject were purely philosophic conjectures. Philosophy always has tended to totalize in its search for an intellectual system, a master key to universal reality. Today the same tendency prevails, not in the intellectual sphere (which, on the contrary, is almost hopelessly fragmented), but in the sphere of reality, all parts of the social body being so conjoined and interconnected as to make that organism all-encompassing and uniform. I do not share Lefèbvre's view of current society as a cluster of practically incoherent subsystems, studded with chinks and gaps, destined to falter and come to a halt. The system, on the contrary, continues to assert and to consolidate itself. The subdivisions operate as one, forming a network of interrelations. The globality is not artificial, forced, or haphazard; it is a systematic development that gradually has absorbed all the social components.[15]

As scientific and technical knowledge expands, a drain-off of residues occurs, a tighter ordering of the social organism, and improved co-ordination of the units. Integration is not complete, to be sure, and the stray ends, the defective parts, the gaps are visible, as is the essential disproportion between the individual and the system. Fortunately. But the rational tendency is firmly incorporated and appears irreversible; it suits our methods and aims all too well. The nature of a global society is such that no single element of it may be touched, or impaired, or questioned without involving the whole. Recipro-

---

[15] Corresponding to the "assimilative power" which I have discussed in *Métamorphose du bourgeois.*

cally, no part is secure once certain elements are challenged. In May 1968, that applied to the university as an institution. No longer can we expect to reject capitalism yet preserve science and technology, or to attack European nationalism while encouraging African nationalism, or to uphold moral standards and still criticize the state. Ours is certainly the first society (since the "primitive" or, let us say for utility's sake, "tribal" era) in which the whole is implied in each part. That requires revolution also to be global. There can be no partial revolution. Marx surely must have shared that view, but by visualizing a process involving a particular type of link, a particular social group (the proletariat), and a philosophy (his own) alien to bourgeois ideology, he distorted his results. But at the very hour when he conceived a process with a particular connection and a human category (the proletariat) that miraculously did not act by his system—in fact was the counter-system and a dogma (his) that did not jibe with the bourgeois ideology—everything fell into contradiction.

This is how socialism began its painful journey toward reformism and vulgarization. The existence of a global society rules out any prospect of sectorial revolutions (for example, a revolution in the sphere of distribution, or participation, or higher education) or of starting a revolution in a specific vein and having it spread throughout the entire society (the underlying mechanism of cultural revolution). In fact, any sectorial or tactically divided revolution will be reabsorbed by the system and integrated into the corporate whole, which is fortified by the added vigor and new blood. Revolution attacking a petty social or national problem, an abuse or impoverishment of one sort or another, is doomed to fail; a global society demands a global revolution. In an institutionalized society, all institutions must be scrutinized and challenged. There is no cultural revolution, only total revolution.

That brings us directly to the phenomenon of integration. Whereas the world appears to be disintegrating despite increasing integration, we should recognize that what have disintegrated are the traditional bonds (morality, formal religion, smaller humanizing groups, reason), and that the seeming incoherence is really the absence of those familiar signs of coherence. We have the impression of a disintegrating society because adult–young relations no longer conform to a family pattern, or because the old culture is decaying and we do not see anything taking its place, so we assume that disintegration is at work. That is not true, however, for integration is occurring through other more rational, voluntary, and complex means, and according to other patterns. Apparently we no longer require deep-rooted and truly collectively evolved "values" and "culture," for the psychosocial instruments of propaganda and advertising supply all the false values and culture needed for integration. What is more, owing to our work methods, our total reliance on consumption, our satisfaction with spectacles, and our administrative foresight, we have reached a unique stage of integration affecting the various social units as well as the individual in relation to those units. That is why structuralism and objectification are flourishing. Revolution therefore cannot restrict its attack to economic or political structures, for it is at the vital center of the assimilative system, the converging point of all mechanisms integrating the individual with the social organism. Psychological factors cannot be divorced from sociological ones, or beliefs from institutions; revolution must be executed on the individual level by the individual's recovery of control over the systems of integration. That is the only antidote to massive assimilation.[16] The individual is the sole antipode of global society, just as individual members of the ancient "primitive communes" were indistinct from the group. We have returned to that state, but with a new armature: the shell has become both skeleton and armor.

Magic has been replaced by conscious design. Global,

---

[16] In *The Political Illusion* [1965; trans. 1967], I took a different approach but concluded the same necessity for resuming political-social life on an individual level, calling it the recovery of citizenship.

assimilative, abstract society: we live in a universe of images and abstract ideas. Countless processes occur before we can apprehend reality. No longer a direct relationship between man and his environment, reality now entails combined operations, some performed by machines, others by institutions or organisms, still others by ideological projections or through the intermediary of "extended relations." We never deal with concrete things any more. Workers never handle their materials, or even the machines themselves. Administrators are in touch not with the decision-makers but with a bureaucratic maze, a labyrinth of official channels. Vacationers do not come in contact with nature, but instead with some advertised image of it, or else with an institutional system (commercial or state-controlled). Abstraction via generalization and mediation: the two operations are companions. Generalization is the result primarily of population growth; mediation, of the multiplicity of means available to accomplish just about anything. Rulers no longer declare war; war breaks out irrespective of anyone's (including Hitler's) decision because certain conditions exist. No employer willfully oppresses his workers; economic necessities exist which are just as imperious as they are abstractly rational and incomprehensible. Revolt is sheer stupidity if it turns soldiers against their commanders, whose hands are tied. Instead it ought to rally all ranks against the necessities that create wars and govern the lives of everyone. The same applies to exploited or unemployed workers who are merely flailing the air when they burn the boss's effigy or lock him in his office. As individuals tormented by abstract necessities, they ought to be probing the question of revolution.

Within a mediated and totally abstract system, no person or persons can be held responsible, no *single* organism can be blamed. Revolution therefore consists in attacking all instruments of mediation which alienate human beings from one another and from society. But resurgent spontaneity, a liberating explosion, or an upheaval is a futile response, a piteous masquerade and barren eroticism passing for revolution. An abstract and mediated world cannot face the ordeal of revolution until theory has superseded abstraction. The nature of our society is such that revolution requires an exact and rigorous system of thought. There again the situationists were right: "Revolutionary organization must present a unitary criticism of society—that is, criticism that does not compromise with any branch of power anywhere, an unrelenting criticism of every aspect of alienated social existence. . . . Proletarian revolution hinges upon the necessity that, for the first time, theory, which is the understanding of human experience, must be acknowledged and acted upon by the masses." It is essential at the outset to establish a critical theory. "Critical theory must speak its own language, the language of contradiction, which is dialectic in form as well as in substance. It is totally and historically critical." Debord [17] rightly relates the indispensability of theory to the inevitably unitary or global nature of revolution reaching out to oppose the entire culture and the entire society. "That unified critical theory alone is capable of confronting the unity of social practice."

One additional feature of our society points to one of the aims of revolution. The world we live in is extraordinarily rigid. On that score, the misconceptions abound. Sociologists and the average person consider society to be in a state of flux, subject to incessant changes, developments, and variations. We see constant technological advance; sudden shifts from agrarian to industrial societies, or rural to urban ones; spectacular demographic or economic expansions; bigger and faster airplanes every year; political regimes running riot and unable to extricate themselves from their own morass; ideologies, philosophies, and aesthetic creeds whose life cycle is but a few years; revolutions erupting everywhere; dissent ruling a society in which values are gone and nothing is sacred. All that is real enough, but significant only in reference to the mounting pace of our own lives and to the barrage of inflammatory information which assaults us. That is, we con-

---

[17] Debord, op. cit., pp. 99 *ff.*; pp. 164 *ff.*

sider the accelerated transformation of our world to be real
and the salient feature of our society because that is what we
are told, that is the fabric and the spectacle of our daily
existence, and that is what feeds our unrest. We live at a faster
pace, see more and more people, have more and more to do,
rush from the telephone to the dictaphone, and because we
"live" faster we interpret the social pace as change and that
change as characteristic. Unfortunately, it is an optical illusion
created by the parade of events.[18] Those rapid changes are
the superficial phenomena of current events. The most obvious
changes occur in that manner, not the most significant ones.
But we always fall back on the notion that what is dramatic is
more important than what is abiding and not immediately
manifest.

Other thoughtful observers maintain that the social structures are malleable if we are determined to alter them and to
utilize the tools of technology.[19] Efficient use of economic or
planning devices thus would elasticize the structures somewhat; the material, institutional, and cultural systems would
become more tangible and operate more smoothly, their added
resources allowing for desired alterations. That position has
the merit of not asserting that we are in a period of great
flux and also of emphasizing the voluntary nature of the
effort. But unquestionably some misunderstanding exists as
to the structures themselves: if we were to ease one or more
of them (which is entirely possible), might not others, perhaps
more pervasive and vital, be fortified? The key is in the facts
themselves. I believe (and have tried to say so often enough)
that the basic structure is technology, upon which the other
equally decisive factors hinge: the state, the city, transpor-
tation, manipulation, and organization. Those phenomena have

---

[18] Which explains why those bold "experts" on the Ecumenical Council,
with their pre-eminent concern for the Christian presence in "a rapidly shifting
society," were totally wrong both from a theological and from a sociological
point of view.
[19] See principally Claude Gruson, *Origines et espoirs de la planification
française*, 1967.

shown no significant change; or, shall we say, the change has been steady, predictable, and always in the same direction. Nowhere has the state become less of a state, less powerful or less managerial. Technology never regresses: it is increasingly the axis of our society. Absolutely nothing supports the notion of a world in flux. Change affects two sectors: one is the Third World, which is fast replacing its institutions, its values, and its customs with the framework of Western civilization: the state, technology, urban life, and the rest. Forms occupy the other sector. Of course, there are many apparent changes, but they are only *transformations*, modified aspects of institutions or ideologies, the basic elements and structures of which remain intact. Whether a state system follows the American or the Russian pattern is of no consequence; the state, not its constitution, is all that matters. Whether technology is decreed or is applied through psychological pressure, through alluring promises of its benefits, or through rational means makes little difference. The exodus of rural populations appears to be a fundamental alteration, but as such is no longer true *at the present time*. Civilization's development was broken in the mid-nineteenth century when populations concentrated in urban and industrial centers, but no distinct change has interrupted its steady evolution since then. The social edifice has not been altered, and everything we now find startling is simply an outgrowth of that mutation. Yet we persist in believing that change occurs constantly and that society's complex operation defies our understanding, whereas in fact it is mere shadow play, orderly and predictable activity, rational development radiating from a century-old impulse, and a visible leveling process affecting the obsolete forms of firmly rooted structures.

We must take cognizance of the extraordinary stability of our institutions. This society rests upon solid girders constantly being reinforced. Every tremor marking an economic, or fiscal, or intellectual, or administrative shift serves to fortify various technical skills, all of which combine to produce the phe-

nomenon of technology. Technology never retreats and is
never challenged. A change unquestionably is taking place:
Gruson, speaking of our potentially malleable structures, calls
them a "shell." For a long time society seemed to be enclosed
in a matrix or sheath—that is, held rigid by external pressures.
I believe that over the past twenty years an internal change
has occurred: the shell has become a skeleton. As a result, we
no longer experience it as a restraint or a constriction, and
now the entire field of technical development seems to be the
essential component, the very core of the change. But that
has not affected the intrinsic stability, inflexibility, or permanence of the structures. As a matter of fact, the internalization
of the social organism, whether it takes the form of psychological manipulation, or of administrative or urban organization, makes our structures more tolerable as well as more
exacting.

Thus no basis exists for saying the world is in upheaval:
revolution is concerned not with the existing turmoil, but with
the purely formal and superficial nature of that turmoil. Revolution must attack the roots of structures, their implacable
development, and their rigidity. A measure of flexibility must
be found, a responsiveness among the specific organs, implying
interference from two sources, both of which are disclaimed
as unreliable: *the arbitrary nature of personal judgment,*
and *the experience of passion.* The two expressions are totally
unscientific and may have a valid bearing on meaningful
revolution. One involves the intellect, the other the emotions.
Both imply a reaffirmation of personal choice, a return to
individualized history, and the obvious risk of mass regression.
Given the extraordinary stability and durability of our social
structures, a revolution that does not attack their roots and
attempt to establish mobility, fluidity, uncertainty, and hence
inefficacy, is not a revolution. The multiple implications need
to be understood. An attack at that level aimed at re-
establishing arbitrary judgment and passionate experience
has nothing to do with the superficial irrationality of modern

poetry or the kind of decorous erotomania practiced in the gathering places of the forward set. Revolution must unhinge the foundations of those structures; otherwise any attempt we make to ease various parts of the system is sheer display and self-indulgence.

Finally, we must consider where this revolution can take place. If, indeed, our society's function is to make it, and if no other revolution can accomplish the same purpose, then it can occur only in the West. If a plan for revolution must be designed to combat the most advanced form of human destruction, then only where such a form and such a society exist is it possible to project and to implement the plan, if feasible. The general view is that revolution most likely will occur in the Third World. Those countries, however, are farthest from a technological, industrial, and statist civilization; a revolution in any one of them therefore stands no chance of getting to the root of the problem. The outcome would be a certain measure of independence, a better way of life perhaps, but not revolution, simply because those countries have not experienced the conditions and the structures that revolution must attack. To visualize revolution, we must see it in the European setting and in terms of Western civilization (including the United States, Europe, and the U.S.S.R., which now has reached approximately the same standard of values and the same economic development and structural penetration). But revolutionary action in such an advanced situation would rule out any hope of rallying the Asian or African peoples to revolutionary aims that they cannot possibly comprehend.

If we narrow the problem to the most advanced sector of Western society, that is where revolutionary thinking must develop: in relation to Western society, as a function of the probabilities existing there and because of their results (visible in Europe, but totally imperceptible, even from afar, in Latin America or Africa). Revolution involving Indian peoples in the American hemisphere, or Africans, is a rear-guard action—

that is, one concerned with events in the past. This does not mean that we should not help Africa or Latin America to solve its own problems; it means that revolutionary action is not the answer to them. They are not the countries in which the single necessary revolution is likely to erupt. However, a revolution designed after the most advanced sector of Western society will also affect African, Asian, and other nations. Not directly or fundamentally (though perhaps on the side, and into the bargain) by easing the strain of their relations with Western technological civilization, but mainly to the extent that those countries already have chosen a European pattern of development and European (revolutionary!) standards of value: Nasser and Fanon are proof of that. But if those values, those achievements, and the whole thrust of that civilization are attacked, the peoples of the Third World may have cause to reconsider their choice.

From the standpoint of basic social structures, all dependent on technology, the West sets the pattern. The rest of the world plainly is developing in relation to that pattern. Even China has been obliged to imitate it, and will continue to do so more and more, though she has tried to find a substitute. In an effort to break the mold, intellectuals are always talking about the primacy of politics and insisting that by changing the political system we can change everything else. That is pure exorcism: they cannot change the facts, so they dream up situations and doctrines totally irrelevant to reality, persuading themselves that political struggle will change something. Until technology's primacy in society shall have been *negated* (and not merely in terms of hypothetical value judgments), Western civilization will remain the prototype of world development. Consequently, the rest of the world will evolve in direct relationship to Western evolution (without reference to neocolonialism, imperialism, or other such superficial factors). Revolution must be conceived in these terms: it will be achieved by the West or not at all.

To summarize the foregoing:

Because revolution must act *against*, and not in response to, an alleged or pseudo-revolutionary situation; because revolution must act against the most advanced sector of civilization, against its most certain course of development, and not against forces already overcome, in defunct situations, it cannot be *conceived* of anywhere but in the West; it has to be envisaged in relation to the most developed sector of our civilization (which is ultimately universal). For we must think about revolution before making it; at least we now realize that today's revolution is not a manifest necessity: it does not arise from a sudden rebellious impulse and is no longer an overwhelming human need. Necessary revolution can result only from careful preparation, conscious awareness, and determined efforts. Today there is no urgent revolutionary imperative. Revolution can be experienced as a necessity only by habitual ascetics and those who have exercised extreme self-discipline—failing that, "revolutionary" action is merely the result of propaganda, or simply "action," and not revolutionary at all.

The Aims of Revolution

Our society has acquired a dozen different names: the industrial society, the consumer society, the Great Society, the affluent society, the repressive society, the society of spectacle, the bureaucratic society, the service society, the bourgeois society, the class society, and many more. It seems to me that all the descriptions are fragmentary, or else incomplete and partial, and that more essential and more decisive features should be considered. Our society is basically technological and statist; all its characteristics point to that, and therefore if a necessary revolution is to be brought about, it will have to be founded upon the realities of technology and the state. Similarly, the social features that determine the nature of revolution are related to technology. Any other revolution of a social or economic type (and, in particular, hinging upon the class struggle) is, *at the present time* (I insist upon that specification, as I am not formulating eternal truths), superficial, inadequate, and inconsequential. No other revolution warrants a mass mobilizing effort because its aims are false and it will not change anything—except the roster of management, the select few who stand to profit from the idyll of technology, and the pace of technological advance. That is all, and is not enough today to make revolution a matter for serious consideration in view of the fundamental difficulties it poses.

But our society is more than technological. As the various techniques developed in one ever-broadening sector, at first along parallel, then along converging, lines, the power of the state also developed. We have indicated Marx's failure to identify that as the true course of history. Because the two phenomena tended to pervade the entire society, they were bound to meet and to become assimilated. We can no longer say that "politics controls technology," or envisage the state dissolved in the class superstructures. Each has been altered by the other. Technology has become the basis of political policy; the state has been technologized extensively.[20] Any revolution attacking the state also would have to attack technology. Any revolution against the perils and the bondage of technological society implies an attempt to disassemble the state. An ordinary political revolution is bound to reinforce the state, as we have asserted at some length. An ordinary revolution involving modes of existence would not weaken the system's coordinating power. For the system has two structural levels: the spontaneous, unconscious one on which the various branches of technology develop and interact, pursuing their own life cycle with no intent to produce a particular type of society; and the conscious and voluntary one on which the state organizes society for the purpose of coordinating and utilizing techniques to the greatest extent possible. The modern state is no longer the symbol of "political power," or of a class or social group: it has become the motor of a globalized, unitary, and all-embrac-

---

[20] Cf. J. Ellul, *The Technological Society; The Political Illusion.*

ing society of which it is also the inseparable expression. Technology and the state combined influence and mold individuals, too—through psychological and psychosociological pressures [e.g., propaganda]. These, then, are the three targets of revolution, the forces and structures against which it must act. It "must": for any other attitude would be futile, or a parody of revolution. The state is the most vital issue today, for it is the only factor in harmony with technological development.

It has been demonstrated often that technological progress challenges economic structures and growth, and that technological rationality can contradict economic rationality. Economic development must relate to technology (the latter accounts for the disappearance of private capitalism). Yet technology always supports the state, bolstering its inherent power and reinforcing it with each new stride in scientific development. In that respect, necessary revolution today should espouse the antistatist tradition. Proudhon, Bakunin, and even Marx in certain passages, have had their say; we are ashamed to criticize the state because its power and influence have increased so greatly in the past century. Marx stated: "The state is a parasite feeding on society and paralyzing its free will" (Paris Commune), and Engels: "A free society cannot sanction the presence of the state dividing it from its members" (Utopian Socialism).

Today it is evident that the state is not a parasite, but is the very keystone of our universe, of our economic existence, of all our satisfactions, and that instead of separating society from its members, it integrates them. A yet imperfect state, but our only wish is to perfect it—that is, to eliminate its failings. There is less evidence than ever of a revolutionary plan directed against the state, and an ever-increasing need for one. Such a plan implies total rejection of the revolutionary state, or of a temporary state destined to wither as socialism develops or a proletarian dictatorship evolves—which is also a state. We saw what came of that. Bakunin [21] was absolutely

---

[21] Bakunin, letter to *La Liberté* (newspaper), October 5, 1872, following the Hague Conference of the First International.

right: "The inevitably revolutionary policy of the proletariat must aim at destroying states. We cannot conceive of international solidarity while states exist—unless it is a vision of the universal state, that is, universal bondage . . . the state's basic impulse being to disrupt that solidarity. Nor can we conceive of proletarian freedom or a genuine liberation of the masses within the state and through its agency. The state means domination, and domination implies the captivity of the masses." Repudiating Marx's projected dictatorship, he said: "I wonder how Marx failed to see that establishing a universal mass dictatorship . . . a dictatorship under the eye of some chief engineer of world revolution whose task it would be to control and to direct mass rebellions in every country . . . that establishing such a dictatorship would be enough to kill revolution." Truer than ever today, and also more difficult, if not impossible, an objective. Because of its nature, the modern state is one of the crucial targets of revolutionary opposition.

Statism in all its forms destroys individuality. The state becomes more tyrannical as it becomes more abstract. Man delegates to the state his responsibility for solving the problems of his society and is trapped thereby in the rigorous and inhuman system. That is the issue, and there is no chance that one day a state will repent and become liberal or personal, the servant of man. It is mortal combat, the outcome of which perhaps already is decided. We must recognize the scope, the odds, and the enormousness of present-day revolution. The growth of nationalism has been a greater factor than state power. "Death to nationalism!" used to be a revolutionary slogan. Its revival is urgently called for today, for the world is more nationalistic than ever. In that respect, socialism failed: national socialism is a thing of the past, and all the so-called socialist countries are hypernationalist. It is remarkable that, in 1944, nations existed wholly fabricated by the treaties of 1918. The U.S.S.R. could have dissolved them easily by taking a revolutionary stand. But they were kept on, with somewhat altered frontiers. Communism has made a practice of reinforcing nationalism. Gomulka was essentially a nationalist; the more independent of the Soviet Union he became, the less liberal he was. In the Socialist Republics, nationalism, bolstered by the U.S.S.R., is now turning against its patron. The Czech crisis was not Marxist in any sense; it had to do with conflicting nationalisms. It is highly amusing to hear the U.S.S.R. issuing grave warnings against nationalism, to Cuba (April 1968) and to Czechoslovakia, while she herself behaves like a rabid nationalist.

Nationalism's triumph in the socialist camp facilitates mass mobilizations in behalf of an abstract ideal. Communism set out to use nationalism as a tool, but underestimated the force of that cult or structure: nationalism became the fundamental reality while communism was being reduced to furnishing the most efficient means of enhancing and developing the nation. In the end, nationalism has destroyed the ideological force and revolutionary impulse of communism. The Communist "summit" reached that bitter conclusion in March 1968. Maoist philosophy also has been shown to derive more from nationalism than from Marxism.[22] North Vietnamese resistance, too, is more nationalist-inspired than communist. Africa provides the best example. No African nations existed; colonialism concocted the various conglomerations of tribes, kingdoms, and territories, mapping out boundaries that are absurd in every respect: geographically, linguistically, ethnologically, and politically. But with independence, those totally artificial groups plunged into an orgy of nationalism. Determined to become nations, they adopted the European ideology and colonialist structures. African nationalism is Europe's most costly gift to Africa and manifests the Africans' utter servility to their former colonizers. They are as passionate as the early nineteenth-century nationalists and will not brook the slightest threat to their "national framework." The war against Katanga,

---

[22] Schramm, in *Preuves*, No. 198.

the repression of separatist maneuvers in Cameroon, the atrocious massacre of the Biafrans and of the South Sudanese peoples, the Palestine conflict—all stem from the delirium of nationalism. They remind us that nationalism is still the same.

People used to assure me that there are two kinds of nationalism, one indefensible, illustrated by the older European nations, the other constructive and an aid to liberating newly decolonized peoples; to which I would reply that the two have identical sociological, psychological, and political features, and that the differences between them are altogether ephemeral and superficial. I also pointed out that the consequences of nationalism are inevitably the same. Unfortunately, the socialist crisis and the Biafran massacres have borne out my predictions all too well. But no one dares attack nationalism directly, and it has become the central belief of our times. To disguise its failure, communists and the current "revolutionary" camp identify imperialism as the target of revolution. We should realize, however, that although imperialism is indeed a *reality* and must be opposed, it has become an alibi in our society—which was not true for Rosa Luxemburg or for Lenin. Calling imperialism the major foe today is a distortion of fact. But the Left has no choice: it cannot question the validity of nationalism, which is now its frame of reference as well as the cornerstone of its architecture. The current Marxist movement, whatever its label, has been defeated by nationalism. Yet today nationalism accounts for a greater share of human alienation than it did when Marx attacked it. Revolution must renew the struggle against it.

In speaking of the expanding state, its unmistakable totalitarianism, and its affiliation with nationalist fervor as the essential element of revolutionary thinking and organization, we include, of course, the familiar society of repression, which is simply one facet of a statist society. My criticism of the idea of a repressive society is the fact that it is an idea: its penetrating analysis provides an escape from the harsh and brutal reality of the modern state, which may be identified far more accurately by its institutions than by its doctrines.

The second phenomenon that should serve as the focal point of revolutionary thinking and determination is the development of technology and the transformation of society into a technological and technologized body.[23] I would simply mention that this implies a society based on consumption, affluence, and organization, and that if the price we must pay for technological progress seems excessive, those positive aspects are the very ones we reject.

A genuine revolution is called for today against increased and improved organization. I prefer that word to bureaucracy. Our pseudo-revolutionary contemporaries are anti-bureaucratic, a typically bourgeois posture in which they specialize. For over a century the bourgeoisie has never ceased to decry the administration, government officials, and the bureaucracy. Do we need to be reminded of the Quibolle legacy? But organizational distortions, malfunctions, and rigidity are not the issue. That attitude is simplistic and obsolete. Organization is precisely what tends to replace bureaucracy, filling the same function, but more versatile, discriminating, intelligent, and visibly adaptive, which serves only to fortify the system and to improve its operation. I have some misgivings about Crozier's efforts to exorcise the hollow specter of bureaucracy and to install a sane and efficient man-made organization, and even more when it comes to the presumptuous reform of the E.N.A. in 1968 aimed at producing a breed of organizational experts.

By challenging technology we also challenge the affluent society (i.e., a society possessing an excess of material things, theoretically useful, but unassimilable and ultimately overwhelming, providing human beings with immediate pleasures and satisfactions, but also with a false sense of security and a false sense of achievement by stifling their ambition) and, to an even greater extent, the consumer society, in which all things are regarded as articles for consumption, and consumption acquires value and meaning as well as justification—the

---

[23] Cf. J. Ellul, *The Technological Society.*

consumption of religion, of leisure, of revolution, for example. The consumer's plight is at issue: he is in a corner and has no choice but to consume. It is simply the other face of the affluent society. We should recognize, however, that rejecting that type of society entails self-denial, a choice, an acceptance of poverty (material as well as spiritual and intellectual), and I am not sure that our young people are prepared to give up their cars, their bathrooms, their phonograph records, or their transistor radios. We cannot avoid the issue by saying that the possession of those objects is not the important thing and that it is *society's* attitude and orientation which forces us into a passive role. I am afraid that individual orientations account for the superabundance of pleasure-giving products; if we did not want them to begin with, they would probably not be produced, and society's orientation would be different.[24] Let us not forget the perpetual connivance between the individual (even the dissenter) and the existing social conditions. Many critics of the consumer society are members of the exclusive intellectual sect and worshippers of the divine Marquis de Sade. Yet his sole accomplishment was to display man as an object of consumption. Invoking Sade is a glaring badge of pseudo-revolution.

Revolution against the technological society is at once a revolution *against the society of spectacle,* so cogently described by the situationists,[25] wherein everything is a spectacle (not films and TV alone). "The spectacle is not just an array of images; it is a social relationship shared by people and mediated by images." But so significant a merger as that between the state and technology requires human intervention, and ultimately it alters only man. The gulf separating the system from its inhabitants must be bridged if they are to stop disrupting and impeding it and, instead, to make it work as

---

[24] Cf. Baudrillart's excellent book, *Le Système des objets*, 1969. In any event, it still does not mean that the consumer would call the tune. If individuals were able to resist the impact of advertising and refused to consume, then they would indeed call it.
[25] Cf. Debord, *La Société du Spectacle.*

efficiently as possible. Man is not ready for that. It has to be done. The over-all technological system is the instrument and the state is the operator, and both are oriented in that direction. It is the true source of man's present alienation and dehumanization. If revolution is to be human, inspired by man's passionate defiance, if its essence is to permit man to exist even for the brief instant of his glory, that alienation (not the alienation Marx defined a century ago) is what revolution must assail, and that dehumanization (not the version cited by those who deride the system of objects and the consumer society and who are rather short-sighted). By attacking the state, revolution is not affirming the age-old view of the state as the *avitum malum, potestatis cupido.* For the latter is an entirely new entity, one that Hobbes and Hegel envisaged but never experienced. If revolution contests the fabric of technological society, that is not because technology is innately evil (an absurd notion, which I have never suggested); the issue is not technology *per se,* but the present structure of society. If revolution orients itself thus, it is because the merger of the modern state and technological society is inevitable—and because the combination inevitably produces alienated and dehumanized members of society, as it *cannot help doing.* The following will summarize the essential points (I have dealt with the subject in detail elsewhere).[26]

In this perspective, revolution must act against *the mounting ascendancy of groups over individuals.* I am concerned here not with the over-all problem of society, but rather with the prevailing attitude that an individual must be part of a group or be nothing: community-mindedness, team spirit (in the individual's immediate circle of existence), group projects, and group leisures. People who claim that intellectual or scientific pursuits now require "teamwork," who set up religious and political action "committees," who hold that individuals can do nothing on their own, are manifesting not a socialist

[26] J. Ellul, *Propaganda,* 1960 (trans. 1965); "Signification des relations humaines dans une société technologique," *L'Année Sociologique,* 1965.

attitude, but the developmental conditions of a technological
society such as ours. They are molding themselves in the image
of their own necessities. Their reasoning is totally confused:
the combining of individuals into groups is represented as a
revolutionary concept (specifically by identifying it with
socialism and hypostasizing the principle that man exists only
through and in his relationships to others), but it is, in reality,
merely a reaffirmation of the imperatives governing the
operation of our structures.

The current view that the public interest supersedes
personal interest, that society's (and not the individual's)
needs are the only relevant ones, and that individual fulfillment can be found only in a group, has all the trappings of
a myth. It is a perfectly rational and even scientific carry-over
from the classic myth of personal sacrifice for the good of the
community—the old story of Iphigenia, or that of the Aztecs
obeying a cosmogony according to which the dying sun
needed fresh blood each evening in order to rise again, whence
the imperative of human sacrifice. The victims did not protest.
Everyone acknowledged the necessity of the sun, and its rising
was of vital concern to the community, so what difference did
one individual's life make? The victim surely was not a
victim because he made it possible for the others to go on
living. It is the old dictum "Better for one man to die than for
a people to perish." It is the same myth-bound reasoning we
encounter in Hitlerites or communists who declare: "At the
cost of one or two generations, we shall have paradise on
earth." It also applies to American social psychologists who
deny the individuality of persons outside a group, or to
socialists who recognize social needs alone. It is myth-making
based on ancient sources and has no rational foundation.

Of course, if revolution occurs, it must oppose all attempts
to integrate individuals into the totalitarian social body by
means of intermediary groups and communities. But that
integration operates through an extraordinarily complex network of psychological devices ranging from harmless public

assistance to tranquilizing propaganda. Revolution must aim at *countering the psycho-sociological manipulation* which is part of the spectacle. A certain spontaneity helps to create the society of spectacle, but also a deliberate effort to absorb the human community through propaganda, psychological pressures, public relations, as well as through a frenzied barrage of information which is not beneficial because it imprisons man (by distorting his perspective) in a purely fictional universe—and, strangely enough, it also arouses hostility to *a society of culture* in which artistic and intellectual creativity has lost its authority and meaningfulness, and in turn has become mere consumption, illusion, triviality, diversion, and mystification.

Revolution's target must not be the distortion of culture, but the culture itself, just as we saw at the end of the eighteenth century. Many ardent rebels would agree, but as they are "for" the Third World and progress, they are bent on educating "underdeveloped" nations—which is sheer conformity. If we contest *our own* culture, we automatically contest the validity of what we write and what we teach. If we repudiate our own culture, we cannot wish to re-create elsewhere the conditions which gave rise to it. A revolutionary attitude demands coherence—not the urge to paint a mustache on the *Mona Lisa*.

Finally, revolution also will have to combat *the tendency of individuals to control one another*. Let us recall just a few facets of our multifaceted modern ideology: it undermines confidence and hope invested in the state, calls on the state to take care of everything, and blames the state when something goes wrong; it condemns nationhood projected as a value and the creed of progress and efficiency; it opposes moral and rational laxity and the indulgence of inclinations, emotions, and tastes (when men lose their inhibitions, they can never gather their wits together for a revolution, let alone a festive one!); it contests the growing need for consumption and for modern conveniences; it is against all ideologies and ideology itself, the world of illusions, "a fantasy of the universe validated by universal abstraction and the effective dictatorship of illusion" (Debord), whether religious or political, philosophic or aesthetic, surrealism or socialism, fascism or productivism, faith in progress or faith in technology, or a nostalgic retreat into happy memories of the past. It also rejects the idea of roles, a widely accredited idea which is the most anti-revolutionary and conformist of all, yet is backed, of course, by overwhelming evidence, namely, that man not only has, but *is,* a role. A neat solution to the problem, for what is dead cannot be revived, and man absorbed in his role ceases to exist. The most elaborate and painstaking psychological studies of roles, said to offer the ultimate definition of the relation of individuals to society, conceal a treacherous assault on humanity and on revolution. Today science serves to disguise everything. Nevertheless, man must refuse to be his role, and revolution must attack all roles.

In other words, it is apparent from the previous remarks that revolution acts not only against organizations, institutions, systems, and structures, but also, and concurrently, against each *member* of this society, his behavior, and his beliefs. Acting at the same time against and for him—to release him from his myths of money, of the nation, of work, of the state, or of socialism—from the chains he worships (gilded perhaps, but still chains). Finally, let us not overlook the ideology of revolution which leads inevitably to terror.[27] It is one thing to hunger spiritually for revolution and to risk one's life for it in an absurd gamble; it is something else to believe in it, to rave about it, to wrap oneself in a dream of it, to talk of nothing else, to join a handful of others in stirring up the fires of hatred and violence; or else to regard it as the most obvious, banal, and ordinary fact of life and a theme for sociologists. When revolution does occur, those dreamers and pseudo-

[27] Cf., among others, Merleau-Ponty, *Humanisme et terreur;* Klossowsky; and the recent book by Lefèbvre, *La Vie quotidienne dans le monde moderne,* 1968.

scientists are the terrorists. The current attitude to terrorism generally fails to account for revolutionary ideology as an inexhaustible source of terrorism fed by the complacency of those who give in to it. If revolution is to come about in our society, it must contest vulgarized revolutionary ideology. "Revolutionary theory is now the alert and declared enemy of revolutionary ideology" (Debord).

I know the type of criticism I have aroused, and the complaints that I have presented only *negative* objectives, the targets of revolution, and nothing else: for what, then, should it be made? The simplest answer might be that whereas I did not specify for *what*, I indicated directly and indirectly (my approach being on both those levels) for *whom* it must be made. Aside from that, I have two reasons for not proposing any positive and constructive plan. The first is this: technology has become the instrument of all action. In other words, just as revolutionary movements spanning the past two centuries frequently have destroyed one power and consistently have created a greater one, culminating in the establishment of the state, so today revolutionary action (because action is now exclusively technique) can serve only to perfect certain techniques (e.g., street-fighting, which effectively integrates individuals by teaching them conditioned reflex actions: the basic principle of Hitler's army) and to advance technological society. Therefore no program of action can help us to discern and to implement necessary revolution.

The second reason should be apparent by now: the global and profound nature of necessary revolution precludes the ordinary political or social approaches to it. No constitutional reform, no party system, no economic reorganization, and no class struggle will bring us any nearer the authentic revolution. We may try the lot of them, of course, and perhaps come up with a few minor transformations to tranquillize our fitful slumber. We can always launch vast movements for the sake of noble ideals and be assured of a gaping audience. And the

lot certainly contains some generous impulses and worthy
values which, when proclaimed, are easier to integrate into
the system. But none of that will bring us anywhere near the
revolution that must be lived now.

Next you will say, With no program and no positive action,
tell us at least the values we strive for. Impossible. The stock-
pile of time-honored values, such as justice and truth, is
already there. What can I add? Formulating values serves
no purpose in any case, and is simply another alibi: a way to
be off somewhere else and not feel concerned. There is no
value to be obtained. There is an organized stand to be made
against a monumental assault, against a mutation that I consider negative. Must we always come back to that? Is a
physician struggling *against* disease doing a negative job
because he is *against*? As I see it, the negative character of
what I ask revolution to combat makes the struggle itself
positive. Yet in order to be positive, no new value or program
is required.

Next you will say that my approach is purely defensive,
hence conservative—lo, that monstrous word is out! Again I
say no, for I see no hope of conserving: only of conquering.
We must move ahead. Think of the physician again: in combatting disease, is he seeking to re-establish the state of health
that preceded it? No, for he is aware that his patient's body
(as well as his state of mind) has changed, and that with
health restored it will gain a *new* equilibrium but will never
be the same. Moreover, the battle against disease stimulates
therapeutic research and the discovery of new remedies,
making that aspect a positive and "progressive" one. Indeed,
it is the only genuinely progressive one. Modern progressivism
is but a faint response to the over-all social situation. Our
sole concern is to be resolved that, in the technostatist assault
on human beings, we shall recover the humanity in each of
us (and not some phantom or futuristic mythical image we
picked up along the way), and shall defend ourselves. We
must recognize the invasion as a plague (instead of as the

supreme gift enabling man "to realize himself," the ultimate
illusion that technology fosters through manipulation). That
is why necessary revolution, although it entails no values,
program, or strategy, has nevertheless a precise focus.

The Focus of Revolution

Nothing short of an explosion will disintegrate the technological society: that is the vital issue. Whatever form the explosion
takes (a federalist community, or self-direction hostile to
planning, for example) will involve, as always, a sacrifice. A
revolution against the technological society (not against technology) implies decreased efficiency in all areas (total yield,
productivity, adaptiveness, integration), a lowered standard
of living, the reduction of large-scale public programs, and the
erosion of a mass culture. If we are unwilling to pay the combined price of those four reductions, then we are not ready for
revolution, the only revolution that is a necessity today. If
we are willing to pay it, we must start by ridding ourselves
of certain ideologies conveyed by commonplaces. For only in
that revolution man can rediscover himself and history. As
Debord has expressed it so well: "When ideology, which is
the abstract desire for the ideal, and its illusion become
justified by abstract universality and the effective rule of
illusion in modern society, it no longer represents the determined struggle against fragmentation, but instead the
culmination of it. . . . [I]deology, heeding its inner totalitarian drive . . . now has achieved its purpose in the motion-
less spectacle of non-history." [28] The issue is not ideology
per se, but the ideology of the technological society, which
alone reflects it. Our revolutionary plan now has three orientations, which I shall merely summarize, having discussed
them elsewhere. First, the rediscovery of individual autonomy.

---

[28] Debord, op. cit., p. 171.

I insist on using that expression despite its general discredit. It is absolutely essential today to restore consciousness in the individual that he *is* an individual, and ought not to feel guilty about rejecting community, collectivity, politics, or social ideals. I know there is value in all of them, but my attitude pertains to a specific historical situation: our own. I maintain that here and now, only one value is essential and efficacious: the redemption of individuality and, to take it a step farther, of uniqueness. Anything else is conformity and is already incorporated into the technological system. We are not concerned with persons, who represent a set of philosophic superstructures, but with the blunt and harsh reality of man's existence in relation to his fellow-men, to his destiny, and to his environment: let him know his isolation and assess things as best he can. Until that focus obtains, nothing can be done— all institutional or economic appraisals being mere evasions and alibis.

In another book,[29] I have dealt with the reasons why, in the political arena, and because of technological penetration of the state, the most hopeful solution, at once concrete and revolutionary, lies in the revival of citizenship, a reawakening to the virtues of individuality, and the cultivation of democratic human beings. As a matter of fact, my opinion has had very little impact because it calls for assuming direct personal responsibility—a distinctly disagreeable affair—instead of invoking a higher authority. Obviously, if we are to break the spell of technology, we will have to use makeshift devices, the real and meaningful value of which is their very lack of efficiency. Yet asking men to be individuals in a society such as ours is like invoking familiar images acceptable to a decadent bourgeoisie afflicted with socialism. I firmly repudiate any kinship with that species, and the individuality we strive for is totally different. But it means defying the mainstream of opinion (i.e., the ideology wedded to technology), and in the

---

[29] *The Political Illusion*, Chapter viii.

end it produces nothing (the young people do not seem to grasp even the meaning of individuality) and causes all sorts of misunderstandings. Everyone assumes he is behaving like a Responsible Person, whereas he is merely a single faithful copy in an edition of thousands off the great cerebral press, or out of the cookie cutter.[30] Thus revolution's only possible focus is upon the development of consciousness.

Technology results from a variety of intellectual processes, scientific discoveries, and planned observations. Technological society goes a step farther by combining involuntarily a multitude of techniques, with unanticipated and startling results. The effort to disintegrate the technological society, and at the same time to master technology, must be a conscious and intelligent one, presupposing a state of mental awareness. However, one of the features of man in a technological society and in a mass culture is his decayed self-awareness—the result of mass imagery, manipulation, a retreat from serious responsibilities, over-specialization, and other factors. Conscious effort [31] alone has no effect whatever on technology and science.

Similarly, revolution cannot result uniquely from individual awakenings to the global nature of society. It is pointless to say that purely spontaneous revolutions have occurred in the past, or that man's continuous social existence accounts for his semi-awareness: yesterday is not today. The aggression he must contend with now is calculated and manifestly willful. Only reason and intelligence can combat it. We have reached the stage of rational organization; a revolution cannot be founded on irrationality, and demands greater discipline than ever. No longer can revolution be made by doing the

---

[30] My combined allusion here is to President Johnson's "Great Society" and Mao's "Theory of Molds."

[31] Le Lannou implies the same thing in speaking of "voluntary geography," which he contrasts with a territorial arrangement that is abstract, theoretical, and technical. "Voluntary geography in terms of artificial projections often has proved its own bankruptcy, and today we can rely on its basic institutions as likely to induce spontaneous industrialization." A countercurrent that could be decisive, aleatory as it is.

opposite. In our present stage of development, technical skill can salvage explosive irrationality, can integrate and utilize it. That would be propaganda's function, for example, to make rational use of spontaneous impulses.

The global society also can turn surrealism or existentialism to its own profit. Anything *less rigorous than that society* is its slave. Without consciousness, we are condemned to the technological system and to be used by it. The obvious risk of adopting such an attitude, however, is that we may take on an efficiency role and thus conform to the society under attack. Cultivating a precise awareness of that society, knowing its mechanics and its tendencies as well as its vulnerable points may induce further adaptation and the desire to reform society. We must go beyond that stage. Consciousness of reality is not enough [32]; no matter how far it takes us, it is only the first step. Consciousness *per se* is a necessity; without it, we can do nothing, but it must promote voluntary acts based on conscious behavior. We must appraise the situation, assess its implication insofar as revolutionary action is concerned, know the price or consequences we may have to pay, rid ourselves of any delusions of guaranteed success, use every ounce of moral fiber at our command—and not stop there.

If we view scientific progress in a revolutionary focus, our awareness and our reasoning must take the form of conscious and deliberate action. Precisely because revolution involves the reaffirmation of individuality, it cannot be assigned to a handful of leaders, to a directive corps, or to an active minority: that would simply reproduce the technological society wherein experts carry out social, economic, and political reform that everyone else has to accept as "the best we can do." Organizing a mass revolutionary party, a nucleus operating by manipulation, a vanguard; using the *coup d'état* as

---

[32] This is the comment I hear so often from students of technology and the state: "Sure, we know all that, but what are we supposed to do?" It is the mark of persons with only a few threadbare, very indistinct, and very detached ideas on technology and politics.

prescribed by Malaparte, Trinquier, or Luttwak,[33] or the revolutionary strategy of Lenin—any one of those merely reinforces the technological system: although opposed to society, such a movement still serves technology, has not altered the over-all orientation, and will be forced to restore society through technology and by rebuilding its power—and the "revolution" will not have happened at all.

In the perspective of revolution, consciousness must be the collective and individual achievement of each member of the revolutionary movement; that is what makes revolutionaries, not their fervor, or courage, or violence, or extremism. I know that the fact is obvious to a great many people. I also know they haven't the faintest notion what it means! They are the ones who believe any and every scrap of information as long as it bolsters their ideas, who give their hearts to a cause, who are swayed by hatred or sympathy, who mouth slogans, who possess an automatic device for testing events (a diagram of the class struggle, for example), and who, in short, display what Lenin called petit-bourgeois behavior. On the other hand, those who know the price of moral integrity and conscious action in our society will say that individual consciousness is an impossibility. It may appear so, but it is that or nothing. Awareness as an individual concern must be associated with another attitude: contemplation.

It would represent a vital breach in the technological society, a truly revolutionary attitude, if contemplation could replace frantic activity. Contemplation fills the void of our society of lonely men. "The art of contemplation produces objects that it regards as signs instead of things—signs leading to the discovery of a different reality. . . . I write to discover," Octavio Paz says, "because contemplation is the art of discovering things that science and technology cannot reveal. Contemplation restores to man the spiritual breadth of which technology divests him, to objects their significance, and to

---

[33] Malaparte, *Technique du coup d'État*, 1936; Trinquier, *Révolte, guerre, révolution*, 1968; E. Luttwak, *Coup d'État: A Practical Handbook*, 1969.

work its functional presence. Contemplation is the key to individual survival today; an attitude of profound contemplation allows actions to redeem their significance and to be guided by something other than systems and objects." That is the way man can recover himself *today*. If you would be genuinely revolutionary *in our society* (I repeat that I am not disclosing a permanent value or an eternal truth), be contemplative: that is the source of individual strength to break the system.

Individual initiative is often cited as a way of making revolution a personal issue. All to the good. But today the usual effort is to arouse irrational, emotional, impulsive, and erotic behavior in a chaotic, explosive, festive, and totally uninhibited atmosphere. The rationale advanced is that if we are to combat a systematized and stultifying society that negates individuality, we should act just the opposite. But it is only a façade. Such explosions have no impact whatever on our society, which is perfectly capable of integrating and absorbing the shock, devitalizing it, diverting its thrust, and molding it into a compensatory system or safety valve. Current erotic or emotional appeals are a retroversion to "primitive" social systems in which festivals acted as social forces. For nine-tenths of the year, life was tightly ordered, each activity, decree, duty, and relationship rigidly detailed. Everything was structured. Because the stringent controls imposed a physical strain, they were lifted and vital energies were restored on the Great Days, the chaos of primitive times.

Whereas those festivals gave license to every excess and irregularity, they were also recognized as occupying a specific time, place, and function. They, too, were a rational element of the system. That is the danger of irrational outbursts for those who regard them as tools of revolution. In reality, our highly touted celebrations are simply a way of consuming objects and time. They serve only to enshrine, within an intellectual and pseudo-revolutionary framework, the supremacy of use and to degrade the value of enduring things.

They express the refined, but also decadent, tastes of the consumer society at its peak. Festivals will no more disrupt society than a bolt on the door will help to open it. They waste time, which all our diversions would have us forget; they have no significance, in a society which drains everything of its significance, and merely help to erode more the distinction between presence and representation, between the atemporal and the historic, between sign and signified object. Far from being revolutionary, therefore, festivals only sanctify the technological society, according it the primacy that makes it liveable and exciting.

Although Freud's work suggests a revolutionary approach to sexual repression, which begins in the family and is perpetuated by a network of social relationships, he was cautious and never indulged in the acrobatic fantasies of Marcuse, not because he was hopelessly bourgeois, but out of recognition of the unreliability of the unconscious, which made repression necessary, and out of a somewhat skeptical view of revolution. He thought that revolution could not "change life," as the reinforced patterns of servility, guilt, and repression would be likely to reappear in seemingly different social surroundings. I accept the logic of that view, whereas "Freudian-Marxist syntheses" strike me as so much haphazard verbiage—but dangerous, still, as all meaningless verbiage is, for they shunt the revolutionary impulse into dead storage, identifying the sexual explosion with revolution, and giving sterile and brutish expression to the whole legacy of revolution.

The triumph of Marcuse merely points to the sterility of the sexual liberation. What he means by "Eros" is never clear to begin with: sexual activity (in the Freudian genital sense), or an aesthetic-sexual mixture of art, sex play, and creative effort, or the whole domain of instinct (which returns us to the age-old problem of reason versus instinct), or else "everything oppressed by civilization." How does one conclude that revolution will occur through Eros and also will liberate it? Of course, the vibrant call for sexual liberty and uninhibited emotions would appeal to young people. But is it not plain that this licensed pan-sexuality, made out to be the highway to revolution, is among the most effective propaganda weapons (the kind that hits below the belt, as Hitler himself put it) and also the most demagogic form of deceit? To redeem spontaneity by that means is senseless regression in terms of revolution—*"Post coitum animal triste"*: that is all we can expect of it, unless an iron fist clamps down on the rampant irrationality, the results of which we have already seen.

We ought not to forget the vast irrational movement of our time which produced public festivals and mindless emotionalism on an incredible scale: National Socialism. The practice of "classifying," and thus dismissing, Nazism should stop, for it represents a real Freudian repression on the part of intellectuals who refuse to recognize what it was. Others lump together Nazism, dictatorship, massacres, concentration camps, racism, and Hitler's folly. That about covers the subject.[34] Nazism was a great revolution: against the bureaucracy, against senility, in behalf of youth; against the entrenched hierarchies, against capitalism,[35] against the petit-bourgeois mentality, against comfort and security, against the consumer society, against traditional morality; for the liberation of instinct, desire, passions, hatred of cops (yes, indeed!), the will to power, and the creation of a higher order of freedom. When I read the following: "The mob disclaims all responsibility, either for those who join it, or for what will happen tomorrow. Their actions and words are free of traditional restraints. They believe what they are doing and saying is simply the truth at the

---

[34] An accurate history of Nazism from A to Z remains to be written. Books such as Shirer's have no value.

[35] The dogmatic and elementary interpretation of Nazism as having been conceived by capitalists to counter communism, and a bourgeois tool in the class struggle, has gained incredibly broad acceptance as a self-evident fact, despite its contradiction of fact. Even after his alliance with certain capitalists, Hitler controlled them as much as they did him. Informed observers of the period between the two World Wars are convinced that National Socialism was an important and authentic revolution. De Rougemont points out how the Hitler and the Jacobin regimes were identical at every level. R. Labrousse, an authority on the French Revolution, confirms that, to cite only two opinions.

moment. . . . I do not represent anyone; I think what I say voices the feelings of the students as a whole. . . . He is a reflection of them just as they are the reflection of science." [36] It takes me back thirty-five years to when I first read Alphonse de Chateaubriant's *Te Deums* to Hitler. I must admit also that the ideas of Marcuse strike me as drenched in the earliest phase of Hitlerist philosophy. There we have the one and only great revolution of irrationality which ever occurred, the great festival (the greatest by far): what it did to reinforce the state, technology, propaganda, and all the rest, is history. Any orientation of that nature will have the same results.

That is why current invocations to irrationalism and to the mystique of revolution fill me with dread. For their only possible outcome was demonstrated by Hitler. The consequences of uncontrolled irrationality are inevitable and predictable. There is no intrinsic virtue in Eros, whereas there is a menace behind those dark forces which were unveiled and used solely for inflicting on mankind the worst disaster it has ever known. What Marcuse has done is sow the seeds of a new Nazism.

We must repudiate all appeals to irrationalism and promises of liberation through the imagination, for one ought not to juggle words and claim that imagination is not the opposite of reason because when imagination *exceeds reverie or ecstasy* its results are enduring and constitute universal forms, whereas reason, in order to be creative, must draw on the imagination.[37] *In theory* that is true, but here imagination is delirium, invoked along with festivals, Eros, desire, and the like. Such appeals are an a priori admission of helplessness and a renunciation of the real revolution. Those who choose that course are convinced that nothing is possible, so they invite everyone to open the floodgates of emotion, to burst the barriers as they see them—hoping that something will come of it. Out of desperation they turn to festivals and Eros,

[36] Claude Lefort, in *La Brèche*, 1968, p. 47.
[37] Coudray, in *La Brèche*, p. 102.

guaranteed losers. It would be to man's credit indeed if he could find true liberty by loosing his emotions and mindless impulses. Consider what the average man has made of countless such opportunities during the past century. Open the doors, eliminate the hierarchies, remove the restraints, call in the unconscious and the irrational, and you invite utter mediocrity and the most contemptible sort of activities.

That ideology, that trust in festivity as an instrument of revolution, may be traced to the notion of revolution as a festival which we discussed earlier. An unconscious belief takes shape: if revolution is a festival, let's start celebrating and we will have a revolution. That is simply a retreat into words, hollow images, trimmings and tinsel, and a pretense that they are real. We already have pointed out the deceit of it.

Irrationality is totally ineffective in contending with our society and can only reinforce the technological system in one way or another. In contrast, necessary awareness means greater self-control, self-denial, intellectual alertness, and persistent determination. There is no place for delirium, only for passion, conviction, and discipline. Today the first step toward revolution should be the battle for reason, which is also an attack on irrationality and on rationalism as well as on all the "cults": Hegel's cult of the state, Fichte's cult of nationalism, and the universal cult of technology. Emmanuel Berl rightly indicates that "we become allies of war [and of man's alienation] in declaring our hostility to reason." [38]

"Peace [and revolution] is a product of wisdom, and wisdom does not reside either in the 'that,' or in the 'superego,' or in the 'pleasure principle,' or in the 'death principle,' but in the principle of reality which acts as a reminder of the world's existence [in its present state] when our impulse and imagination fail to recognize it."

---

[38] Emmanuel Berl is a French left-wing author, very important between the two World Wars, very independent. He is known particularly for his *Mort de la pensée bourgeoise*.

Man must face the facts of the technological society and, in his private self, go beyond them. He must create values, therefore, not artificial values but common ones that can be shared, and the values he creates should not be the products of revolution: they should be the motive, the source, and the meaning of it. His revolution will be motivated and oriented by the values he chooses. Today's revolution is not open confrontation of society, for the very things we contest there are already decayed. It is absurd to challenge the authority of fathers, cops, priests, and profs, for they, by virtue of this technological and mass producing-consuming society, have lost all but the semblance of authority.[39] The May 1968 revolutionists tore at an empty husk, leaving not a mark on the concrete bastion. In reality, all values are at issue; we need to create fresh ones. Imagination has a function there, but nowhere else, and no demonstrations of collective unconsciousness can help us determine them: more courage and less conformity are called for. We must find a sovereign indisputable principle that is outside the rigid existing structure but will enable us to confront it and to pierce its armor instead of the phantom shells of decayed values.

Historically, few doctrines have attempted to follow the thread we have been pursuing. I know of only two: personalism and, in the contemporary scene, situationism. We ought to add a word about the revolution in daily life and the modern slogan of self-direction. I shall not attempt to summarize personalism, on which a vast literature already exists. I would point out simply that at its source and in its early years when it was revolutionary,[40] it tried to attack society

---

[39] See the important book by Mitscherlich, *Vers la Société sans pères,* 1969.
[40] Personalism originally was quite different from what it became under the impetus of the magazine *Esprit* and the new approach gradually developed by Mounier. It used to be a revolutionary doctrine, unlike the philosophic one we see emerging more and more clearly. It did not always focus on Mounier's ideas, on *Esprit,* and on the group consisting of Davenson, Lacroix, Touard, and Philipp. From 1932 until 1937, the magazine *Ordre Nouveau* (founded in 1930; *Esprit* was founded in 1932) played an equally important role and at-

as a whole, singling out technology as the key factor (a view supported by Aron, Dandieu, Charbonneau, A. Ollivier, and others). It repudiated both the Right and the Left, fascism, communism, liberal democracy, capitalism, and standard socialism.

Personalism had the commendable distinction of challenging the authenticity of any revolution that was self-validating, i.e., an end in itself. That type of revolution, wherein the phenomenon exists for its own sake, inevitably introduces brutality, dehumanization, and, when the movement ends, a totalitarian society; whereas the essence of revolution is an ethical relationship, consideration for others, and the acknowledgment of another man's (anyone's, and not just a select person's) rights and dignity.

Personalism tried to put revolution into proper focus: "Our task is not to re-enact past revolutions or to preserve accepted spiritual values, but to revive, gradually and with understanding, the spirituality congealed in an anachronistic society and to cultivate in whatever time it takes the kind of periodical reawakening which refreshes the human spirit as well as human institutions. . . . [W]hoever is concerned with our spiritual destiny is tempted in these times to concentrate solely on preserving truth and justice, as if they should be isolated from a world askew instead of being woven into the fabric of it" (Mounier, 1944). That is a far cry from the trite

---

tracted such personalities as Robert Aron, A. Dandieu, D. de Rougemont, Chevalley, A. Marc, A. Ollivier, and G. Izard.

The two movements differed, of course. The *Esprit* forces tended to be more "spiritual," the *Ordre Nouveau* group more skeptical and astringent. The former were outspokenly democratic and statist; the latter examined democracy and tried to cut a fresh path by weeding out political decay. Both movements were distinctly personalist.

Personalism's early phase cannot be identified with the contents of *Esprit* after 1944, or even after 1940. The following is a list of basic references on personalism: Mounier, *La Technique des moyens spirituels*, 1934 (probably the best thing he wrote); Dandieu, *Discours contre la méthode*, 1929; Aron and Dandieu, *La Révolution nécessaire*, 1933 (previously cited); De Rougemont, *Politique de la personne*, 1934; Charbonneau and Éllul, "Directives pour un manifeste personnaliste," in *Cahiers des Amis d'Esprit*, 1934; "Pour la Liberté," *Manifeste de l'ordre nouveau*, 1936. Also by Mounier, *Le Manifeste personnaliste*, 1936.

and standard Leftist approach that took over the movement. Personalism aimed at action that is revolutionary yet dependent somewhat on the status of a person (at that time there was reason to differentiate between "person" and "individual") in relation to the community. Revolution was seen as a rigorous human attack on institutions, based on a precise theory of political and economic reality.

In June 1932, De Rougemont wrote: "Humanism in the year 1932 is revolution . . . the only climate that allows and encourages spiritual adventure. . . . What defense have we other than attack? other than to try to create a way of life founded on spiritual and temporal identity, and to establish values that are at once supreme and ordinary." The conclusion is simple: Do as you think, and think as you do. Whereas bourgeois ethics would urge: Do what everyone else does, and think what you would never dare *do*. Later on, Bernanos became associated with the movement, though he never espoused personalism. In *La France contre les robots, La liberté pour quoi faire?* and other works, he called for building a totally new society, saying that the two poles of revolutionary action should be "Liberty and Reason."

Revolution was seen to embrace everything: the spirit, the person, and the community. It was intended to be carried out on the personal level. "This adventure, beginning each time with a false understanding of revolution, with an inner rebellion questioning our own share in the established disorder, or our complacency in the face of it, the gulf we will tolerate between what we are and what we must serve, reaches a new stage, a steady conversion of our whole person, speech, actions, and principles, into a single indissoluble commitment" (Mounier, 1936). Commitment was the aim. And long before Sartre, that necessity was the core of personalism. Its general orientation may be seen in the dichotomy posed by Dandieu: man's goal is the creation and affirmation of his own identity; his means are various systems of thought and of energy which are called rationalism, automatism, etc. The means must not be allowed to mask or to replace the goals. The rational sector therefore must be separate from the creative one. That applies to the whole of society: certain areas of activity would be rationalized and highly systematized, yet would not interfere with the area of creativity. In that perspective, eliminating the proletarian condition would mean that no one would work exclusively at the first type of activity but that everyone would participate in both types—that each individual would be responsible for the meaningless automatism yet would retain the incentive to do creative work. Those principles are still valid, and indeed have been adopted and presented as new ideas by a number of modern authors. In its time, personalism was alone in discerning the specific problems of revolution and of contemporary society. Its failure unquestionably was caused by the lack of commitment, the drift toward culture and ideological protest, and the inability to initiate revolutionary action on a day-to-day basis. But due acknowledgment should be given to the awareness created by that movement, which far surpasses anything Marxism has achieved between 1914 and the present.

The other movement deserving mention is contemporary international situationism.[41] Built on ideological premises utterly opposed to those of personalism (the latter is strongly influenced by Christianity, which situationists reject), the movement actually advances (despite its criticism) the tenets of surrealism, which were genuinely revolutionary at the start and closely resembled those of situationism. Surrealism now appears to have become integrated, just as personalism did. What inner force could revive it? Situationism, however, is a live movement. It is aware that the global nature of technological society implies a global revolution, and that self-styled revolutionary political movements do not approach

---

[41] The movement began in 1958 with the founding of the *Internationale Situationniste* magazine. Its doctrine developed steadily between the publication of the first and ninth issues, presenting a fresh formulation of its views. The basic texts are: Debord, *La Société du Spectacle*, 1967; Vaneigem, *Traité de savoir vivre à l'usage des jeunes générations*, 1967.

the current revolutionary imperative. In particular, Debord's critique of communism, socialism, and anarchism is terribly pertinent. Situationism should be credited for advocating individual decision-making and the exercise of imagination free of the irrationality we have discussed. The individual is committed to scrutinize his daily existence and to create a potential new one. In an organized, rationalized, totalitarian society, he will have to eliminate the disorder and reorganize its elements. The concept of a "constructed situation" conveys that: "a moment of existence, concretely and purposefully constructed by the collective ordering of a consistent climate and a series of events." Situationists insist on challenging "basic banalities," which include most of the beliefs of our society.

"A revolutionary movement radically changes the organization of time and space (relative to the individual and his immediate environment) and even the means of deciding its permanent future pattern; it does not merely change the legal status of property or the social structure of power." The necessity of a rigorous theoretical basis of revolution is explained, and its close relationship to action, as well as the potential role of initiative in each situation, the rejection of compromise, cultural integration in revolutionaries, and the need for constant criticism. Situationists have focused attention on such basic concepts as the society of spectacle, drift, deflection, and the distinction between survival and living. The movement appears to be developing in a different direction, fortunately, from that of *Esprit*, i.e., situationism has dissociated itself from the center of cultural activity, realizing that concentrated interest in culture, films, and its own publication could make it appear the mouthpiece of a rebel faction of the Paris intelligentsia. The cultural factor is becoming integrated in its total perspective, and its theoretical approach is increasingly revolutionary.

The situationist movement stresses the analysis of life-style. That position requires clarification. We have already indicated that revolution begins with the recovery of individuality, implying criticism of the pattern of life and the need for a revolutionary additive. In the modern era of revolution, retreat into a private existence has always been a goal. The citizen of those revolutions became the private individual of nineteenth-century society whose passion for political freedom found refuge in the inner recesses of conscience, the "heart" or "conscience" being the safest abode for liberty—it was easier that way. Saint-Just declared: "the people's liberty is in the privacy of their lives; respect it." Goebbels was equally eloquent on the subject.

The concept is open to a good deal of misinterpretation. On the one hand, we can interpret it as a retreat into the past. With society as it is, and revolution impossible, I shall make my own revolution in the safe surroundings of my own person. Each individual carries on his private revolution—which may simply entail not buying the same newspaper as his neighbor. For Christians, the retreat to an inner life affords even greater privacy, the experience of which leaves no marks at all. That interpretation is too obvious to concern us. Another aspect is more pernicious: as systematic restraints multiply, man becomes a mechanism in the "social-political-economic" pattern, and the more he insists on being regarded and treated as a person, the louder are his demands for independence in his private or inner life—and the more services he requires. After that, he looks for autonomy, but his autonomy will relate solely to the increased services he uses and to his desire to *exceed certain limits* that he finds extremely confining. The barriers he chooses to defy, however, are relatively frail. That is why I distrust all so-called revolutionary activity in the cultural sphere, for it attacks only what has surrendered already. The individual may attempt to assert his autonomy in the areas of sex, or drugs, or the Pill, having been led to believe that he can thus reach beyond himself (through drugs), defy morality and society, or cast off restraints. It is only an illusion: all such activities are elements of one aspect of technological society (spectacle and consumption), for they represent consumption, products put out for the same purpose as every other product, be it TV or cars. To look for freedom in drugs or pills is to perpetuate the pattern of society, which could not care less about traditional morality and the preservation of individuality.

On the subject of revolution through criticism of life-style and in private life, A. Molès makes an even greater mistake. He says that "interstitial mobility is reduced to nought as the technocrats of cybernetics proceed to classify 300,000,000 insects," and thinks that the field of technology and the adoption of what he calls new situations should be the focus of man's private search for a new freedom. The situations would be devised partly by psychosociological analyses, partly by highly perfected techniques. Freedom would reside in a multiplicity of odd but feeble deviations, e.g., non-observance of taboos. That whole line of thought is absolutely meaningless in relation to the problem posed by technological society, not only to the individual, but to the entire society, from which the individual cannot be separated as if he were a self-sustaining entity. What Molès is proposing is simply a flawless American gadget and the "do it yourself" method (cf. *Internationale Situationniste*, No. 9).

We attack nothing by taking this imaginary escape route from society. What is more, the escapism induces even greater adaptation, for once man has had his fling at freedom, he will accept other forms of restraint more readily. As a revolutionary act, it is totally sterile; it leads not toward greater freedom, but away from it. Sex or drugs can be an act of liberation the first time around, but have no permanent connection with a revolutionary process or a free style of life. They can only degenerate into broader expressions of compliance under the illusion of mechanical autonomy. The concept of a revolution in life-style (as a beginning and a means) is highly ambiguous and questionable. We must define the exact terms of it and explain why the critique of ordinary existence [42] demands

---

[42] H. Lefèbvre, *Critique de la vie quotidienne* (2 vols.), 1948–63; *Introduction à la Modernité*, 1954; *La Vie quotidienne dans le monde moderne*, 1968.

strict discipline and implies a rejection of everything society
has to offer. It is a step toward revolution, but has nothing to
do with meaningless psychosociological analyses of the im-
personality of relationships purporting to rectify the im-
balanced man/groups/society relationship. The importance
of life-style here stems from the fact that our technological
society has abolished style and instituted routine, and that all
the social threads ultimately end in/are reflected in/are
echoed by/cause repercussions in/are expressed by/the
pattern of life: to start at this level is a direct attack on
civilization, both in respect to all its consequences and to its
specific impact on human beings.

"Is the ordinary man still a man? he is a virtual automation,
and what is to be done to repossess him of the qualities and
properties of a human being, or to enable him to transcend
the ordinariness of which he is the epitome?" And the following
strikes a sympathetic chord: "The primary and fundamental
requisite of cultural revolution is the redemption in full of
these concepts: work, creativity, freedom, appropriateness,
style, useful value, human being, which cannot be achieved
without scrupulously reassessing the productivist ideology,
economic rationality and economism, as well as the myths and
half-truths of participation, integration, creativity." [43] Yes, and
then how discouraging it is to be told next that the access to
day-to-day revolution lies in urban living and to read thrilling
tributes to its encounters, its lack of barriers, its thwarting of
natural cycles, and the assertion that urban life is an interval
of mystery, the abode and season of desire, a confrontation
with terrorism, and the absence of stifled creativity. The
festivity and gallop of urban life is seen in contrast to the
consumption of spectacles and signs.[44] That strikes me as a

[43] H. Lefèbvre, *La Vie quotidienne dans le monde moderne.*
[44] In this regard, Le Lannou's approach seems much more revolutionary in
the perspective of a revolution in daily life. He says, for example: "Voluntary
geography has greater respect for human inhabitants than for producers," and,
in criticizing "regionalization": "Regionalization is readily adopted, not in pursuit of human values, but as an occasional method of stimulating the major

bizarre ideology or fable, a city-dweller's mystique of his own environment. It is not an overture to revolution, and its conclusions, although eloquently expressed, are untenable. Basically, however, this inquiry into the nature of everyday life is essential to an understanding of what revolution means today and how we should reflect upon it. We have examined three doctrines, three trends, three visualizations of present society, all of which evidence mobile values, equivocal responses, and the absence of practical experience. But in view of the relentless "imposition of severe penalties on human beings" in the name of tender humanity and of eternal principles, the revival of conscious awareness is in itself a miracle, and its spread sustains our hopes and our dignity.

Our lengthy exploration of "definitions" was not an intellectual exercise. It was an effort to grasp an experience, not a word, and to interpret it intelligently. It gave us a perplexing encounter with two images of revolution, one hot, one cold. The first responds to naked emotion, to impulse, to a sense of tragedy and of romance, but it is "blurred," as that word applies to televised images: [45] vague and indiscriminate, its design is incoherent, its tactics wavering. The second image is "sharp," accurate, and uncompromising; it is planned and premeditated like a game of chess, the sacrifices anticipated, the sentiment suspended. The first can raise rebellions, but in the name of what, and against what? It is always late in recognizing social transformations, and hurls itself against the ghosts of memory or of inheritance. The second expoits entire nations; it is among the primary realities, but has abandoned forever the ultimate truths; undaunted by the harsh climate

---

sectors of the economy." Here he states the problem directly: "Man gives less and less thought to living, and more and more to gaining the anonymity of the sheepfold" [in perpetual motion]. He shares the situationist view, probably inadvertently, for the two have little else in common, when he says: "Each situation calls for a unique approach." That is precisely the problem of a revolution in daily existence.

[45] The sharp definition is factually informative, explicit, and rigorous; the blurred one is the reverse.

of our times, it has lost sight and track of man—and perhaps can do without him altogether. In the end, the first is no longer revolution, for though it moves us, it does not involve us; nor is the second, as all its calculations are lost in the new wasteland of human existence, and its efficiency allows no margin for error.

From there we went on to discover an attitude of dull familiarity wholly inappropriate to the mighty wrath, now tamed, of rebellious peoples. It leads ultimately to a purely abstract revolution achieved by technical means. If that is what we must accept, then Marshall McLuhan is right, and if we pursue that argument to its end, we are forced to conclude that the only vital revolution today is the mutation of our brain and our perception and view of the world through the displacement of language by televised images, the relentless army of electric impulses. If that is so, what can we do about it? Still, it makes us uneasy, and gives rise to the vulgar appeals to revolution which distort and annihilate its meaning. Instead of solving matters, it has brought us to the brink of the final revolution. Final because no other will be possible if this one fails. Final because it confronts us with penultimate realities. We are torn between the lure of a vain political revolution and the necessity of a technological revolution against which, precisely, we must rebel. We need every spark of defiance and self-assertion we can muster, a new spirit wholly distinct from traditional individualism and from everything heretofore described as revolution. We have no legacy to fall back on; everything must be initiated.

Jacques Ellul was born in Bordeaux, France, in 1912. He studied at the University of Bordeaux and the University of Paris; from the latter he holds a doctorate in law. He has been professor of the history of law and of social history at Bordeaux since 1946. His European reputation is immense, and his reputation in America has been firmly established by the publication here by Alfred A. Knopf of *The Technological Society* (1964), *Propaganda* (1965), *The Political Illusion* (1967), and *A Critique of the New Commonplaces* (1968). Professor Ellul is married and has seven children.

A NOTE ON THE TYPE

The text of this book is set in *Caledonia,* a Linotype face designed by W. A. DWIGGINS, the man responsible for so much that is good in contemporary book design and typography. Caledonia belongs to the family of printing types called "modern face" by printers—a term used to mark the change in style of type-letters that occurred about 1800. Caledonia borders on the general design of Scotch Modern but is more freely drawn than that letter.

Composed, printed and bound by
Kingsport Press, Inc. Kingsport, Tenn.